History of How the Spaniards Arrived in Peru

History of How the Spaniards Arrived in Peru

Dual-Language Edition

Titu Cusi Yupanqui

Translated, with an Introduction, by
Catherine Julien

Hackett Publishing Company, Inc.
Indianapolis/Cambridge

12 11 10 09 08 07 06   1 2 3 4 5 6 7

For further information, please address:

Hackett Publishing Company, Inc.
P.O. Box 44937
Indianapolis, IN 46244-0937

www.hackettpublishing.com

Cover design by Abigail Coyle
Text design by Meera Dash
Maps by Bill Nelson
Composition by Agnew's, Inc.
Printed at Edwards Brothers, Inc.

Library of Congress Cataloging-in-Publication Data

Yupangui, Diego de Castro, titu cussi, 16th cent.
   [Ynstruçion del ynga don Diego de Castro titu cussi Yupangui. English
& Spanish]
   History of how the Spaniards arrived in Peru : dual-language edition /
titu cusi Yupanqui ; translated, with an introduction, by Catherine Julien.
         p.   cm.
   Includes bibliographical references and index.
   ISBN-10: 0-87220-828-1 (pbk.)
   ISBN-10: 0-87220-829-X (cloth)
   ISBN-13: 978-0-87220-828-5 (pbk.)
   ISBN-13: 978-0-87220-829-2 (cloth)
   1. Peru—History—Conquest, 1522–1548. 2. Peru—History—
1548–1820. 3. Incas—History. I. Julien, Catherine J. II. Title.
   F3442.Y8513 2006
   985′.02—dc22

                                                    2006010681

∞

Contents

Acknowledgments

The work for this project was supported by a National Endowment for the Humanities Fellowship at the John Carter Brown Library and by a John Simon Guggenheim Memorial Fellowship. Travel funding for archival research in Spain was provided by the Burnham-Macmillan Fund of the History Department at Western Michigan University. I thank the staff in the library of the Escorial for their assistance in allowing me to see the original manuscript and for making a copy of it. My greatest debt is to Kenneth Mills for his thorough reading of the manuscript and suggestions for revision.

Introduction

In the *History of How the Spaniards Arrived in Peru* (1570), Titu Cusi offers Philip II, king of Spain, an account of all that had happened following the arrival of Francisco Pizarro and his men on the coast of the Inca empire—the largest native polity in the Americas. What motivated the creation of the *History* can only be guessed. Titu Cusi may have been trying to secure the implementation of the agreement he had negotiated with the king's representatives as the recognized head of the Inca dynasty. The work involves much more than diplomacy, however. Titu Cusi narrates the story of the alliance made between his father, Manco Inca, and Francisco Pizarro just as the latter arrived in Cusco in late 1533. In Cajamarca, Pizarro had executed Atahuallpa, who had just won a fratricidal war that left deep divisions in the Inca dynastic elite. When Pizarro met Manco Inca, a half-brother of Atahuallpa's, the two joined forces out of mutual need to defeat Atahuallpa's remaining armies. Titu Cusi also tells about his own dealings with the Spaniards after Manco's death in 1544, but the centerpiece of the story is how the alliance between his father and Francisco Pizarro unraveled. In it, he combined the forms of the Spanish historical narrative with what appears to be an Inca rhetorical genre. The result is a unique literary and historical achievement that forces us to reconsider how the story of the conquest has been told.

The *History* is one of only a handful of historical narratives to be authored by native Andeans in the century after the Spanish arrival. The scarcity of such narratives probably stems, at least in part, from the absence of an Andean alphabetic writing system prior to that time. Of these narratives, Titu Cusi's stands out because it is the earliest; it is the only narrative authored by an Inca; its author was *the* Inca (the recognized head of the dynastic line); and it was written from Vilcabamba, a province then only tenuously subject to Spanish authority. Though the full title of Titu Cusi's narrative—*History of how the Spaniards arrived in Peru and what happened to Manco Inca during the time he lived among them*—is taken from the heading of the first chapter about his father, the story actually begins with the arrival of the Spaniards on the coast of the Inca empire. During the time covered in the *History,* the Spaniards overthrew the Inca

elite and usurped authority over the largest native state in the Americas, establishing the de facto rule of Spain in the Andes. Although we still use the word "conquest" to refer to this period of initial engagement between Europeans and native Andeans, we now realize that the capture of Atahuallpa was an initial salvo in a much longer war, and that the Incas may not have even guessed at Spanish intentions for some two years after the events at Cajamarca. Interestingly, Titu Cusi does not use the term "conquest." Instead, he says that the Spaniards "arrived" and events "happened" during the time his father "lived among them." He portrays his father as naïve and foolish, a man who ignored his closest advisers' calls for resistance and inadvertently allowed the Spaniards to take the Inca empire away from him. His story is another telling of the traditional story of the conquest, containing truths as well as new forms of bias.

In the traditional version of the "conquest" of Peru, control passed from Inca to Spanish hands with the capture of the Inca Atahuallpa in Cajamarca in November 1532. The official accounts, written by Pizarro's secretaries, represent Atahuallpa's capture as a battle between Spaniards and Incas. Spanish domination was decisively established when the Incas lost the fight. A long period of rooting out pockets of resistance followed, finally ending with the campaign against the Vilcabamba Incas in 1572. When relating the history of the period, modern scholars tend to use language that reflects their basic acceptance of the story told in the official accounts: control over the Andes effectively passed to Europeans upon Atahuallpa's capture; the Incas appointed by Pizarro after Atahuallpa's death were "puppets"; the ensuing military events were "rebellions." But, as Titu Cusi's *History* makes clear, there are other ways to tell the story.

One account situates the events of the Spanish arrival within the broader context of Andean history (Rowe, "Como se apoderó"). A war had broken out after the death of Huayna Capac, Manco Inca's father, about 1528. Huayna Capac had been campaigning in Ecuador at the time of his death, and his son Atahuallpa took effective control of the army. Another son, Huascar, was named Inca ruler in Cusco, the center of the empire and homeland of the Incas. War soon broke out between the two brothers. Atahuallpa's army, led by some of his father's most capable generals, outmaneuvered Huascar near Cusco and took him captive. At the very moment Pizarro captured Atahuallpa, Huascar was a prisoner of Atahuallpa. Atahuallpa, afraid that Pizarro might prefer to ally himself with Huascar, had

his brother killed. When Tupa Huallpa, another of Huayna Capac's sons, arrived in Cajamarca, Pizarro found someone from Cusco to ally with and had Atahuallpa put to death. Pizarro then left with Tupa Huallpa for Cusco to arrive in the Inca capital as its liberator. Tupa Huallpa died en route, but when Pizarro met Manco Inca just before arriving in Cusco in late 1533, in the town of Jaquijaguana, he had found another Inca that the Inca elite of Cusco would recognize. The two joined forces and immediately returned to the business of campaigning against Atahuallpa's remaining armies.

That the Spaniards were the real enemy was not apparent to Manco at first. It would be two years before he would plan to oust the Spaniards from his territory. When the decision was made, he called up an army from Tahuantinsuyu, the four regions into which the Inca empire was divided. He then attacked Cusco in April 1536 and launched a concurrent campaign against Lima. Both campaigns failed; Manco was forced to abandon Cusco and retreat to the remote region of Vilcabamba, northwest of Cusco, and Peru was left to the Spaniards. Manco lived in Vilcabamba until approximately 1544, by which time any real hopes of ousting the Spaniards had disappeared. The conquest qua conquest—that is, the period of military action that lasted from Manco's attack on Cusco in 1536 to the loss of his best captains in 1539—had happened. Following Manco's death, Vilcabamba was ruled first by a regent, then successively by his three sons— Sayre Tupa, Titu Cusi, and Tupa Amaru—until 1572. Titu Cusi governed Vilcabamba himself from 1559 to 1571. He would tell Manco's story in 1570, drawing on what his father and members of his father's inner circle told him about the early years of the Spanish presence in the Andes. Titu Cusi would be the only person to represent the conquest from his father's point of view: the point of view of the Vilcabamba Incas.

Titu Cusi and Vilcabamba

The exact date of Titu Cusi's birth is unknown. If he was the oldest of Manco's three sons (as is likely), he might have been born around the time the Spaniards arrived in Cusco, in November 1533, or just afterward. Titu Cusi describes himself as "a boy" (f. 53) and "small" (f. 53v),[1] at the time

---

1. Folio references omit the notation *recto* for the front side and abbreviate the notation *verso* as "v" for the reverse.

of his father's death, about 1544, he would have been about ten. We know that Titu Cusi spent his entire life in the Vilcabamba province, save for a period of perhaps two years (sometime between 1539 and 1541) when he was captured in a Spanish attack on Vitcos and taken to live in Cusco in the household of Pedro de Oñate, a Spanish resident (f. 47). He and his mother (whom he does not name) were later secreted out of Cusco by his father's men and returned to Vilcabamba. If 1533 is a good estimate for his birth date, Titu Cusi would have been forty-seven when he composed the *History* and forty-eight when he died.

Though Vilcabamba may seem like an inaccessible place to non-Andeans (as it did to the Spaniards), it had been a fully incorporated province of the Inca empire. A sizeable settlement at Vitcos and a number of fortresses had been built by Inca rulers in the region prior to the Spanish arrival. Though the highland region surrounding Vitcos allowed Manco to keep a large herd of Andean llamas and alpacas requiring high-altitude pasture, he feared that the settlement was too vulnerable to Spanish attack. So Manco developed a second urban settlement at the site of Vilcabamba, in the heavily forested lowlands. The Vilcabamba province was bordered by lowland Inca provinces that were not incorporated into Spanish Peru, and these peoples continued to recognize the Incas of Vilcabamba. It was situated just over the mountains from the main highland road between Cusco to Lima, facilitating attacks on the highlands north of Cusco. The terrain in Vilcabamba was difficult to navigate effectively on horseback, limiting reprisals. In short, it was the perfect place from which to frustrate Spanish efforts to hold the former Inca heartland.

Titu Cusi says nothing about how Vilcabamba was governed just after his father's death, but Juan de Betanzos, a Spaniard who wrote an account that covers the same period, the *Suma y narración de los Incas* (1551–1557), relates that one of Manco's captains, Pumasupa, succeeded Manco as head of the Vilcabamba Incas. Betanzos was married to Angelina Yupanqui, a cousin of Atahuallpa's, and got his information from Inca sources. He was also sent into Vilcabamba as an interpreter in 1557 to negotiate with Manco's sons and could have learned on his own about how Vilcabamba was governed in the period after Manco's death. Betanzos was part of an effort made by the viceroy Marquis of Cañete (1555–1559) to negotiate with Sayre Tupa, Titu Cusi's brother, and coax him to leave Vilcabamba. The Spaniards thought—rightly or wrongly—that Sayre Tupa

had been chosen to succeed Manco. They awarded him an *encomienda* (a grant from the Spanish crown to the tribute owed to the crown by a particular group) that incorporated some of the estates that had been the personal property of the Inca rulers but had been alienated from their descendants when Pizarro granted them as *encomiendas* in August 1535. The most important of the estates granted to Sayre Tupa was Yucay, which had been the estate of the eleventh ruler, Huayna Capac, Manco Inca's father, and which Francisco Pizarro had awarded to himself. This estate, located in the agriculturally rich Urubamba valley, was the main source of support of Huayna Capac's royal corporation (*panaca*), and also included a region in the adjacent tropical lowlands where the finest coca leaf in the Andes was grown. From an Inca point of view, these estates were essential to a life outside of Vilcabamba.

Sayre Tupa left Vilcabamba in 1557. Titu Cusi (who was probably thirty-four at the time) and his younger brother Tupa Amaru stayed behind. In a letter of 1559 to Polo de Ondegardo (the Spanish *corregidor*, or royal magistrate, and author of several important treatises on native Andean organization), Titu Cusi mentions that Tupa Amaru—and not himself—had been chosen to be the next Inca. Though Titu Cusi's later negotiations with the Spaniards clearly indicate that he is acting as Inca, just who was in line to succeed or how this might have changed is unknown.

Titu Cusi's letter to Polo is the first of his surviving letters, and in them he consistently tries to negotiate with the Spaniards for additional *encomiendas*. There were other *encomiendas* in the Cusco region that included the retainer populations of Inca estates that had been the property of the Inca rulers and were intended to maintain their descendants. Titu Cusi was clearly trying to negotiate the return of these properties. When Sayre Tupa died (in 1560 or 1561), he left an infant daughter, Beatriz Coya. Marriage to Beatriz would secure title to her father's *encomienda*, so later negotiations between Titu Cusi and royal officials turned on the marriage between this little girl and Titu Cusi's son, Felipe Quispe Titu.

The death of Sayre Tupa temporarily ended any possibility of negotiations, however. Titu Cusi describes some of the events of this period in the second part of the *History*, where he deals with the period of his own rule, and in the *Memorial* of 1565 (see Appendix). Relations between the Vilcabamba Incas and Spanish authorities in Cusco deteriorated steadily to a point where Gregorio González Cuenca, *corregidor* of Cusco in 1562,

threatened war, and Titu Cusi launched retaliatory attacks. After 1563, however, there were no more attacks from Vilcabamba, and although there were rumors about a possible uprising, it did not materialize. Some of these rumors arose because of the discovery of a movement known as Taqui Onqoy, which prophesied the defeat of the Spaniards and their God by Andeans and their *huacas,* or sacred beings. Concurrent with the discovery of this movement in 1565, the Licentiate Lope García de Castro's negotiations with the Vilcabamba Incas began in earnest, and an agreement called the Capitulations of Acobamba was drafted. In exchange for a full pardon for Titu Cusi and his captains, property and revenue for Titu Cusi, and the marriage between Beatriz Coya (Titu Cusi's niece) and Felipe Quispe Titu (his son), Titu Cusi would accept baptism, swear his loyalty as a vassal to Philip II, allow civil and religious personnel into Vilcabamba, and live in Spanish Peru. Between the properties granted and the *encomienda* of Beatriz, Titu Cusi and his son would be able to support themselves outside of Vilcabamba.

At the time the *History* was drafted by Titu Cusi in 1570, the negotiations between the Spanish administration and the Vilcabamba Incas had reached an impasse. Sabotage of the talks by Spaniards and, very likely, Incas in Cusco and the distance between Vilcabamba and Spain contributed to the stalemate. In accordance with the terms of the Capitulations of Acobamba, Titu Cusi had accepted baptism for himself and his son, had allowed a *corregidor* and Dominican missionaries into Vilcabamba, and had sworn the required oath to be the vassal of Philip II by early 1566. The linchpin of the agreement for the Vilcabamba Incas was the marriage of Titu Cusi's niece, Beatriz Coya, to his son, Felipe Quispe Titu. In December 1565 a prominent Cusco Spaniard named Arias Maldonado arranged with Beatriz's mother and guardian to have the seven-year-old removed from the convent where she lived and married to his younger brother, Cristóbal. Spanish authorities caught up with the couple— although the marriage was reportedly consummated—and returned Beatriz to the convent. Both an annulment and a papal dispensation so that Beatriz could marry her first cousin were being obtained. Despite the apparent removal of obstacles to the fulfillment of the accord, Titu Cusi did not leave Vilcabamba. Although he does not explain in the *History* his reasons for remaining, he writes to viceregal authorities at various points noting that he cannot live outside of Vilcabamba without some kind of

income. None of the income streams he was to receive under the terms of the agreement had been paid to him.

This was a sufficient reason to hold out, but the *History* itself may provide a clue about his intentions. He describes the words his father had spoken to his people when he left for Vilcabamba:

> First, you must not believe a thing these bearded people—who have offended me so deeply because I placed so much faith in them—tell you, because they lie a great deal as they have in all my dealings with them. They will lie to you, too. What you can do is act as if you consented to what they order. . . . (f. 44v)

Spaniards may have doubted whether Titu Cusi intended to hold up his end of the bargain. But, as Titu Cusi's father had already told him in no uncertain terms, they would not live up to theirs.

And they did not. Though the viceroy Francisco de Toledo (1569–1581) arrived in Peru with instructions to carry out the Capitulations, both his actions and his correspondence make it clear that he did not intend to negotiate with the Incas. In 1571 he wrote to Cardinal Espinosa, then an important figure at court and a confidante of Toledo's, that he had come to understand that the Inca line was illegitimate even before he left Spain for Peru in 1569. As Toledo traveled from Lima to Cusco in 1570, he began to collect testimony from native witnesses on the way to prove that the Incas were tyrants and had been wrongly recognized by the Spanish crown. In addition to trying to convince the king that Spanish policy was wrong, he tried to derail the agreement made in the Capitulations of Acobamba. Toledo sent an embassy headed by Tilano de Anaya to Vilcabamba to meet with Titu Cusi. Anaya was someone Titu Cusi had dealt with, and he may have been told that if he returned to Vilcabamba he would be killed. He was killed, but Titu Cusi was also dead, so it may have been the closure of the province in the wake of the Inca's death that brought about the failure of the viceroy's embassy. No matter what, the time for negotiation had ended. Toledo sent a small army into Vilcabamba, under the command of Martín García de Loyola, the nephew of Ignatius de Loyola (founder of the Jesuit order) and a member of the viceroy's personal entourage, to capture Titu Cusi. When the army found that Titu Cusi was dead, it captured his younger brother Tupa Amaru

instead; it also seized Punchao, the most important Inca cult object, a gold image the size of a child (Julien, "Punchao en España," 709–12). Tupa Amaru was taken to Cusco. He arrived September 21, 1572 and was baptized and beheaded in the main square on September 24, 1572. Toledo had put an end to the Vilcabamba Incas.

The Creation of the *History*

Titu Cusi's *History* was written two years earlier by his mestizo (mixed Spanish and Indian) scribe, Martín de Pando, about a year before Titu Cusi's death. Pando had arrived in Vilcabamba with Betanzos in 1557 and had been kept there ever since. An Augustinian friar, Marcos García, also assisted in composing the work, or as Pando wrote, "related and organized" the account "on the insistence" of Titu Cusi (ff. 63v–64). The account was written in his own voice. It was probably delivered orally, possibly in Spanish, and translated or corrected as it was being recorded. (Since Titu Cusi had been taken from Vilcabamba as a boy and spent two years living in a Spanish home in Cusco, he probably had some competence in Spanish. He had known a number of Spanish residents of Vilcabamba and had worked with Martín de Pando over more than a decade in the preparation of at least a dozen letters in Spanish and two historical narratives. There is no reason to assume that he could not have worked in Spanish, but there is no way of knowing how Titu Cusi, Pando, and García communicated.)

The text clearly borrows from a Christian discursive tradition and includes references to European political theory (for example, the concept of "natural lords"). Although both García and Pando can have influenced the text in subtle ways, the language and ideas represented cannot easily be dismissed as theirs alone; at the very least, Titu Cusi and his Inca sources should be credited with having told his father's story.

The *History* can be divided into two halves corresponding to the rulerships of Manco Inca and Titu Cusi. The entire account is narrated by Titu Cusi, who inserts himself into the account of his father by referring to him as "my father" and by narrating his own story in the first person. A great deal of the *History* is related through the recreation of verbal encounters between Manco and Francisco Pizarro or one of Francisco's brothers (Hernando, Juan, or Gonzalo) or between Manco and his inner circle of

followers. (These encounters are discussed in greater detail below.) Although there are descriptions of action where no direct speech is involved, the speeches are central to the story and essential to conveying Titu Cusi's representation of his father's treatment by the Spaniards. Titu Cusi supplies numerous subheadings; these subheadings frequently separate one speech from the next. The focus of the narrative shifts from Manco to Titu Cusi in the second part of the *History*. When the subject is Titu Cusi's own relationship with the Spaniards, there are no speeches or subheadings; these features are found only in those passages related to his father. The Incas' engagement with the Spaniards remains the main topic throughout, however, and neither half offers much information on what was transpiring outside of the Inca's immediate presence.

The manuscript reached Spain with Licentiate Lope García de Castro, governor of Peru (1563–1569) under whom the Capitulations of Acobamba had been negotiated. It was copied in 1574, and the copy is now kept in the Escorial library. Though the original appears to have consisted of two documents, the copying has effectively turned them into a single text. The first element in the text is Titu Cusi's Instruction to the Licentiate Castro; the *History* is embedded in this Instruction. The second element is Titu Cusi's Power of Attorney. Some earlier publications of the manuscript have used the heading of the Instruction (*Instrucción al licenciado Lope García de Castro*) as a general title for the whole text.[2] This title is not entirely misleading, but the overall thrust of the narrative is to tell the story of Inca dealings with the Spaniards. Titu Cusi calls the text a *relasción* (f. 2v) in a subheading, a narrative format for reporting that developed from the letter form. The manuscript is essentially a narrative history, accompanied by certain features related to its authentification and formal transmission (the Instruction, notarizations of the *History,* and the Power of Attorney).

Soon after beginning his own story, Titu Cusi addresses the Licentiate Castro directly, referring to him as "Your Lordship," as in the first part of the Instruction. The *History* appears to end at folio 62, without a chapter or paragraph break; the Instruction then begins again with the word "therefore" (*por tanto*).

2. See Titu Cusi Yupanqui 1985, 1988, 1992, 2001.

Therefore, because Your Lordship understands and will make His Majesty understand, I have tried to tell above and in summary form, without going into great detail, how my father lived his life and the content and purpose of my own actions to the present moment. If it should be necessary to explain anything in greater detail than it has been explained here, you can let me know and I will do what you tell me. What I have written seems to me at the moment to be sufficient. (f. 62)

Whether Titu Cusi intended the Licentiate Castro to give the king a written copy of the *History,* or simply wanted him to "explain" his situation to the king, is not clear.

Both the Instruction and the Power of Attorney are notarized. The notarization of the Instruction is complex and includes important information on the composition of the *History.* Pando, the notary, wrote:

All of what was written above (providing information about the actions of our illustrious lord Don Diego de Castro Titu Cusi Yupanqui, son of Manco Inca Yupanqui, natural lord who ruled these lands) was done and ordered by the reverend father Friar Marcos García, a friar of the order of our lord Saint Augustine. . . . (f. 62v)

The document was witnessed by the other Augustinian friar assigned to Vilcabamba, Diego Ortiz, and three Inca captains, in the town of San Salvador de Vilcabamba on February 6, 1570. The lack of Christian baptismal names for the captains indicates that they had not been baptized. Since the extant version of the text is a copy, there are no actual signatures. The copy, however, indicates that only the friars and the notary were signatories. Following the notarization is a statement in the voice of Titu Cusi, and apparently signed by him, reiterating what Pando has said about the production of the *History* and affirming that he had commissioned it:

Because it is necessary for me to relate to King Philip II, our lord, what is in my interest and in the interest of my successors, and I do not know the phrases and the manner Spaniards use for such enterprises, I requested that the very reverend father Friar Marcos García and Martín de Pando order and compose the above narrative, according to their custom, so that it could be sent to the kingdoms of

Spain to [sic: with] the very illustrious lord the Licentiate Lope García de Castro, so that he, for me and in my name, and taking with him my Power of Attorney, as he has, could do me the favor of showing and communicating it to His Majesty the King, Philip II, our lord. . . . (ff. 63v–64)

The Instruction was ordered and composed by the Augustinian friar and the notary, but it was constructed from source material supplied by Titu Cusi.

The Power of Attorney was also notarized, and on the same day. The same two Augustinian friars and three different Incas served as witnesses. (Christian baptismal names are listed for these Inca witnesses, indicating that they had been baptized.) This time Martín de Pando notes that he signed in the name of Titu Cusi. Since the document is not an original, there is no possibility of examining the two signatures of Titu Cusi to determine whether or not he could sign his name.

Authorship and Textual Matters

Titu Cusi understood the value of writing. As he says at the beginning of the Instruction, he is recording some "important matters" because "the memory of men is weak and fragile"; without writing, "the complex and important events that occur will be impossible to remember in detail." Titu Cusi wanted his story to be told, and he found an appropriate form in which to accomplish his purpose.

The *History* was not committed to paper by Titu Cusi himself. It was customary for Spaniards in positions of high authority to dictate their letters, decrees, and other writings. In this practice, Titu Cusi was on equal footing with kings, viceroys, and governors. He was clearly familiar with Spanish forms of communication, and regardless of whether he could write or not, he was the "author" of more than a dozen letters and one other historical narrative, even though these were also written by Pando. The letters are known either from references made to them in other documents or from actual copies found in archives. The first of the known letters was dated June 20, 1559; the last, February 8, 1570. The *Memorial*, his other historical narrative written in 1565 (see Appendix), is a briefer account of his father's and his own dealings with the Spaniards (the same

literary territory he would later tread in the *History*). Though it was also recorded by Martín de Pando, it was created prior to the arrival of Marcos García or any other friars or priests to Vilcabamba and cannot be credited to their influence.

There are significant differences between the *Memorial* and the *History*. Some of the difference is due to what happened in the five years after the *Memorial* was written: Titu Cusi has more to say about the events of his own life in the *History*. But some of the difference is also due to the religious instruction Titu Cusi had received and his contact with Augustinian missionaries after 1565. For example, "the Viracochan" and the "Supay" are thinly disguised Andean stand-ins for God and the devil. In the *History*, the devil himself is an agent of the discord that developed between Manco and the Pizarros; after the Spaniards had been in Cusco for some time, "greed reigned in their hearts to such an extent that, deceived by the devil (who is friend to all evil and enemy to all virtue), they entered into an accord with each other about how to harass my father" (ff. 13v–14). Though Manco was not a Christian, the Spaniards were something worse, and Titu Cusi was quick to note the hypocrisy of the Christianity practiced by the Spaniards. Titu Cusi was baptized in the period between the creation of the *Memorial* and the *History* and professed to be a Christian (whether or not he was entirely sincere is another matter). In the *History* he explains that he had only recently come to understand that earlier Spanish efforts to make peace were motivated by the possibility of his conversion (f. 57v).

Manco's story is the link between the *Memorial* and the *History*. In both narratives, Titu Cusi makes it clear that Manco had initially accepted the authority of the crown; it was the mistreatment he suffered at the hands of the Pizarros that caused him to turn against the Spaniards. The *History* carries another, subtler message: had Manco chosen to fight the Spaniards immediately—as he was encouraged to do by such important figures as his general Vila Oma—Pizarro and his followers would have been killed. Manco's behavior, by this logic, made Spanish success possible.

Both the *History* and the *Memorial* used formats commonly used for reporting to the king of Spain, and there are many examples of these reporting genres in Spanish archives. Titu Cusi's *History* departs from Spanish generic models in at least one significant feature, however: the incorporation of oral discourse (between individuals or between individuals

and groups) sets Titu Cusi's *History* apart from these models. Whereas some of the interchanges reproduced in the text are brief, most are long and could be called speeches. They are represented as verbatim, in the voice of the individual or the group speaking. This kind of verbal interchange is reminiscent of the Renaissance literary tradition, in which two characters with opposing views explored ideas through conversation. In Titu Cusi's time, this dialogic form would be employed by such authors as Juan Ginés de Sepúlveda (*Demócrates secundus,* 1550) and Pedro de Quiroga (*Coloquios de la Verdad,* c. 1563), to air controversial views. But Titu Cusi's use of direct speech in his *History* differs from the Renaissance dialogic form in that it relies on verbal encounters between diverse individuals and groups to advance the plot and to portray aspects of character or emotional states, not to explore abstract concepts. As a result, Titu Cusi's account often reads like the text of a dramatic performance.

What must be considered is whether or not Titu Cusi's use of speeches in the *History* reflects some sort of Inca practice. The various historical narratives the Spaniards created about the Inca past drew from several Inca genres. The Spanish narratives are not characterized by lengthy verbal citations. They may incorporate direct speech (or traces of it), but not to the degree that Titu Cusi's narrative does. His retelling of his father's story resembles a genre of life history that appears to have its origins in a pre-Hispanic Inca narrative tradition. It begins in his father's youth and ends with the event of his death. Precisely in the case of the account that is closest to a translation from an Inca genre (Juan de Betanzos' *Suma y narración de los Incas,* which incorporates a life history of Pachacuti, the ninth Inca), there are traces of direct speech. Then again, Titu Cusi's biography of Manco lacks many of the details that characterize the pre-Hispanic Inca life history genre: we learn nothing about his father's principal wife and children, or the name of his lineage, or of the image that served as his surrogate (*huaoque*).

Of the Spanish narratives of the Inca past, the one that bears the greatest literary resemblance to Betanzos' account is Pedro Sarmiento de Gamboa's *Segunda parte de la historia índica* (in *Geschichte des Inkareiches*) (1572). Originally appointed as a cosmographer to write a description of the Viceroyalty of Peru, Sarmiento was asked by Viceroy Toledo to collect an account of Inca history from members of the Inca dynastic lineages (*panacas*) in Cusco. What he collected includes an account of Pachacuti's

dealings with his father, Viracocha,[3] after Pachacuti miraculously repelled the Chanca attack on Cusco. The dramatic action in Sarmiento's narrative revolves around Pachacuti's three failed attempts to win his father's acceptance of the victory over the Chancas. (Other versions of this story recall fewer attempts.) Similarly, Titu Cusi tells of Manco's having been imprisoned by Hernando and Gonzalo Pizarro (we know he was imprisoned by Juan). Similarly, in Sarmiento's story, Pachacuti's anguish can be understood from his repeated attempts to approach his father. In the *History,* Manco's anguish at being shackled is dramatized through the speeches incorporated in the text. One can only wonder if Sarmiento's account drew from an underlying genre that was dramatized through the use of direct speech and repetition.

While it is possible that Titu Cusi's incorporation of speeches simply followed Inca "literary" models, it is also possible that these speeches reflect a kind of formalized internal political discourse between the Inca and his advisors. The Inca addressed his inner circle as "sons and brothers"; these terms would have accurately reproduced the appropriate ways of addressing members of one's *panaca* (patrilineage). The term "Sapay Inca" (which Titu Cusi glosses elsewhere as "you, only lord") was the standard form of address when speaking with the Inca. The Inca used a particular form of address when speaking to his people, and they responded in a similarly formal manner. This much, at least, may reflect actual practice. Garcilaso Inca de la Vega, who was descended from a Spanish father and Inca mother and was probably Titu Cusi's contemporary, wrote that pre-Hispanic Incas recorded speeches on *quipos* (knotted string records). The formality may have been there in the original, and the appearance of this genre in the *History* may be a case of art imitating life.

The appearance of verbatim speeches in the *History* provokes questions about when and how such speeches were composed. Titu Cusi includes no direct speech in the *Memorial,* yet he incorporates it at every turn in the *History,* from brief interchanges to his father's long speeches to his people and their responses to him. He first uses direct speech in Atahuallpa's initial address to the Spaniards. Several brief interchanges involving Atahuallpa follow, but all of the longer speeches involve Manco

---

3. The eighth Inca ruler, not to be confused with the creator deity of the same name that Titu Cusi mentions in his text.

Inca. There are no speeches in Titu Cusi's account of his own dealings; perhaps his use of first person obviates the need for them. It seems unlikely that all of these speeches were recorded and remembered in a systematic way in the years following the Spanish arrival; instead, they were probably composed for Titu Cusi's purposes with help from people in Vilcabamba who had been with Manco and could remember what had been said on particular occasions (if not the exact language used). The content of the speeches may have been truer to the emotions of the speakers and the meaning behind the words than to the words themselves.

Although the *History* was created for oral communication (between the Licentiate Castro and Philip II) and, as such, may have drawn from some kind of historical genre that incorporated direct speech, we cannot assume that it was ever performed, except, perhaps, in the act of transmission to Martín de Pando. The presence of three Inca captains at the notarization is worth noting here. In contrast to the witnesses to the Power of Attorney, the three men who witnessed the transmission of the *History* had not been baptized. Though we do not know how old they were or whether they were eyewitnesses to the events dramatized by Titu Cusi, the inclusion of these men as witnesses suggests that they may have been Titu Cusi's sources for the early parts of his *History*. The complexity of his *History* is evident here. Titu Cusi chose forms for communication that had no connection to Inca practice. The *History* follows the same form as the letters and reports (called *relaciones* and *memoriales*) that passed from royal officials in the Americas to Spain. It was written for essentially the same purpose: to inform the king. At the same time, it incorporated forms of indigenous oral discourse. It may have incorporated these oral forms even though the written text would have been read by the king or his officials, rather than performed. In attempting to breach a cultural divide, Titu Cusi created an entirely new and original literary genre.

Telling the Story of the Conquest

Titu Cusi told one version of the story of the "conquest." His version represents the point of view of the Vilcabamba Incas at a particular moment in time. It is not the only "Inca" account of what happened in those years, nor should it be assumed that the Spaniards who were there or who had

access to eyewitness testimony do not offer insight into the initial engagement between Incas and Spaniards from different points of view.

One of the most important accounts of "what happened" in those years
was written by Juan de Betanzos, as noted earlier. Betanzos was married
to Cusi Rimay, a cousin of Atahuallpa and a member of Capac Ayllo, the
lineage of Tupa Inca Yupanqui, the tenth Inca on the Inca genealogical
list. Because of his wife's connection to this lineage, Betanzos represents
a story told by the members of the Inca elite most closely connected to
the Inca expansion. These individuals had better pedigrees than the Incas
of Vilcabamba, but the Spaniards had not recognized their line. They had
made an accommodation with the Spaniards, and when Betanzos wrote
about the events following the Spaniard's arrival in the Inca territory,
probably around 1551, they had different concerns than their Vilcabamba
cousins. Betanzos was a Spanish interpreter, and his account appears to be
a translation of the story told by well-informed Inca sources about what
was going on in Atahuallpa's camp before and after his capture. Betanzos'
version of the events in Cajamarca is closer to the Spanish accounts:
Atahuallpa had won the civil war and was Inca in his own right; Manco
was only named Inca after Atahuallpa's death. Titu Cusi had claimed that
his father had been named Inca and that Atahuallpa and Huascar attempted to take advantage of his father's youth and usurp his rule. There
was no monolithic Inca perspective on what happened in the years after
the Spaniards arrived in Andean territory.

Some Incas would assert that the events of Cajamarca, when Atahuallpa
was captured and put to death by the Spaniards, formed the defining moment of the conquest. Titu Cusi's *History*, however, forces us to question
that representation. As Titu Cusi reminds us, the skirmish in Cajamarca
must be considered in the context of the war between Atahuallpa and his
brother Huascar, a war that Atahuallpa had effectively won before Pizarro
entered Peru. When Pizarro captured and killed Atahuallpa, he restarted
the war. When he named Tupa Huallpa, then Manco, as Inca, he gave the
Cusco faction a second chance to consolidate the power of Cusco.

How the capture of Atahuallpa came to be seen as the central event of
the conquest of Peru is a story worth telling. By the time Betanzos wrote
his account (before 1557), Incas in Cusco were beginning to remember
Atahuallpa as the member of a respected Inca lineage, not as the winner
of a war that resulted in the commission of many atrocities on the inhab-

itants of Cusco. Atahuallpa's relatives attributed his capture and execution to the treacherous behavior of an interpreter who had slept with one of Atahuallpa's wives (the story told in Betanzos). The injustice done by Pizarro to Atahuallpa is clearly evident in Betanzos' retelling of the conquest. Betanzos' extremely unflattering portrait of Huascar also indicates that the elite Incas he consulted in Cusco told the story of the Inca civil war from Atahuallpa's point of view in the decades following the Spanish arrival.

What is at the heart of the difference between the accounts of Titu Cusi and Betanzos? The difference appears to grow out of differences in status within the Inca dynasty. In Betanzos' version of Manco's story, Manco's mother was from Anta, a town near Cusco. She was Inca, but not a descendant on both her father's and mother's side, as were the elite Inca lineages of the upper moiety of Cusco, called Hanancusco. Atahuallpa's mother, as Betanzos records, traced her descent from Pachacuti, the ninth Inca ruler, whose descendants were from Hanancusco. A status passed through the Inca dynastic line that made them *capac*. This status was inherited through both the mother's and father's lines, and it was most concentrated when both the mother and father were descended from the dynastic lineages of Hanancusco (Julien, *Reading Inca History,* 27–35). Although other authors, notably Cieza de León in the second part of the *Crónica del Perú* (c. 1554), cast aspersions on Atahuallpa's pedigree (Cieza says Atahuallpa's mother was from Quito, in what is now Ecuador), Betanzos is an excellent source of information about such things, and the best conclusion that can be drawn is that Atahuallpa was held in higher regard among the Cusco Incas than Manco and his descendants.

Titu Cusi and Betanzos are the best sources to read for an Inca point of view, but there is a third, although much later, account that should be mentioned. Called the *Discurso,* it was drawn from the descendants of Paullu Inca, another son of Huayna Capac and an important non-Inca woman called Añas Collque from the region of Huaylas. Paullu had no claim to succeed as Inca following Inca rules, but he very quickly realized that the Spaniards were operating with a different rulebook. He accompanied Francisco Pizarro's partner, Diego de Almagro, to Chile in 1535, arriving in Cusco again after Manco had laid siege to Cusco in 1536. Almagro gave Paullu the title of Inca before returning to Cusco. But Almagro and Pizarro were soon at war, and Paullu quickly shifted his allegiance

to the winning side after Hernando Pizarro executed Almagro in 1538. Paullu's story, written by his descendants in the early seventeenth century, highlights his collaboration with the Spaniards. In the beginning, he was very much Manco's man. It is too bad that we do not have an account of the events from Paullu's point of view, from either the time he was subordinate to Manco, or in the years just following, when he had hopes of becoming Inca himself.

The Spaniards, of course, also wrote about the events following Francisco Pizarro's arrival in Cusco, and their accounts are characterized by differences in perspective, especially given the emerging conflict between Francisco Pizarro and his partner, Diego de Almagro. Especially interesting is an anonymous letter called the *Sitio del Cuzco* by its publishers, written in April 1539 by someone inside Pizarro's camp. This letter offers great insight into what was going on in the Pizarro camp during the time Manco laid siege to Cusco. A careful reading of this Spanish text alongside Titu Cusi's results in a deeper understanding of how Manco lost Peru to the Spaniards. The *Relación de muchas cosas acaescidas* (c. 1552), another anonymous Spanish account, offers still another perspective on the events of those years. The author was a Spanish cleric and a follower of Almagro. Historians suspect that he was either Cristóbal de Molina (often called "the Almagrist," to distinguish him from another cleric of the same name who wrote about the Incas, who was called "the Cuzqueño") or Bartolomé de Segovia, but his identity has never been adequately confirmed. In any case, there have been few careful comparisons of these Spanish accounts, and nothing at all has been done to explore the central event of the Spanish conquest from their differing points of view.

One reason why so little has been written about the Inca effort to oust the Spaniards from Peru is that this effort has not been seen as the central event of the Spanish conquest, but rather as some sort of rebellion. The capture of Atahuallpa at Cajamarca has been portrayed as the event that established Spanish power and effectively subjugated the Incas. When all of the different narratives—Spanish and Inca—are considered together, however, a different picture of the events in Cajamarca emerges. Betanzos' account suggests that the Incas of Cusco thought the Spaniards would eventually return home: only after Pizarro made *encomienda* grants (a regranting of the tribute owed to the Spanish crown in August 1535) did Manco realize that they were staying. Titu Cusi says that the Spaniards understood

that the true Inca lived in Cusco and, casting Atahuallpa aside, traveled there to meet him. Though the loss of the war by the Cusco faction is not a topic that Titu Cusi dwells on at any length in his *History,* he does put Pizarro's support for the beleaguered Cusco faction on record; and Manco was not subordinate to Francisco Pizarro or his brothers at first. Titu Cusi writes that Pizarro's freedom of movement was restricted upon his arrival in Cusco; it took some time for the Spaniards to turn the tables on Manco. To Titu Cusi, it was the siege of Cusco—not the events in Cajamarca—that led to the defeat of the Incas and the loss of Peru.

The Forgotten Inca

That several different versions of the Spanish conquest exist comes as no surprise; such diversity of perspectives is to be expected when a country is torn apart by civil war. But we might wonder how subsequent historio-graphical research singled out the death of Atahuallpa as the defining mo-ment in the takeover of the Inca empire. After all, Pizarro recognized Manco Inca—not Atahuallpa—as the ruler of Peru and the heir to the royal line de-scended from Manco Capac, the first Inca; this recognition, which extended to Manco's sons, was acknowledged in both Peru and the uppermost levels of royal administration in Spain. Following this line of reasoning, represen-tatives of the crown sought Titu Cusi's acquiescence in 1565; King Philip II himself ratified his agreement with Titu Cusi in 1569. Viceroy Toledo ex-ecuted Tupa Amaru in 1572 because he was next in line to be Inca. Two centuries later, in 1780, a man calling himself Tupa Amaru led a rebellion against Spanish authorities and attempted to restore Inca rule; he traced his descent back to the first Tupa Amaru through a daughter. Thus Manco and his heirs remained, in both Spanish and Inca memory, the legitimate native lords of the Andes. How, then, have modern historians overlooked their centrality to the story of the conquest of Peru? The answer seems to lie with Titu Cusi's own contemporaries and the politics of memory.

Though the memory of Tupa Amaru lingered, oddly enough, Titu Cusi was forgotten after the fall of Vilcabamba. Neither of the two most im-portant indigenous historians—Felipe Guaman Poma de Ayala and Gar-cilaso Inca de la Vega—mention him in their narratives, written in the early seventeenth century. The identification of the "last Inca" was a contentious matter. Viceroy Toledo did what he could to establish that Huascar had

been the last legitimate Inca, and that neither the Vilcabamba Incas nor the descendants of Atahuallpa had legitimate claims to rule. Guaman Poma rejects this Toledan view in his *El primer nueva corónica y buen gobierno* (c. 1615); that is, he does not exclude the Vilcabamba Incas from his story. He follows the story of Manco Inca and his retreat to Vilcabamba, the Spanish recognition of Manco's son Sayre Tupa as Inca ruler following his father's death, and Sayre Tupa's marriage to María Cusi Huarcay. Guaman Poma also relates the capture of Tupa Amaru by Martín García de Loyola, Toledo's captain, and his subsequent execution in Cusco. Curiously, Guaman Poma draws visual parallels in his descriptions of the executions of Atahuallpa and Tupa Amaru, showing both as having been garroted, even though the former was garroted and the latter beheaded. Guaman Poma's account may already reflect an ambiguity as to which event truly represented the end of the Inca line.

Even though *El primer nueva corónica* mentions the Vilcabamba Incas, Guaman Poma curiously neglects to mention Titu Cusi. But Guaman Poma's history was not widely read until its publication in the twentieth century; it therefore had little effect on later authors. On the other hand, Garcilaso Inca de la Vega's 1617 history of the first decades of Spanish contact—the *Historia general*—was widely read; it, too, omitted any mention of Titu Cusi, and an omission by Garcilaso requires explaining. As noted, Garcilaso was born in Cusco to a Spanish father and an Inca mother at about the same time as Titu Cusi. Garcilaso's father later married a Spanish woman, who bore him two daughters and then died abruptly. Garcilaso, unrecognized in his father's will, left Peru in 1559 to seek his fortune in Spain. Though it is possible that Garcilaso had not heard of Titu Cusi before leaving Peru, it is almost impossible that he did not hear of Titu Cusi in subsequent years, especially since he maintained contact with people in the Andes and received visitors from Cusco. One of his visitors was Juan Arias Maldonado, the son of Diego Maldonado and an Inca mother and a contemporary of both Garcilaso and Titu Cusi. Juan Arias Maldonado left for Spain at the end of the 1560s and visited Garcilaso at least twice. He must have told Garcilaso about the negotiations with Titu Cusi in 1564 and 1565 as well as other events that occurred in Peru in the years following Garcilaso's departure; since Juan Arias had been mixed up in the events related to the plot to marry Beatriz to Cristóbal Maldonado, he certainly knew about the bargain that had been made with Titu Cusi regarding her marriage to Titu Cusi's son.

Because Garcilaso was accepted as an authority on Peru, his failure to mention Titu Cusi in the *Historia general* had serious repercussions on how other historians wrote about the Incas in subsequent years. When the Spanish historian Andrés González de Barcía y Carballido y Zúñiga republished Garcilaso's *Comentarios reales* in 1723 (a work first published in 1609), he noted that Garcilaso had not mentioned Titu Cusi at all and tried to add what he could about the life of this Inca to his prologue. The title page included the following notation: "Second printing, corrected, with the life of Inti Cusi Titu Iupanqui, penultimate Inca, added" (*Segunda impresión, enmendada: y añadida la vida de Inti Cusi Titu Iupanqui, penultimo Inca . . .*). Barcía had read the chronicle of the Augustinian Antonio de la Calancha, published in 1638. Calancha provided detailed information on the time Titu Cusi governed Vilcabamba; he also had a good deal to say about the Augustinian friars in Vilcabamba, since one of them, Diego Ortiz, had been killed in the wake of Titu Cusi's death, and an effort was being made to represent him as a martyr and to seek his canonization. Titu Cusi played heavily in Calancha's account of the Augustinian mission.

An Inca History in 1570

Though the portrait Titu Cusi paints in his *History* of the Spaniards who arrived in Peru was necessarily an ugly one—they had, after all, killed his father and brought about the destruction of the Inca empire—he cannot hide a certain admiration for them. He took every opportunity to learn from them: his own private Augustinian tutors taught him the tenets of Christianity, and he had learned how to communicate in the Spanish language from the notary who was his constant companion for a decade. And whether or not his conversion to Christianity was sincere, he had at least become thoroughly acquainted with the beliefs of the Spaniards.

Defeat was not Titu Cusi's central theme. He dealt with present circumstances in a constructive, optimistic, forward-looking way. Beyond the story of how his father lost Peru to the Spaniards, the story should be read as the effort of an individual deeply involved in negotiating a place for himself and his family in a changing world. Titu Cusi made heroic efforts to communicate across a cultural divide in a foreign medium. His account impresses the reader with its ability to address a Spanish king in terms the king would understand. Titu Cusi's *History* succeeds in its endeavor

to explain his father's and his own actions, and although his efforts were not repaid in his own time, there is no reason they should not be repaid in ours.

The Manuscript and Prior Publication

The manuscript of Titu Cusi's *History* is kept in the library of the Escorial, bound with other documents in a volume that bears the signature L.I.5. The volume has 346 folios, and the manuscript occupies folios 132 recto to 196 verso. Folio 197 is blank. On folio 198 recto, the following is written: "History of the Incas. This is the instruction that the Inca Don Diego de Castro Titu Cusi Yupanqui gave to the Licentiate Lope García de Castro. It belongs to the lord Licentiate Castro and should be returned to His Lordship" (*Historia de los yngas. Es la instruccion que el Inga D. Diego de Castro Titu Cussi Yupangui dio al licenciado Lope García de Castro. Es del señor licenciado Castro y ase de uoluer a su Señoria*). On folio 199, another note is written in the same hand: "This copy of the Incas was made from another that the lord Licentiate Castro gave to me in Madrid, in the year [15]74" (*Saco esta copia de los yngas de otra del señor licenciado Castro que me dio en Madrid, año de 74.*). Castro took the manuscript back to Spain and presented it to the king, although perhaps not until the year 1574. The manuscript in the Escorial appears to be the copy mentioned on folio 199. The note on folio 198 suggests that Castro allowed his copy of the manuscript to be copied for the king, but wanted it returned. The manuscript was written in a sixteenth-century hand, entirely consistent with a date of 1574.

If the manuscript became part of the king's library in those years, it sat there for three centuries before any part of it was published. Marcos Jiménez de la Espada included folios 182 verso to 193 verso in an appendix to his edition of *Las guerras civiles del Perú* by Pedro de Cieza de León (1877).

The first complete edition of the *History* was published in Lima in 1916 by Horacio H. Urteaga.[4] It was based on a transcription of the Escorial manuscript in the possession of Manuel González de la Rosa, who had intended to publish it himself. The transcription was incomplete, so Urteaga

---

4. All editions of the *History* appear under Titu Cusi's name in the Selected Bibliography.

had someone transcribe the missing parts from the manuscript at the Escorial (Romero, 1916, p. xxvii). A second edition, based on the Urteaga edition, was published in Lima in 1973.

Since then, three new Spanish transcriptions have been made from the Escorial manuscript—two were published in Peru (*Ynstruçion del ynga Don Diego de Castro Titu Cussi Yupangui*, 1985; and *Instrucción al licenciado don Lope García de Castro*, 1992) and one in Spain (*En el encuentro de dos mundos*, 1988). The newest Spanish-language edition, based on the 1916 and 1985 Lima editions, appeared in Mexico, in modernized Spanish (*Instrucción del Inca don Diego de Castro Titu Cusi Yupanqui*, 2001). Translations based on the Escorial text have appeared in German (*Die Erschütterung der Welt: ein Inka König berichtet*, 1984) and Japanese (*Inka no hanran*, 1987). Brief excerpts from the manuscript were also published in English in a collection by Parry and Keith. After the translation presented here was submitted, an English translation by Ralph Bauer was published (*An Inca Account of the Conquest of Peru*, 2005) based on the Escorial manuscript. A second English translation by Nicole Delia Legnani was published shortly afterward (*Titu Cusi: A 16th Century Account of the Conquest*, 2005); a modernized Spanish version, based on one of the Peruvian editions (1985), was also included with Legnani's translation.

The Spanish transcription presented here is based directly on the Escorial manuscript. It reproduces the section titles and paragraph breaks of the original. I have also divided the translation into four sections to mark the beginnings of different parts: [1] the Instruction, [2] the time of Manco Inca's rule, [3] the time of Titu Cusi's rule, and [4] the Power of Attorney. The *History* technically begins with section [2] and ends near the end of section [3], where a break has been introduced with a line of asterisks to mark the return to the Instruction. The transcription of the text from the Spanish original and its translation into English appear on facing pages to facilitate a critical reading, which is one of the major virtues of this edition. In the translation, I have attempted to adhere as closely as possible to the meaning of the original, while striving for readability in English. The Spanish transcription follows the sixteenth-century original closely. The major editorial intrusion is the addition of punctuation to clarify meaning; there is no punctuation in the original. Anything appearing in square brackets is mine.

Selected Bibliography

Adorno, Rolena, ed. *From Oral to Written Expression: Native Andean Chronicles of the Early Colonial Period.* Syracuse, N.Y.: Maxwell School of Citizenship and Public Affairs, Syracuse University, 1982.

Betanzos, Juan de. *Suma y narración de los Incas* [1551–1557]. Edited by María del Carmen Martín Rubio. Madrid: Ediciones Atlas, 1987.

———. *Narrative of the Incas by Juan de Betanzos.* Translated and edited by Roland Hamilton and Dana Buchanan. Austin, Tex.: University of Texas Press, 1996.

Calancha, Antonio de la. *Corónica moralizada del orden de San Agustín en el Perú con sucesos egenplares vistos en esta monarquia.* Barcelona: P. Lacavallería, 1638.

Campos y Fernández de Sevilla, Francisco Javier. *Catálogo del fondo manuscrito americano de la Real Biblioteca del Escorial.* San Lorenzo: Estudios Superiores del Escorial, 1993.

Chang-Rodríguez, Raquel. "Writing as Resistance: Peruvian History and the *Relación* of Titu Cusi Yupanqui." In *From Oral to Written Expression: Native Andean Chronicles of the Early Colonial Period,* edited by Rolena Adorno, 41–64. Syracuse, N.Y.: Maxwell School of Citizenship and Public Affairs, Syracuse University, 1982.

———. *La apropiación del signo: tres cronistas indígenas del Perú.* Tempe, Ariz.: Center of Latin American Studies, Arizona State University, 1988.

Cieza de León, Pedro de. *Tercero libro de las guerras civiles del Perú, el cual de llama La guerra de Quito* [c. 1554]. Edited by Marcos Jiménez de la Espada. Madrid: Imprenta de M. G. Hernández, 1877.

———. *Crónica del Perú, primera parte* [1553]. Lima: Pontificia Universidad Católica del Perú, 1984.

———. *Crónica del Perú, segunda parte* [1554]. Lima: Pontificia Universidad Católica del Perú, 1985.

Cook, Noble David, ed. *Tasa de la visita general de francisco de Toledo* [1583]. Lima: Universidad Nacional Mayor de San Marcos, Seminario de Historia Rural Andina, 1975.

D'Altroy, Terence. *Provincial Power in the Inka Empire.* Washington: Smithsonian Institution Press, 1992.

"Discurso sobre la descendencia y gobierno de los Incas" [1602–1608]. In *Colección de Libros y Documentos referentes a la Historia del Perú,* vol. 3 (series 2), edited by Horacio H. Urteaga, 3–53. Lima: Imprenta y Librería Sanmartí y Cía., 1920.

Espinoza Soriano, Waldemar. "Los huancas aliados de la conquista: tres informa-

ciones inéditas sobre la participación indígena en la conquista del Perú, 1558, 1560 y 1561." *Anales científicos de la Universidad del Centro* (Huancayo, Peru) 1 (1971): 9–692.

Garcilaso Inca de la Vega. *Primera parte de los Comentarios reales, que tratan, de el origen de los Incas, reies, que fueron del Peru, de su idolatria, leies, y govierno, en paz, y en guerra: de sus vidas, y conquistas: y de todo lo que fue aquel imperio, y su republica, antes que los Españoles pasaran, a el* [1609]. Edited by Andrés González Barcía Carballido y Zúñiga. Madrid: Oficina Real, 1723.

———. "Historia general del Perú." In *Obras completas del Inca Garcilaso de la Vega*, edited by Carmelo Saenz de Santa María, vols. III–IV. Biblioteca de Autores Españoles, vols. 134–35. Madrid: Ediciones Atlas, 1960–65.

González Holguín, Diego. *Vocabulario de la lengua general de todo el Peru llamada Qquicchua, o del Inca* [1608]. Edited by Raúl Porras Barrenechea. Lima: Imprenta Santa María, 1952.

Guaman Poma de Ayala, Felipe. *El primer nueva corónica y buen gobierno* [c. 1615]. 3rd ed. Edited by John V. Murra and Rolena Adorno. Mexico City, Mexico: Siglo Veintiuno, 1992.

Guillén Guillén, Edmundo. "Documentos inéditos para la historia de los incas de Vilcabamba: La capitulación del gobierno español con Titu Cusi Yupanqui." *Historia y Cultura* (Lima) 10 (1977): 47–93.

———. "Titu Cusi Yupanqui y su tiempo: El estado imperial inka y su trágico fin." *Historia y Cultura* (Lima) 13–14 (1981): 61–99.

———. *La guerra de reconquista Inka*. Lima: R. A. Ediciones, 1994.

Hampe Martínez, Teodoro. "Relación de los encomenderos y repartimientos del Perú en 1561." *Historia y Cultura* (Lima) 12 (1979): 75–117.

Hemming, John. *The Conquest of the Incas*. New York: Harcourt Brace Jovanovich, 1970.

Jákfalvi-Leiva, Susana. "De la voz a la escritura: La Relación de Titu Cusi Yupanqui." *Revista de Crítica Literaria Latinomericana* (Lima) 19, no. 37 (1993): 259–77.

Jiménez de la Espada, Marcos, ed. *Tercero libro de las Guerras Civiles del Perú, el cual se llama la guerra de Quito, hecha por Pedro Cieza de León coronista de las cosas de las Indias*. Madrid: Biblioteca Hispano-Ultramarina, Imprenta de M.G. Hernández, 1877.

Julien, Catherine. "Inca Decimal Administration in the Lake Titicaca Region." In *The Inca and Aztec States, 1400–1800, Anthropology and History*, edited by George A. Collier, Renato I. Rosaldo, and John D. Wirth, 119–51. New York: Academic Press, 1982.

———. "How Inca Decimal Administration Worked." *Ethnohistory* 35, no. 1 (Summer 1988): 257–79.

———. "La Encomienda del Inca." *Actas del IV Congreso Internacional de Etnohistoria* 2. Lima: Pontificia Universidad Católica del Perú, 1998.

Julien, Catherine. "La organización parroquial del Cuzco." *Tawantinsuyu* (Canberra, Australia) 5 (1998): 82–96.

———. "Francisca Pizarro, la cuzqueña, y su madre, la *coya* Ynguill." *Revista del Archivo Regional del Cusco* (Cusco) 15 (June 2000): 53–74.

———. "Inca Estates and the Encomienda: Hernando Pizarro's Holdings in Cusco." *Andean Past* 6 (2000): 229–75.

———. *Reading Inca History.* Iowa City: University of Iowa Press, 2000.

———. "Las tumbas de Sacsahuaman y el estilo Cuzco-Inca." *Ñawpa Pacha* (Berkeley, Calif.) 25–27 (1987–1989), 2004: 1–125.

———. "Punchao en España." *El hombre y los Andes, Homenaje a Franklin Plase G. Y.,* edited by Javier Flores Espinoza and Rafael Varón Gabai, 2, 709–15. Lima: Pontificia Universidad Católica del Perú, 2002.

Lee, Vincent R. *Forgotten Vilcabamba: The Stronghold of the Incas.* Jackson Hole, Wyo.: Sixpac Manco Publications, 2000.

Levillier, Roberto. *Don Francisco de Toledo, supremo organizador del Perú: su vida, su obra (1512–1582).* 2 vols. Buenos Aires: Espasa-Calpe, 1940.

Lienhard, Martin. "La épica incaica en tres textos coloniales: Juan de Betanzos, Titu Cusi Yupanqui y el Ollantay." *Lexis* (Lima) 9, no. 1 (1983): 61–85.

Loaysa, Jerónimo de. "Carta del Arz. fr. Jerónimo de Loaysa, Arzobispo de los Reyes, Lima, 25 mayo 1572." *La iglesia de España en el Perú,* edited by Emilio Lissón, 2, no. 9, 609–10. Seville: Editorial Católica Española, 1944.

Lockhart, James. *The Men of Cajamarca.* Austin, Tex.: University of Texas Press, 1972.

Lohmann Villena, Guillermo. "El Inca Titu Cusi Yupanqui y su entrevista con el oidor Matienzo 1565." *Mercurio Peruano* (Lima) 23, no. 167 (1941): 3–18.

———. "Propuestas de solución de juristas y políticos." In *La ética en la conquista de América,* edited by Demetrio Ramos et al., 631–58. Corpus Hispanorum de Pace, 25. Madrid: Consejo Superior de Investigaciones Científicas, 1984.

Mackenhenie, Carlos A. "Apuntes sobre don Diego de Castro Titu Cusi Yupanqui." *Revista Histórica* (Lima) 3 (1909): 371–90.

Mannheim, Bruce, and Krista Van Vleet. "The Dialogics of Southern Quechua Narrative." *American Anthropologist* 100, no. 2 (1998): 326–46.

Martín Rubio, María del Carmen. "Dos fuentes andinas en la biblioteca del Real Monasterio de El Escorial: Suma y Narración de los Incas y la Instrucción de Titu Cusi Yupanqui." In *Catálogo del fondo manuscrito americano de la Real Biblioteca del Escorial,* edited by Francisco Javier Campos and Fernández de Sevilla, 235–51. San Lorenzo del Escorial: Ediciones Escurialenses, 1993.

Matienzo, Juan de. *Gobierno del Perú* [1567]. Edited by Guillermo Lohmann Villena. Travaux de l'Institut Français d'Etudes Andines, 40. Lima, 1967.

Medina, José Toribio, ed. *Colección de documentos inéditos para la historia de Chile desde el viaje de Magallanes hasta la batalla de Maipó, 1518–1818*. 30 vols. Santiago: Imprenta Ercilla, 1886–1902.

Mills, Kenneth. "Bad Christians in Colonial Peru." *Colonial Latin American Review* (Basingstoke, England) 5, no. 2 (1996): 183–218.

Molina, Cristóbal de. "Relación de las fábulas i ritos de los Ingas." In *Fábulas y mitos de los incas*, edited by Henrique Urbano and Pierre Duviols, 49–134. Madrid: Historia 16, 1989.

Moliner, María. *Diccionario de Uso del Español*. 2 vols. Madrid: Editorial Gredos, 1992.

Niles, Susan A. "The Provinces in the Heartland: Stylistic Variation and Architectural Innovation near Inca Cuzco." In *Provincial Inca: Archaeological and Ethnohistorical Assessment of the Impact of the Inca State*, edited by Michael Malpass, 145–76. Iowa City, Iowa: University of Iowa Press, 1993.

———. *The Shape of Inca History*. Iowa City, Iowa: University of Iowa Press, 1999.

Nowack, Kerstin. "Las provisiones de Titu Cusi Yupangui." *Revista Andina* (Cusco) 38, no. 1 (2004): 159–79.

Nowack, Kerstin, and Catherine Julien. "La campaña de Toledo contra los señores naturales andinos: el destierro de los Incas de Vilcabamba y Cuzco." *Historia y Cultura* (Lima) 23 (1999): 15–81.

Oviedo, Gabriel de. "Relación de lo que subcedió en la ciudad del Cuzco, cerca de los conciertos y horden que su Magestad mandó asentar con el Inca Titu Cuxi Yopanqui y del cuso [sic] que tovo la guerra que en razón de esto se le hizo." *Revista Histórica* (Lima) 2 (1907): 66–73.

Parry, John, and Robert C. Keith. "Instrucción del inga Don Diego de Castro Titu Cusi Yupangui, 1570." In *New Iberian World: A Documentary History of the Discovery and Settlement of Latin America to the Early Seventeenth Century*, vol. 4 of *The Andes*, edited by John Parry and Robert C. Keith, 135–45, 268–72. New York: Times Books, 1985.

Porras Barrenechea, Raú. "Tres cronistas del Inkario; Juan de Betanzos, Titu Cusi Yupanqui (1529–1570), y Juan Santa Cruz Pachacuti." *La Prensa* (Lima) January 1, 1542, p. 5.

Quiroga, Pedro de. *Libro intitulado Coloquis de la verdad, trata de las causas e inconvinientes que impeden la doctrina e conversión de los indios de los reinos del Pirú, y de los daños, e males, e agravios que padecen* [c. 1563]. Edited by Julián Zarco Cuevas. Seville: Tipografía Zarzuela, 1922.

Regalado de Hurtado, Liliana. "*La Relación* de Titu Cusi Yupanqui: valor de un testimonio tardio." *Histórica* (Lima) 5, no. 1 (1981): 45–61.

———. *El Inca Titu Cusi Yupanqui y su tiempo: los incas de Vilcabamba y los primeros cuarenta años del dominio español*. Lima: Pontificia Universidad Católica del Perú, Fondo Editorial, 1997.

"Relación de muchas cosas acaescidas" [c. 1552]. Conquista y población del Perú. In *Colección de documentos históricos para la historia de Chile,* edited by José Toribio Medina, 4: 428–82. Santiago: Imprenta Elzeviriana, 1895.

Rowe, John Howland. "What Kind of a City Was Inca Cuzco?" *Ñawpa Pacha* 5 (1967): 59–76.

———. "An Account of the Shrines of Ancient Cuzco." *Ñawpa Pacha* 17 (1979): 1–80.

———. "El barrio de Cayau Cachi y la parroquia de Belén." In *Horacio H. Villanueva Urteaga, La casa de la moneda del Cuzco, homenaje de la facultad de ciencias sociales y los amigos del autor,* 173–87. Cusco: Universidad Nacional de San Antonio Abad, 1994.

———. "Como se apoderó Francisco Pizarro del Perú." *Actas del IV Congreso Internacional de Etnohistoria,* vol. 2, 517–34. Lima: Pontificia Universidad Católica del Perú, 1998.

Salomon, Frank. "Chronicles of the Impossible." In *From Oral to Written Expression: Native Andean Chronicles of the Early Colonial Period,* 9–39. Syracuse, N.Y.: Maxwell School of Citizenship and Public Affairs, Syracuse University, 1982.

Salomon, Frank, and George L. Urioste, eds. *The Huarochirí Manuscript: A Testament of Ancient and Colonial Andean Religion.* Austin, Tex.: University of Texas Press, 1991.

Sarmiento de Gamboa, Pedro. *Geschichte des Inkareiches* [1572]. Edited by Richard Pietschmann. Abhandlungen der Königlichen Gesellschaft der Wissenschaften zu Göttingen, philologisch-historische Klasse, new series, 6, no. 4. Berlin: Weidmannsche Buchhandlung, 1906.

Sepúlveda, Juan Ginés de. *Democrates segundo; o, De las justas causas de la guerra contra los indios* [1550]. Edited by Angel Losada. Madrid: Consejo Superior de Investigaciones Científicas, Instituto Francisco de Vitoria, 1951.

"Sitio del Cuzco." In *Relación del sitio del Cusco y principio de las guerras civiles del Perú hasta la muerte de Diego de Almagro, 1535–1539.* Colección de libros españoles raros o curiosos, vol. 13. Madrid: Imprenta de Miguel Ginesta, 1879.

Temple, Ella Dunbar. "Notas sobre el virrey Toledo y los Incas de Vilcabamba." *Documenta* (Lima) 2, no. 1 (1950): 614–51.

Titu Cusi Yupanqui, Diego de Castro. *Relación de la conquista del Perú y hechos del Inca Manco II por D. Diego de Castro Tito Cussi Yupangui Inca.* Edited by Horacio H. Urteaga. Colección de Libros y Documentos para la Historia del Perú, 2. Lima: Imprenta y Librería Sanmartí, 1916.

———. *Relación de la conquista del Perú.* Edited by Francisco Carrillo. Colección Clásicos Peruanos. Lima: Ediciones de la Biblioteca Universitaria, 1973.

———. *Die Erschütterung der Welt: ein Inka König berichtet über den Kampf gegen die Spanier.* Edited and translated by Martin Lienhard. Olten and

Freiburg on Breisgau: Walter-Verlag, 1985.

———. *Ynstruçion del ynga Don Diego de Castro Titu Cussi Yupangui para el muy ilustre Señor el licenciado Lope García de Castro, governador que fue destos reynos del Piru, tocante a los negoçios que con su magestad, en su nombre, por su poder a de tratar; la qual es esta que se sigue* [1570]. Edited by Luis Millones. Lima: El Virrey, 1985.

———. *Inka no hanran: hiseifukusha no koe.* Edited by Hidefuji Someda. Iwanami bunko. Tokyo: Iwanami Shoten, 1987.

———. *En el encuentro de dos mundos: los incas de Vilcabamba: Instrucción del inga Don Diego de Castro Tito Cussi Yupangui* [1570]. Edited by María del Carmen Martín Rubio. Madrid: Ediciones Atlas, 1988.

———. *Instrucción al licenciado don Lope García de Castro* [1570]. Edited by Liliana Regalado de Hurtado. Colección Clásicos Peruanos, 9. Lima: Pontifica Universidad Católica del Perú, Fondo Editorial, 1992.

———. *Instrucción del Inca don Diego de Castro Titu Cusi Yupanqui.* Edited by Alessandra Luiselli. Mexico City, Mexico: Universidad Autónoma de México, Coordinación de Difusión Cultural, Dirección de Literatura, 2001.

———. *An Inca Account of the Conquest of Peru by Titu Cusi Yupanqui.* Edited and translated by Ralph Bauer. Boulder: University Press of Colorado, 2005.

———. *Titu Cusi: A 16th Century Account of the Conquest.* Edited and translated by Nicole Delia Legnani. Cambridge, Mass.: Harvard University Press, 2005.

Verdesio, Gustavo. "Traducción y contrato en la obra de Titu Cusi Yupanqui." *Bulletin of Hispanic Studies* (Liverpool) 72 (1995): 403–12.

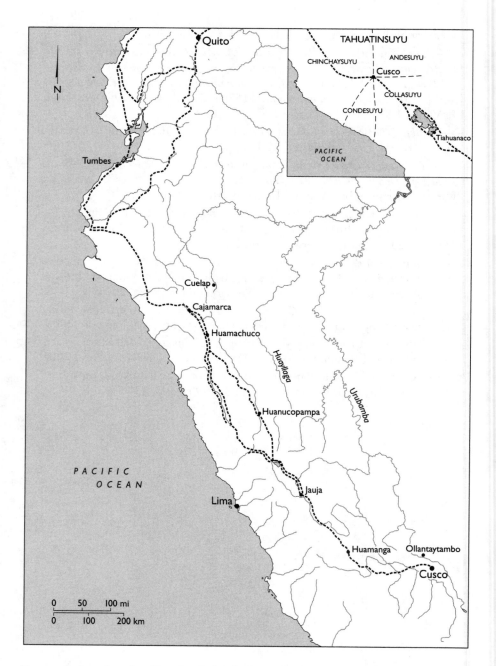

Routes taken by the Spaniards in their early travel in the Inca empire

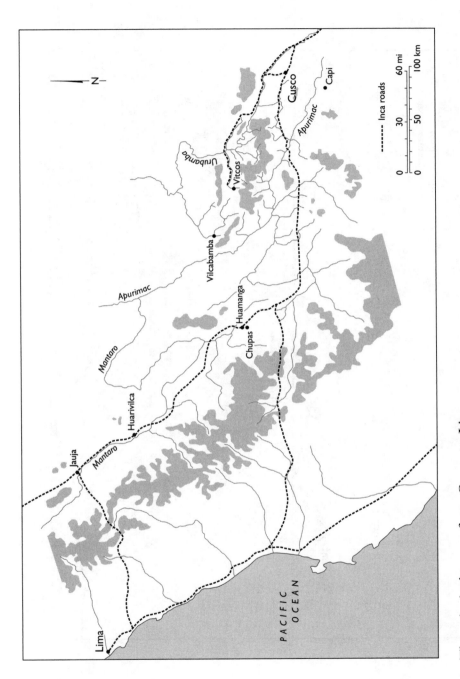

The principal routes from Cusco to Lima

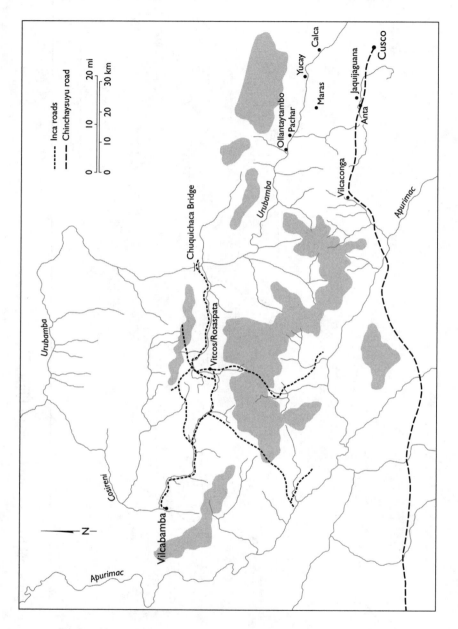

The Vilcabamba region

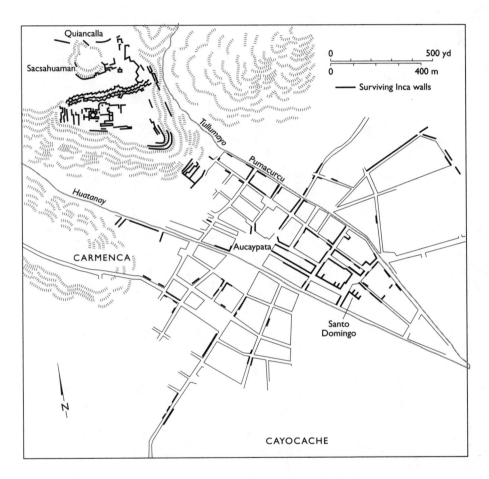

Cusco

History of How the Spaniards Arrived in Peru

(Relasçion de como los españoles entraron en el Peru)

[1]

**Ynstruçion del ynga don Diego de Castro Titu Cussi Yupangui
para el muy Yllustre señor el liçençiado Lope Garçia
de Castro, gouernador que fue destoss rreynos del Piru,
tocante a los negoçios que con Su Magestad
en su nonbre por su poder a de tratar,
la qual es esta que se sigue:**

Por quanto yo, don Diego de Castro Titu Cussi[1] Yupangui, nieto de
Guaina[2] Capac e hijo de Mango Ynga Yupangui, señores naturales que
fueron de los rreinos[3] y prouinçias[4] del Piru, he rreçiuido muchas merçedes
y fauor del muy yllustre señor el liçençiado Lope Garçia de Castro, gouernador que fue destos rreynos por su Magestad del rrey don Phelipe nuestro señor, me a[5] pareçido que, pues su Señoria ba destos rreynos a los de
España y es persona de balor y gran cristiandad, no podria yo hallar quien
con mejor titulo y voluntad me faboresçiese en todos mis negoçios que
ante su Magestad aya de presentar y tratar ansy en cosas a my neçesarias
como a mys hijos y deçendientes, para lo qual por el gran credito que de
su Señoria tengo no dexare de ponerlos todos en su mano para que ansy en
vno como en otro, pues en todo hasta aqui me a hecho tanta merçed, en
esta tan prençipal me la haga como yo espero de su muy yllustre persona.

---

1. [The scribe (whose name is unknown) sometimes doubles the letters *f* and *s* where modern
Spanish uses the single letter (as in *Cussi; fflaca* and *gratifficarme* on f. 1; *ffalesçio* and *ffue* on
f. 2; *esso* and *elloss* on f. 1v).]

2. [The scribe uses all three orthographic variants of the Spanish vowel *i* interchangeably: *i latina*
(the letter *i* in English), *i griega* (the letter *y* in English), and *i larga* (no equivalent in English,
but similar to the letter *j*). The letters *i latina* and *i larga* are written as the English *i* in the text;
i griega has been written as "*y*."]

3. [Double *r* (*rr*) is a separate phoneme from *r* in Spanish. Modern Spanish orthography uses
a single *r* to represent this sound when it occurs at the beginning of a word. In this text *rr* is
written as "rr" wherever it occurs, except when it begins a proper noun where it is transcribed
as "R."]

4. [The letters *u, b,* and *v* are also used interchangeably (as in *prouinçias, fauor, ba, balor,* and
vno in this paragraph). Two phonemes may be represented by any of these letters: one similar to
the English vowel *u*, and the other, intermediate between the English consonants *b* and *v*. The
three letters have been transcribed as in the original, and their value must be understood from
the context.]

5. [The letter *h* is often dropped in sixteenth-century Spanish, most notably in conjugations of
the verb *haber* (*a* and *aya* on f. 1; see also *auito* for *hábito* on f. 2v; *vbiese* for *hubiese* on f. 3v;

[1]

Instruction of the Inca Don Diego de Castro Titu Cusi Yupanqui, given to the very illustrious lord, the Licentiate Lope García de Castro (who was governor of these kingdoms of Peru), with regard to the business that he is to conduct with His Majesty in the Inca's name and under his Power of Attorney, as follows:

I, Don Diego de Castro Titu Cusi Yupanqui, grandson of Huayna Capac and son of Manco Inca Yupanqui, natural lords of these kingdoms and provinces of Peru, have received many grants and favors from the very illustrious lord, the Licentiate[1] Lope García de Castro,[2] who was governor of these kingdoms in the name of His Majesty the King Philip II,[3] our lord. It has therefore seemed to me that since His Lordship is leaving these kingdoms to go to those of Spain—and since he is a person of valor and great Christianity—I could not find anyone of better title nor more disposed to represent me in the business that I wish to present and negotiate with the King, regarding what is necessary for me and my children and descendants. For these reasons, and because of the great regard that I have for His Lordship, I do not hesitate to place all of my affairs in his hands. He has always treated me very well and will do what I would expect his very illustrious person to do in such an important matter as this.

---

1. The title Licentiate indicates a professional law degree.
2. Governor of Peru (1564–1569).
3. King of Spain (1556–1598).

Y porque la memoria de los honbres es devil y fflaca e si no nos acu-
rrimos [ocurrimos] a las letras para nos aprouechar dellas en nuestras
neçesidades hera cosa ynposible podernos acordar por estenso de todos
los negoçios largos y de ynportançia que se nos ofresçiesen; y por esso,
vssando de la breuedad posible, me sera neçesario hazer rrecopilaçion de
algunas cosas neçesarias en las quales su Señoria, lleuando mi poder para
ello, me a de hazer merçed de fauoresçerme ante su Magestad en todas
ellass como a la clara de yuso yra declarado y rrelatado, la rrecupilasçion[6]
de las quales cosas es esta que se sigue:

Primeramente, que su Señoria me haga merçed, llegado que sea con
bien a los rreynos de España, de dar a entender a su Magestad del rrey
don Phelipe nuestro señor, debaxo de cuyo anparo yo me he puesto, quien
soy y la neçesidad que, a causa de poseer su Magestad y sus vasallos la tierra
que fue de mis antepasados, en estos montes padezco.

Y podra su Señoria dar la dicha rrelaçion, siendo dello seruido, por
esta via, començando lo primero por quien yo soy e cuyo hijo para que le
conste a su Magestad mas por estençо la rrazon que arriua he dicho para
gratifficarme.

Bien creo que por nuebas de muchas personas se abra publicado quien
fueron los señores naturales antiguos desta tierra y de donde y como
proçedieron, y por esso no me quiero detener açerca desto; solo me hara
su Señoria merçed de avisar a su Magestad de como yo soy el hijo ligitimo, digo el primero y mayorazgo, que my padre Mango Ynga Yupangui
dexo entre otros muchos, de los quales me mando tubiesse cargo e mirase
por ellos como por my propia persona, lo qual yo he hecho desde quel
ffallesçio hasta oy, e lo hago e hare mientras Dios me diere vida, pues es
cossa tan justa que los hijos hagan lo que sus padres les mandan, en espeçial
en sus postrimeros dias.

1v

2

---

aueis for *habeis* on f. 5). It may also be inserted where modern Spanish does not use it (*hera* on
f. 2v; *horden* on f. 12v; *thiene* on f. 14v).]

6. [At times the scribe uses the letter *u* to represent the vowel *o*, and vice versa (*mochacho* for
muchacho on f. 3v; *cochillos* for *cuchillos* on f. 4; *obsurpandole* for *usurpandole* on f. 8). This may
be because Pando was bilingual and the Inca vowel is intermediate between Spanish *o* and *u*.]

The memory of men is weak and fragile, and if we do not rely upon writing to satisfy our needs, the complex and important events that occur 1v will be impossible to remember in detail. For this reason, it is necessary for me to record some of these important matters—trying to be as brief as I can—so that His Lordship, taking my Power of Attorney with him for this purpose, will do me the favor of representing all of them favorably to His Majesty, as will be clearly declared and related herein. My list of instructions is as follows:

First, after His Lordship arrives safely in the kingdoms of Spain, I ask that he do me the favor of making it clear to His Majesty King Philip, our lord (under whose protection I have placed myself), who I am and the suffering I undergo in this wilderness because His Majesty and his vassals have taken possession of the land that belonged to my ancestors.

His Lordship, if he would, could present the following history to the King in the same way. His Lordship could begin with an explanation of who I am and whose son, so that His Majesty has a more complete understanding of why he should gratify my wishes.

I am certain that many people have already taken word to His Majesty about who the natural lords[4] of this land were and where and how they originated.[5] For this reason, I will not say much about these matters.

I ask only that His Lordship do me the favor of advising His Majesty that 2 I am the legitimate son—that is, the firstborn and the son with the right of succession[6]—of the many children left by my father Manco Inca Yupanqui. My father ordered me to take charge of his children and to look after them as I would myself, as I have done from the time he died until now. I have looked after his children and will continue to look after them so long as God grants me life, since it is only right that sons do what their fathers order them to do, especially when their fathers are on their deathbeds.

---

4. Titu Cusi refers to the Incas here as "natural lords" (*señores naturales*), a claim to legitimacy in European terms. There was an argument then being forcefully made that the Incas were not natural lords, but tyrants who had gained ascendancy through conquest by force in the recent past. Spanish usurpation of sovereignty was thus justified (Letter of Francisco de Toledo, Cusco, March 1, 1572, in Levillier, vol. II, 3–13; Matienzo, pt. 1, chs. 1–2: 3–14; Lohmann Villena, "Propuestas," 631–47).

5. Titu Cusi clearly thought saying something about earlier Inca history was important, but he excuses himself from this task since others have already told this story.

6. Here again, he discusses legitimacy in European terms.

Tanbien que su Magestad sepa que mi padre Mango Ynga Yupangui, hijo que ffue de Guaina Capac e nieto de Tupa Ynga Yupangui, y ansy por sus abolengos deçendiendo por linea rrecta ffue el señor prençipal de todos los rreynos del Piru señalado para ello por su padre Guaina Capac y tenido y obedeçido por tal en toda la tierra despues de sus dias, como yo lo fuy, soy y he sido en esta despues quel dicho mi padre ffallesçio.

Y tanbien dar a entender a su Magestad la rrazon por donde yo agora estoy con tanta neçesidad en estos montes, en los quales me dexo mi padre con ella al tienpo que rreinaua y gouernaua el Piru y toda su tierra, que fue en el tienpo que los españoles le desbarataron y mataron.

Y tanbien que sepa su Magestad por estenço como abaxo yra declarado
2v   la manera y como y en que tienpo los españoles entraron en esta tierra del Piru y el tratamiento que hizieron al dicho my padre todo el tienpo que en ella biuio hasta darle la muerte en esta que yo agora poseo, ques la que se sigue.

It is also necessary for His Majesty to know that my father, Manco Inca Yupanqui, son of Huayna Capac and grandson of Tupa Inca Yupanqui—and directly descended from this lineage—was the principal lord of these kingdoms of Peru. He was chosen to rule by his father Huayna Capac[7] and was regarded and obeyed as principal lord by all of the inhabitants of this land, just as I am now and have been since the time my father died.

Your Lordship should also make His Majesty understand why I am suffering from such need in this wilderness. My father left me here in these straits when he was defeated and killed by the Spaniards, while he still reigned and governed over Peru and all its territory.

His Majesty should also know in detail, as will be declared below, of the manner, and of how and when the Spaniards entered the land of Peru, and of how they treated my father while he lived until they killed him in the territory I now possess. This is told in the following account.

2v

---

7. Only Titu Cusi argues that Huayna Capac named his father as successor, and it is unlikely in the extreme. Distortions related to genealogy and succession appear to be more common in accounts that drew from Inca sources because of the importance of these matters to the Incas. Spanish accounts distort the story in predictable ways, as well; for example, Spanish accounts of the conquest seldom mention the participation of native allies or even their existence.

[2]

**Relasçion de como los españoles entraron en el Piru y el subçeso
que tubo Mango Ynga en el tienpo que entre ellos biuio,
ques esta que se sigue:**

En el tienpo que los españoles aportaron a esta tierra del Piru, que llegaron al pueblo de Caxamarca çiento y nobenta leguas [950 km] poco mas
o menos de aqui, my padre Mango Ynga estaua en la çiudad del Cuzco;
en esa hera con todo su poderio y mando como su padre Guaina Capac se
lo auia dexado, donde tubo nueba por çiertos mensajeros que vinieron de
alla de vn hermano suyo mayor avnque bastardo llamado Atavallpa,[7] y
por vnos yndios *yungas* tallanas que rresiden a la orilla del mar del sur
quinze o beynte leguas [75–100 km] del dicho Caxamallca, los quales
dezian que abian bisto llegar a su tierra çiertas personas muy differentes
de nuestro auito y traje que pareçian *viracochas,* ques el nonbre con el qual
nosotros nonbramos antiguamente al criador de todas las cossas, diziendo
tecsi viracochan, que quiere dezir "prençipio y hazedor de todo"; y
nonbraron desta manera a aquellas personas que auian visto, lo vno porque
diferençiauan mucho en nuestro traje y senblante, y lo otro porque beyan
que andaban en vnas animalias muy grandes, las quales tenian los pies
de plata; y esto dezian por el rrelunbrar de las herraduras, y tanbien los

3

7. [Elsewhere, the name Atavallpa appears as "Atauallpa," an expected orthographic variation.
The sound represented by the letters *v* and *u* in these spellings is like the English *w,* which can
also be rendered as "hua" (or "gua") in Spanish, as in Atahuallpa (or Ataguallpa). The same sound
appears at the beginning of words, as in the names Huayna (or Guayna) Capac, Tupa Huallpa
(or Guallpa), and Huascar (or Guascar).]

[2]

History of how the Spaniards arrived in Peru and what happened to Manco Inca during the time he lived among them, as follows:

At the time the Spaniards first arrived on the coast of Peru—and when they later arrived in the town of Cajamarca, about 190 leagues [570 mi] from here—my father Manco Inca was in the city of Cusco. My father was there exercising all the power and authority that his father Huayna Capac had conferred upon him. It was there that he received a message from his older (though bastard) brother named Atahuallpa,[8] in Cajamarca, and from some Tallanas *yungas*,[9] who inhabit the Pacific coast some fifteen or twenty leagues [45–60 mi] from Cajamarca. The Tallanas said that they had seen some people arrive in their land who dressed very differently from our people; these new people seemed to be *viracochas*.[10] This is the name we used long ago to refer to the creator of all things, calling him Tecsi Viracochan,[11] which means "beginning and maker of everything." The   3 Tallanas *yungas* called the people they had seen by this name because the Spaniards were very different in their dress and appearance from the people who live here, and also because the Spaniards rode very large animals with silver feet (the Tallanas *yungas* thought this because of the light given off by the Spanish horseshoes). The Tallanas *yungas* also used the

8. Atahuallpa was one of two contenders for succession after the death of Huayna Capac. He successfully defeated the other contender, his brother Huascar, just before the Spaniards took him hostage.

9. Inhabitants of the Tumbes region (Betanzos, *Narrative*, pt. 2, ch. 17: 235–36; Sarmiento de Gamboa, ch. 67: 123). The term *yungas* is a general reference to people from the coast, or from the lowland valleys east of the Andes. It was defined by González Holguín both as plains or valleys and as the inhabitants of "that region" (*Yunca o yuncaquinray. Los llanos o valles. Yunca. Los Indios naturales de alli;* 371).

10. González Holguín defines *Viracocha* as an epithet for the sun, "the honored name of the God that the Indians adored," and proceeding from this understanding "and equating the Spaniards with their god, they called them by the name viracocha" (*Viracocha. Era epicteto, del sol honrroso nombre del Dios que adorauan los indios y de ay ygualandolos con su Dios llamauan a los españoles viracocha;* 353).

11. Here and elsewhere, Titu Cusi is giving an Andean name to the Christian God. *Tecsi* is defined as "origin, beginning, foundation, basis, cause" in the dictionary of

llamavan ansy porque les auian visto hablar a solas en vnos paños blancos como vna persona hablaua con otra, y esto por el leeer [sic: leer] en libros y cartas; y avn les llamauan *viracochas* por la exçelençia y paresçer de sus personas y mucha differençia entre vnos y otros, porque vnos heran de baruas negras y otras bermejas, e porque les veyan comer en plata, y tanbien porque tenian *yllapas,* nonbre que nosotros tenemos para los truenos, y esto dezian por los arcabuzes porque pensaban que heran truenos del çielo.

Destos *viracochas* traxeron dos dellos vnos yugan [sic: *yungas?*] a mi tio Ataguallpa que a la sazon estava en Caxamarca, el qual los resçiuio muy bien; y dando de beuer al vno dellos con vn vasso de oro de la beuida que nosotros vsamos, el español en rresçibiendolo de su mano lo derramo, de 3v lo qual se enojo mucho mi tio; y despues desto, aquellos dos españoles le mostraron al dicho my tio vna carta o libro o no se que, diziendo que aquella hera la *quillca* de Dios y del rrey; e mi tio, como se sintio afrentado del derramar de la *chicha,* que ansy se llama nuestra beuida, tomo la carta o lo que hera y arrojolo por ay, diziendo "¿que se yo que me dais ay? ¡anda, bete!"; y los españoles se boluieron a sus conpañeros, los quales yrian por bentura a dar rrelaçion de lo que auian visto y les auian pasado con mi tio Ataguallpa.

D[e] ay a muchos dias, estando my tio Ataguallpa en guerra e differençias con vn hermano suyo Vascar Ynga[8] sobre qual dellos hera el rrey verdadero desta tierra, no lo siendo ninguno dellos por auerle osurpado

---

8. [The scribe is employing *v* where he could have used *u,* an orthographic variant. The sound represented in the Inca language is often rendered as "hua" (or "gua") in Spanish, so this name is also written as Huascar (or Guascar).]

name [*viracocha*] to refer to the Spaniards because they heard the Spaniards speaking, all by themselves, to some white sheets just as one person would speak to another (what they were observing was the reading of books and letters). The Tallanas *yungas* also called the Spaniards *viracochas* because of the excellence of their appearance and the great differences between them: some Spaniards had black beards and others had red ones; and because they were seen to eat on silver dishes and because they had *yllapas*.[12] This is the name we use to refer to the thunder, but in this case it referred to the harquebuses[13] that the Spaniards carried, because the Tallanas *yungas* thought the harquebuses were thunder from the sky.

Two of these *viracochas* were brought by some *yungas* to my uncle Atahuallpa, who was in Cajamarca at the time. He received them very well. When my uncle gave one of these *viracochas* a golden cup containing our customary drink, the Spaniard spilled some of it as he took the cup from Atahuallpa's hand. My uncle became very angry. Afterward, the two 3v Spaniards showed my uncle a letter or a book or some such thing, saying that this was the *quillca*[14] of God and the King. Since my uncle was still offended by the spilling of the *chicha*[15] (which is what our drink is called), he took the letter (or whatever it was) and threw it down, saying "What do I know about what you would give me? Go on, get out of here!" The two Spaniards returned to their companions and then left to give an accounting of what they had seen and what had happened with my uncle Atahuallpa.

At that time, and for some time afterward, my uncle was at war with his brother Huascar Inca over which one was the true lord of the land.[16] Neither of them had a real claim to the honor since they had usurped the

---

González Holguín (*Ticci. Origen principio fundamento cimiento caussa;* 340). Titu Cusi's equation is spurious and almost certainly due to well-intentioned efforts to create parallels between Andean ideas and Christian ones.

12. *Yllapa* was defined as "lightning, arquebus, artillery" by González Holguín (*Yllappa. Rayo arcabuz, artilleria;* 367).

13. Matchlock guns.

14. Defined as "paper, letter, or writing" by González Holguín (*Quellca. Papel carta, o escriptura;* 301).

15. A fermented corn beverage. The term *chicha* is Spanish. In the Inca language, the term is *aka* or *açua* (González Holguín. *aka. El açua o chicha;* 18).

16. As mentioned in note 7, it is extremely unlikely that Huayna Capac named Titu Cusi's father as his successor.

[usurpado] a mi padre el rreyno a causa de ser mochacho en aquella sazon
y querersele levantar con el por los muchos tios e parientes que tenian el
vno y el otro, los quales dezian que por que auia de ser rrey vn mochacho,
avnque su padre en sus postrimeros dias le vbiese nonbrado por tal, que
mas rrazon hera lo ffuesen los grandes y no el chico, la qual rrazon no se
pudo llamar tal syno passion de cobdiçia y anbission, porque ellos deçen-
dian, avnque hijos de Guaina Capac, de parte de las madres de sangre suez
4   [soez] e baxa, e my padre ffue hijo ligitimo de sangre rreal como lo ffue
Pachacuti Ynga, aguelo de Guayna Capac; y estando estos en estas differençias, como dicho tengo, vno contra otro avnque hermanos, en differentes asientos, llegaron a Caxamarca, pueblo arriua nonbrado, dizen que
quarenta o çinquenta españoles en sus cauallos bien adereçados; y sauido
por mi tio Ataguallpa, que çerca de alli estaua en vn pueblo llamado Guamachuco haziendo çierta ffiesta, luego leuanto su rreal, no con armas para
pelear ny arneses para se deffender, syno con *tomes* y lazos, que ansy llamamos los cuchillos nuestros para caçar aquel genero de nuevas *llamas*,
que ansy llamamos el ganado nuestro, y ellos lo dezian por los cauallos que
nueuamente auian aparesçido; y lleuauan los *tomes* y cochillos para los des-
ollar [degollar] y desquartizar, no haziendo casso de tan poca jente ni de
lo que hera.

Y como my tio llegase al pueblo de Caxamarca con toda su jente, los
españoles los rresçibieron en los baños de Conoc, legua y media [7.5 km]

kingdom from my father (who had been only a boy at the time).[17] [They usurped my father's rule] because they wanted it for themselves, and because they were supported in this by many uncles and relatives who questioned why the king should be a boy (even though Huayna Capac had named the boy as his successor at the end of his life), and because it made more sense to them that the older brothers should succeed before the boy.[18] But the real reasons [for their usurpation] were passions like envy and ambition. After all, though Atahuallpa and Huascar were both sons of Huayna Capac, they were descended from mothers of low birth;[19] my father was the legitimate son of royal blood just as Pachacuti Inca, the grandfather of Huayna Capac, had been. Atahuallpa and Huascar were involved in this war against each other, as I have already said, even though they were brothers. They were each at different places when the forty or fifty Spaniards arrived in Cajamarca, the town mentioned above. The Spaniards were well-armed and rode on horseback. When my uncle Atahuallpa, who was nearby in the town of Huamachuco celebrating a certain fiesta, learned of the Spaniards' arrival, he left his camp taking neither arms for battle nor defensive armor but *tumis*[20]—our knives—and lassos to hunt the new type of *llamas*,[21] the name we call our livestock, which was used to describe the horses that had just been seen for the first time. My uncle and his men took the *tumis* (or knives) to kill and butcher the horses, showing no concern for such a small number of Spaniards nor about who they were.

As my uncle approached Cajamarca with all of his people, the Spaniards went out to receive them in the baths of Conoc, a league and a half [about

17. There was no fixed rule of succession. Ideally, a ruler named his successor from among his sons with the principal wife, but divination had to show that the choice would be fortunate. Succession through a brother is known in the case of local nobility in the colonial period, but not in the case of the Inca dynastic line.

18. A qualification for succession was to be closely related to the Inca dynastic line on both the side of the father and the mother (Julien, *Reading Inca History*, 23–48).

19. Titu Cusi is casting aspersions on his brothers' claims.

20. González Holguín defines *tumi* as a copper knife used by the Indians, "like an axe with no handle" (*Tumi. Cuchillo de indios de cobre a manera de segur sin cabo;* 346).

21. The Andean camelid used for burden-bearing, glossed by González Holguín as "sheep of the land" (*Llama. Carnero de la tierra;* 208).

de Caxamarca, y ansy se ffueron con el hasta Caxamarca; y llegados que fueron, les pregunto que a que benian, los quales les dixieron que benian por mandado del Viracocha a dezirles como le an de conoçer; y my tio, como les oyo lo que dezian, atendio a ello y callo y dio de beuer a

4v   vno dellos de la manera que arriua dixe para ver sy se lo derramavan como los otros destos; y ffue de la misma manera que ny lo beuieron ny hizieron caso; e bisto por mi tio que tan poco caso hazian de sus cosas, [dijo] "pues vosotros no hazeis caso de my ni yo lo quiero hazer de vosotros"; y ansy se lebanto enojado y alço grita a guisa de querer matar a los españoles; y los españoles, que estauan sobre auisso, tomaron quatro puertas que auia en la plaça donde estavan, la qual hera çercada por todas partes. Desque aquella plaça estubo çercada y los yndios todos dentro como ouejas, los quales heran muchos, y no se podian rrodear a ninguna parte ny tanpoco tenian armas porque no las auian traido por el poco caso que hizieron de los españoles sino lazos e *tumes,* como arriua dixe, los españoles con gran ffuria arremetieron al medio de la plaça donde estaua vn asyento del Ynga en alto a manera de ffortaleza, que nosotros llamamos *vsnu,* los quales se apoderaron del y no dexaron sibir [sic: subir] alla a my tio, mas antes al pie del le derrocaron de sus andas por ffuerça y se las trastornaron e quitaron lo que tenia y la *borla,* que entre nosotros es corona; e quitado todo lo dicho le prendieron, e porque los yndios daban grita los mataron a todos con los cauallos, con espadas, con arcabuzes,

5   como quien mata a ouejas, sin hazerles naidie rresistençia, que no se escaparon de mas de diez mill dozientos; y desque ffueron todos muertos, lleuaron my tio Ataguallpa a vna carçel donde le tubieron toda vna noche en cueros atada vna cadena al pescueso; y otro dia por la manaña

4.5 mi] from Cajamarca;[22] from there they accompanied him to Cajamarca. Once they arrived Atahuallpa asked them why they had come. The
Spaniards answered that they had been sent by the Viracochan to tell the
people of the land how they could know Him. My uncle listened to what
they said. Then he became quiet and gave one of them a cup to drink from,
in the same manner that I described above, to see whether they would   4v
again spill its contents as the others had. And the same thing happened
again: the Spaniards neither drank from the cup nor paid any attention to
the gesture. When my uncle understood what little regard they had for his
gesture, he said, "Well, you do not have any regard for my gesture, and I
do not have any regard for yours." And rising up angrily, he yelled as if he
wanted them to be killed. The Spaniards, who were prepared for an attack, immediately seized the four gates of the plaza in which they found
themselves. Because the plaza was entirely enclosed, the people were
locked in just like a lot of sheep. They had no weapons because they had
not brought any; they did not think of the Spaniards as a threat. All they
had with them were knives and lassos, as I said before. The Spaniards furiously attacked the center of the plaza where there was a seat of the Inca—
up high, as if it were a kind of fortress—that we call *usnu*.[23] They were able
to gain control of the *usnu* and prevented my uncle from getting to the
top of it. They pulled him out of his litter at the foot of the *usnu* and took
away what he had, including the *borla*,[24] which is like a crown. Once they
had taken everything from him, they took him as well. Then, because the
people began to shout, the Spaniards killed them all with their horses, their
swords, and harquebuses, just as if they were slaughtering sheep. No one   5
put up any kind of resistance. Of the more than 10,000 people who were
there, not more than 200 escaped. Then, after all the people were dead,
the Spaniards took my uncle Atahuallpa to a jail, where they held him
overnight, naked, with chains around his bare body. The next morning

22. Conoc is the the site of natural hot springs, near Cajamarca (Hemming, 33).

23. According to González Holguín, an *usnu* was an erected stone where a judge held
court, or a boundary marker, when the erected stone was a large one (*Vsnu. Tribunal
de juez de vna piedra hincada. Vsnu. Mojon quando es de piedra grande hincada;* 358).

24. The Inca ruler wore a band that wrapped around the head with a deep fringe
across the forehead. It was similar to the headdress worn by other members of the dynastic lineage, but no one else wore the fringe across the forehead.

le dieron su rropa e su *borla* diziendo "¿heres tu el rrey desta tierra?"; y el rrespondio que sy; y ellos dixieron "¿no ay otro ninguno que lo sea syno tu? porque nosotros sabemos que ay otro que se llama Mango Ynga; ¿dondesta este?"; y mi tio rrespondio "en el Cuzco"; y ellos rreplicaron "pues, ¿adonde es el Cuzco?"; a esto rrespondio my tio "duzientas leguas [1,000 km] de aqui esta el Cuzco"; y mas, tornaron a dezir los españoles "pues luego, ese que esta en el Cuzco, porque como nosotros tenemos por nueua es la caueça prençipal desta tierra, deue de ser el rrey"; y my tio dixo "de ser, sy es, porque mi padre le mando que lo ffuere, pero porque es muy moço gouierno yo la tierra por el"; y los españoles dixieron "pues, avnque sea moço sera justo que sepa nuestra llegada y como venimos por mandado del Viracochan; por eso, auisaselo"; y mi tio dixo "¿a quien quereis que enbie?, pues me aueis muerto toda my jente e yo estoy desta manera"; y esto dezia porque no estaba bien con my padre e temia que, sy le auisaba de la llegada de los *viracochas,* por ventura se harian con el, porque le paresçian gente poderosa y avn pensaban que heran *viracochas,* por lo que arriua dixe.

Los españoles, como bieron que my tio Ataguallpa se detenia de dar auiso a my padre de su llegada, acordaron entre sy de hazer mensajeros; y en este medio tienpo que los españoles enbiauan o no, entendieronlo los tallanas *yungas,* y porque temian mucho a my padre, porque le conosçian por su rrey, acordaron entre si, syn dar auiso a los españoles ny a my tio, de yr ellos a dar la nueua a my padre; y ansy lo hizieron e se partieron luego para el Cuzco; e llegados que ffueron alla, dixieron a mi padre estas palabras:

"Çapay Ynga" (que quiere dezir "tu, solo señor"), "beniemos [crossed out] a dezir como a llegado a tu tierra vn genero de jente no oyda ny bista en nuestras nasçiones, que al paresçer sin dubda son *biracochas*" (como dize "dioses"); "an llegado a Caxamarca donde esta tu hermano, el qual les a dicho y çertifficado que el es el señor y rrey desta tierra, de lo qual nosotros como tues [sic: tus] vassallos rresçeuimos gran pena; y con ello, por no poder suffrir a nuestros oydos semejante

they gave him his clothes and the *borla,* saying, "Are you the king of this land?" He responded that he was. They asked, "Isn't there anyone else who is king? We have heard there is another called Manco Inca. Where is he?" My uncle answered, "In Cusco." The Spaniards replied, "Where is this Cusco?" To which my uncle responded, "Cusco is 200 leagues [600 mi] from here." The Spaniards said, "Of course! The one in Cusco is king, because we have heard that it is the principal place in this land.[25] He must be the one who is king." My uncle said, "That he is king is true, because my father ordered that he should be. But I am governing the land in his name because he is very young." The Spaniards said, "Even though he is young, he should know of our arrival and of how we came by order of the Viracochan. So tell him." My uncle said, "Who would you have me send, since you have killed all of my people, and I am in this fix?" Atahuallpa said this because he was not getting along with my father at the time. He thought that if he let his brother know about the arrival of the *viracochas* they would deal with him instead, because they seemed like powerful people and because the people still thought the Spaniards were *viracochas,* as I mentioned above. 5v

When they saw that my uncle Atahuallpa was taking his time in sending a message to my father about their arrival, the Spaniards decided to send their own messengers. The Tallanas *yungas,* who understood what was happening at the time, agreed among themselves (without telling the Spaniards or my uncle) to give the news to my father, whom they regarded and feared as their king. They left for Cusco immediately after making this decision. When they arrived, they told my father the news in these words:

"Sapay Inca"[26] (which means "you, only lord"), "we come to tell you how a kind of people that has never been heard of or seen by our peoples has arrived in your land. By all signs these strangers are certainly *viracochas*" (the way we say "gods"). "They have arrived in Cajamarca where your brother is, and he has told them and certified to them that he is the lord and king of this land. As your vassals, we were saddened [by what your brother told them]. Because we could not bear to hear such

25. Cusco was the center of the Inca empire, called Tahuantinsuyu.
26. Titu Cusi translates a form of address used when speaking with the Inca ruler himself.

ynjuria syn le dar parte, te benimos a dar auiso de lo que passa porque no seamos tenidos ante ti por rreueldes ni descuydados a lo que toca a tu seruiçio".

6   E my padre, oyda su enbaxada, quedo ffuera de sy, diziendo "pues ¿como en my tierra a sydo assada [sic: osada] a entrar semejante jente syn mi mandado ni consentimiento? ¿que ser y manera tiene esa jente?"; y rrespondiendo los mensajeros dixieron "señor, es vna jente que syn dubda no puede ser menos que no sean *viracochas,* porque dizen que bienen por el viento y es jente barbuda muy hermosa y muy blancos; comen en platos de plata, y las mismas ouejas que los traen a cuestas, los quales son grandes, thienen çapatos de plata; echan *yllapas* como el çielo; myra tu sy semejante jente, y que desta manera se rrije y gouierna, sy seran *viracochas;* y avn nosotros los auemos visto por nuestros ojos a solas hablar en paños blancos y nonbrar a algunos de nosotros por nuestros nonbres syn se lo dezir naidie, no mas de por mirar al paño que tienen delante; y mas, ques gente que no se les pareçen otra cossa sino las manos y la cara; y las rropas que traen son mejores que las tuyas, porque tienen oro y plata; e gente desta manera y suerte ¿que pueden ser syno *viracochas?*"

A esto my padre, como honbre que de hecho se deseaua çertifficar de lo que hera, torno a amenazar los mensajeros diziendoles asy: "mirad, no me mintais en lo que me aueis dicho, que ya sabeis y abreis entendido quales mis antepasados e yo solemos parar a los mentirosos"; y ellos, tornando a rreplicar con algun temor y grima, dixieron "Sapay Ynga, si no lo

6v   ovieramos visto por nuestros ojos y te tubieramoss el temor que tenemos, por ser como somos tus vasallos, no te osaramos ver ny benir a ti con semejantes nueuas; y si no nos quereis creer enbia tu a quien tu quisieres a Caxamarca y alli beran a esta jente que te hemos dicho, que esperando estan la rrespuesta de nuestro mensaje".

Y biendo my padre que aquellos tan de beras se çertifficauan en lo que dezian, y dandoles en ello algun credito, les dixo "pues, que tanto me

injurious words without informing you, we came to tell you about what is happening so that you will not think we are rebels or that we have not done all we can to serve you."

When he heard their words, my father became distraught and said: "Well, how is it that such people have dared to enter my lands without my orders or consent? What manner of people are they?" In response, the messengers said: "Lord, they are a kind of people that—without doubt—cannot be anything less than gods since they say they arrived with the wind, and they are bearded and very beautiful and white. They eat on silver dishes, and even the sheep[27] that carry them on their backs are large and have silver shoes. They emit bolts of thunder like the sky itself. Don't you think that people like this, who behave in this manner, must be *viracochas?* With our own eyes we have seen them speaking by themselves using white sheets; they have called some of us by our names without their having been told our names, but simply by looking at the sheet they have before them. You cannot see any part of them except for their hands and face.[28] The clothing they wear is better than yours, because they use gold and silver. How could people of this sort be anything other than *viracochas?"*

Since he was a man who wanted to be sure of what he was being told, my father began to berate the messengers. He said, "Look, do not lie to me. You know very well what my ancestors and I usually do to those who lie." The *yungas* answered him in fear and terror, saying, "Sapay Inca, if we, your vassals, had not seen it with our own eyes and did not have the respect for you that we do, we would not have dared to appear before you or bring you such news. If you do not want to believe us, send whoever you like to Cajamarca. There they will see these people we have told you about, as they are waiting there for you to respond to our message."

When he saw how earnestly they believed what they had told him, my father gave them some credit. He told them: "Well, since you have taken

6

6v

27. Here, the word "sheep" refers to the horses of the Spaniards. There is a paradox, as Titu Cusi probably said "llamas," which was translated with the Spanish word "sheep," when what was being described was horses.

28. Another way to read this phrase is: "they do not resemble each other, except for their hands and face," since Spanish clothing did not identify the affiliation of the wearer in the same way that Inca dress did.

ahincais en çertificarme la llegada desa gente, andad y traedme aqui algunos dellos para que, biendolos yo, lo crea a ojos vistas"; y los mensajeros hizieron lo que les mandaua my padre y boluieron a Caxamarca con no se quantos yndios, que my padre enbio a la çertificasçion de lo dicho y a rrogar a los españoles se llegase alguno dellos dondel estaua porque deseaua en estremo ver tan buena gente, que con tanto ahinco los *yungas* tallanas le hauian çertificado que hera; y ffinalmente todos los mensajeros, vnos y otros, se partieron del Cuzco por mandado de my padre para Caxamarca a ber la gente que hera aquellos *viracochas;* y llegados que fueron al Marques don Ffrançisco Piçarro, los rresçiuio muy bien y se holgo con saber de mi padre y con no se que cosillas que les enbio, el qual, como dicho tengo, les enbiaua a rrogar se biniesen con el algunos dellos, los quales lo tubieron por bien y acordaron de enbiar dos españoles a besarle las manos, llamados el vno ffulano Villegas, y el otro Antano, que no le supieron los yndios dar otro nonbre; y salieron de Caxamarca por mandado del Marques y consentimiento de los demas y llegaron al Cuzco syn temor ni enbaraço ninguno, mas antes my padre, desque supo mucho antes que llegasen su benida, les enbio al camino mucho reffresco y avn auia mandado a los menssajeros que fueron al Cuzco a llamarlos que los truxiesen en hamacas, los quales lo hizieron ansy; y llegados que fueron al Cuzco y presentados delante de my padre, el los rresçibio muy honrradamente y los mando aposentar y proueer de todo lo neçesario; y otro dia les hizo benir adonde estaua, y haziendo vna gran fiesta con mucha gente y aparato de baxillas de oro y plata en que auia muchos cantaros y vasos e librillos[9] y barrañones[10] de lo mesmo; y los españoles, como vieron tanto oro y plata, dixieron a my padre que los diese algo de aquello para lo lleuar a enseñar al Marques y sus conpañeros y les signifficar la grandesa de su poderio; e my padre tubolo por bien y dioles muchos cantaros y basos de oro y otras joyas e

9. Lebrillo, "barreño o palangana pequeños" (Moliner, vol. II, 230); palangana, "recipiente redondo de loza, etc., con el fondo mucho más pequeño que el borde y el perfil de las paredes en forma de ese, que se utiliza para lavarse" (Moliner, vol. II, 610).
10. Barreño, "recipiente de barro cocido, redondo, más ancho por el borde que por el fondo" (Moliner, vol. I, 352).

such trouble to tell me about the arrival of these people, go and bring some of them to me so that, by seeing them myself, I can believe what you say." The messengers did what my father told them and returned to Cajamarca with a great number of Indians.[29] My father sent these Indians to confirm what he had been told and to ask the Spaniards to send some of their men to where he was, because he urgently desired to see the wonderful people the Tallanas *yungas* had told him about. Finally, all of the messengers left Cusco for Cajamarca on my father's orders to see the people who were said to be *viracochas*. The Marquis Don Francisco Pizarro[30] received them very well when they arrived. He was pleased to learn about my father; he was also pleased with the little things my father sent him. As I have said, my father sent the messengers to ask Pizarro to send some Spaniards to him. The Spaniards thought well of this idea and agreed to send two Spaniards—one called Villegas and another called Antano[31] (the only name the Indians knew for him)—to pay their respects to Manco in Cusco. These Spaniards left Cajamarca on the Marquis' orders and with the consent of all the other Spaniards. They arrived in Cusco without incident or upset along the way. In fact, since my father knew the Spaniards were coming a long time before they actually set out, he had provisions sent to them along the way. He even ordered the messengers who went out from Cusco to meet the Spaniards to bring them back in hammocks, which was done. When the Spaniards arrived in Cusco and were brought before my father, he received them very honorably and ordered that they be given lodgings and everything they needed. The next day, he had them brought to where he was and gave them a large party with many people and an elaborate display of gold and silver service, including pitchers and cups and basins and other containers. Upon seeing all that gold and silver, the Spaniards told my father to give some of it to them; they would show it to the Marquis and his companions so that they would know what a powerful lord my father was. My father, who thought this was a good idea, gave them many pitchers and gold cups and

7

29. Note that Titu Cusi uses the term "Indians" to describe Andean people.

30. Francisco Pizarro received the title of Marquis in 1537, and he was frequently referred to simply as "the Marquis" (*el marqués*) afterward.

31. Other authors name Martín Bueno and Martín García de Moguer (Hemming, 64).

7v   pieças rricas que lleuasen para sy e ssus conpañeros; y despacholos con mucha gente al gouernador diziendoles que pues le auian benido a beer y benian de parte del Biracochan, que entrasen en su tierra, y sy querian venir adonde el estaua, viniesen mucho de enorabuena.

Entretanto que estos dos españoles fueron a besar las manos a mi padre y a berse con el en el Cuzco, my tio Ataguallpa, lo vno por temores que lo pusieron aquellos *viracochas* y lo otro de su grado, por tenelles de su mano para que le ffauoreçiesen contra Mango Ynga, mi padre, y Guascar Ynga, su hermano, les dio gran suma de tesoro de oro e plata, que todo pertenesçia al dicho mi padre; e por el rreçelo que tenia avn de my tio Guascar Ynga, desdel lugar donde estaua enbio çiertos mensajeros a que se conffederasen con su jente y le matasen para tener por aquella parte las espaldas seguras, pensando que las tenia por la parte de los españoles, como digo, por el tesoro que syn ser suyo syno de my padre les auia dado, los quales mensajeros lo hizieron tanbien que mataron a Guascar Ynga en vna rrefriega que tubieron en vn pueblo llamado Guanucopanpa; y sauido por el Ataguallpa la muerte de Guascar Ynga, su hermano, rreçiuio dello sumo contento por pareçerle que ya no tenia a quien temer y que lo tenia todo se-

8   guro, porque por la vna parte ya el mayor enemigo tenia destruydo y muerto y por la otra por el cohecho que avia hecho a los *viracochas* pensaua que no auia mas que temer; y saliose al rreues de su pensamiento, porque, llegados que fueron los dos españoles adonde estaua el Marques don Françisco Piçarro y sus conpañeros con la enpresa que my padre les enbiaua y con las nueuas de my padre, ffue çertificado el [al] Marques, que nosotros llamamos *macho capitu*, de como my padre Mango Ynga Yupangui hera el rrey verdadero de toda la tierra, a quien todos rrespetauan, tenian y acatavan por señor, y que Ataguallpa, su hermano mayor, poseya el rreino tiranicamente,

other precious pieces to take with them. He sent many bearers with these　7v
gifts back to Pizarro. My father said that, since he knew that the Spaniards
had come to see him, and since they had come on behalf of the Viracochan, they could enter his land. If they wanted to come to where he
was, they would be welcome.

While these two Spaniards were paying their respects to my father in
Cusco, my uncle Atahuallpa gave the *viracochas* a large treasure of gold
and silver, all of which belonged to my father. Atahuallpa did this, in part,
because he was afraid of the *viracochas;* he also did it to keep them in his
power so they would favor him over my father, Manco Inca, and his
brother, Huascar Inca.[32] Because he was still being cautious about my uncle Huascar Inca, Atahuallpa sent out certain messengers to conspire with
some of Huascar's people and kill him, so that he himself would be secure.
Huascar's death would ensure his safety. Atahuallpa also gave no mind to
any threat he might face from the Spaniards because of the treasure he had
given them (even though it was not his treasure but my father's, as I have
said). Atahuallpa's messengers did their job well and killed Huascar Inca
in a skirmish in a town called Huanucopampa.[33] When Atahuallpa learned
of the death of Huascar, his brother, he was very pleased, because it
seemed to him that he had no one left to fear and that he was now secure:　8
on the one hand, he had destroyed and killed his worst enemy; on the
other, he had given the *viracochas* a great gift. But everything turned out
just the opposite of what he thought. As soon as the two Spaniards [Vil-
legas and Antano] delivered my father's gifts and news to Pizarro and his
companions, it was evident to Pizarro (whom we called *machu capitu*)[34]
that my father, Manco Inca Yupanqui—whom all of the people respected,
held, and served as lord—was the true ruler of all the land and that
Atahuallpa, his older brother, ruled the land tyrannically. When Pizarro

32. Huascar was the brother engaged in a war of succession with Atahuallpa. He, not
Atahuallpa, had been recognized in Cusco as his father's successor and given the *borla*
(royal insignia). He had lost to Atahuallpa and was captured on the eve of the Spanish arrival in Cajamarca.

33. Others say that Huascar was executed in Andamarca, a town on the highland road
between Huamachuco and Huaylas (Hemming, 54).

34. This term is an early Quechua-Spanish composite, meaning "old captain."
González Holguín glosses *machu* as "old, in reference to persons, animals or plants"
(*Machu. Viejo en personas, o animales, o plantas;* 223).

de lo qual, lo vno por saber tan buenas nueuas de mi padre y que hera persona tan prençipal y lo otro por tan buen presente como le enbiauan y tan de boluntad, rresçiuio mucho contento y gran pena de ber que su hermano tan syn justiçia le procurase de veexar y molestar, obsurpandole su rreyno syn justiçia, el qual, segund despues pareçio, no quedo sin castigo, porque fue castigado segund su meresçido.

Ya que fueron llegados, como arriba dicho tengo, los españoles mensajeros que ffueron a mi padre a su rreal y los demas yndios que my padre enbiaua con el presente de oro y plata, que ffue mas de dos millones, arriba dicho, rrepresentaron su enbaxada los españoles por sy y los yndios por la suya, segund que por my padre Mango Ynga Yupangui les ffuera mandado, al gouernador, diziendo que my padre Mango Ynga se auia holgado mucho con la llegada de tan buena gente a su tierra, que le rrogaua que si lo tubiese por bien se llegasen al Cuzco adondel estaua y quel los rresçibiria muy honrradamente, y les daua su palabra de hazer todo lo que le rrogasen, pues venian por mandado del Viracochan, que les hazia saber como por aquellas partes donde ellos auian aportado estaua vn hermano suyo llamado Ataguallpa, el qual se nonbraua rrey de toda la tierra, que no le tubiesen por tal, porque el hera el rrey y señor natural della, señalado para ello en sus postrimeros dias por su padre Guaina Capac, y quel Ataguallpa se le auia leuantado con el rreyno contra su voluntad.

Sauido todo esto, lo vno y lo otro, por el gouernador y toda su gente, rresçibio a los mensajeros de my padre con grand alegria juntamente con el presente arriba dicho, y mando que los ospedasen y honrrasen como a mensajeros de tal señor; y de ay a algunos dias los yndios mensajeros de my padre se boluieron con la rrespuesta; y se quedo en Caxamarca el Marques, teniendo como tenia todabia preso a Ataguallpa desde que llegaron el e sus conpañeros a la tierra por la sospecha que tenia del, porque le paresçia que sy le soltaua se alçaria contra el y lo otro porque tubo sienpre sospecha, diziendo que no hera el el rrey natural de aquella tierra y queria se çertificar dello con la rrespuesta que de my padre viniese, y por esto le tubo

8v

9

received the good news from my father (who was such an important lord), along with the great gift Manco had freely sent, he was content. Pizarro was also very saddened to see that my father's brother Atahuallpa had unjustly tried to vex and upset my father by usurping his authority. As it turned out later, this injustice did not go unpunished, and Atahuallpa got the punishment he deserved.

Once the Spanish messengers and the Indians sent by my father had arrived with the gift of gold and silver mentioned above (worth more than two million *pesos*),[35] each group conveyed their messages to Pizarro. The Spaniards conveyed their messages and the Indians told him what my father, Manco Inca Yupanqui, had told them to tell the Governor. They said that Manco was very happy with the arrival of such good people in his land and that he begged them, if they were agreeable, to come to Cusco where he was; there he would receive them very honorably. My father gave his word that he would do all that they asked since they had been sent by the Viracochan. My father also told the Spaniards that in the area where they were there was a brother named Atahuallpa who had named himself king of all the land where they were, but that they should not treat him as king because he, Manco, was king and natural lord, having been designated to rule by his father, Huayna Capac, in that Inca's last days; Atahuallpa had attempted to take Manco's kingdom away against his will.

Once all of this had been made known to the Governor and his men, Pizarro received my father's messengers, and the gift mentioned above, with great joy. He ordered that the messengers should be lodged and treated with the respect that messengers of such an important lord deserved. A few days later, my father's messengers returned with Pizarro's response. Pizarro remained in Cajamarca, where he and his companions kept Atahuallpa prisoner just as they had since they first arrived. Pizarro did not trust Atahuallpa: it seemed to Pizarro that Atahuallpa would rebel if he were released.[36] Pizarro also kept Atahuallpa prisoner because he suspected that Atahuallpa might not be the rightful ruler of the land; he was waiting for my father's response to confirm this suspicion. Pizarro kept

8v

9

35. Hemming, 73.
36. Another possibility is that Pizarro chose to ally himself with Huascar's faction because most of the empire had supported Huascar.

tanto tienpo presso hasta que por my padre le fuese mandado otra cosa.

E visto por my tio Ataguallpa que my padre auia enbiado mensajeros e tanto oro y plata a los españoles, rresçiuio dello gran pena, lo vno por ver que con tanta breuedad se auia confederado con ellos y ellos rresçiuidole por rrey y señor y lo otro porque sospechaua que de aquella conffederasçion le auia de benir algun daño, y estando con esta sospecha y temor que de vna parte y otra le çercaua, determino de hazer juntar toda la gente y capitanes suyos que por ay a la rredonda estubiesen para sygnificarles la affliçion en que estaua puesto; y desque los tubo juntos les dixo estas palabrass: "*Apoes*" (que quiere dezir "señores"), "esta gente que a benido a nuestras tierrass es muy contraria a nuestro opinion y se a conffederado y tienen mucha paz con my hermano Mango Ynga; si os pareçe demosles en la cabeça, y muertos todos estos, porque me pareçe que avnque es poca jente es valerosa, no dexaremos de tener la suprema en toda la tierra como antes teniamos, pues ya es muerto my hermano Guascar Ynga; y si no los matamos y estos se hazen con my hermano Mango Ynga, a causa de ser jente tan balerossa y que al pareçer son *viracochas,* podria ser que nos ffuese mal del negoçio, porque my hermano esta muy enojado contra my, e si haze llamamiento de toda la tierra hara capitanes a estos, y el y ellos no podrian dexar de matarnos; por eso, si os pareçiese, ganemosle nosotros por la mano"; los capitanes y gente, como oyeron el rrazonamiento de my tio Ataguallpa, paresçioles muy bien lo que les dezia lo que les dezia [repetition in the original], y dixieron todos a vna boz "*hu çapay ynga*" (que quiere dezir "muy bien as dicho señor"), "bueno sera que matemos a estos porque ¿que gente es esta para con nosotros?; no tenemos en todos ellos vn almuerzo"; e ya que entre todos ellos estubo conçertado el dia y la ora en que los auian de matar, no tardo mucho, que no se porque bia lo supo

Atahuallpa prisoner for so long because he was awaiting different orders from my father.

When my uncle Atahuallpa saw that my father had sent messengers and a great deal of gold and silver to the Spaniards, he was very upset—in part because he saw how quickly the Spaniards had allied themselves with Manco and acknowledged him as king and lord, and in part because he suspected that this alliance would bring him harm. Enveloped in this suspicion and fear, Atahuallpa decided to gather all of his nearby people and captains to let them know about the situation in which he found himself. After calling them together, he said the following words:

"*Apoes*"[37] (which means "lords"), "the people who have come to our land have not favored our side; they have aligned themselves with my brother Manco Inca and reached some accord. If you are willing, we will strike them head on, and when they are dead—and it seems to me that though there are only a few of them, they are very valiant—we will regain supremacy over all the land since now my brother Huascar Inca is dead. If we do not kill these people—who are so valiant and appear to be *viracochas*—and if they join up with my brother Manco Inca, it could go very badly for us because my brother is very angry with me. If he calls the people together against me, he will make these men captains, and together they will not fail to kill us. For these reasons, and if you are agreeable, let us try to capture them." The captains and the people, when they heard my uncle Atahuallpa's reasoning, were convinced by what he said, and all replied in one voice: "Hu Sapay Inca"[38] (which means "how well you have said it, my lord"), "it would be good to kill them, because who are they to do this to us? There aren't enough of them for a decent lunch."[39] But soon after they had all agreed on a day and time for killing the Spaniards, the Marquis discovered their plan (though I do not know how

9v

37. A Spanish plural of the Inca word *apo*, defined by González Holguín as "a great lord or superior judge; or a principal cacique" (*Apu. Señor grande o juez superior, o Curaca principal;* 31). When modified by *sapay*, it was synonymous with the form used to address the Inca (*Çapay Inca çapay apu, El rey desta tierra;* González Holguín, 78).

38. The addition of *hu* signifies approval (*Hu ari o hu hu. Sea así que me plaze o norabuena.* "It pleases me if it is so," or "in good time"; González Holguín, 163).

39. This appears to be a Spanish usage and not a reference to any sort of cannibalism (see note 40).

el Marques; y sauido por el Marques la traiçion que estaua armada para
10 matarles, antes que los comiesen los almorzo el, porque mando poner espias por todas partes y que estubiesen a punto, syn dilasçion ninguna
mando sacar a la plaça a Ataguallpa, my tio, y en medio de la plaça en vn
pala syn ninguna contradiçion le dio garrote, y desque se le vbo dado
lebanto su rreal para benirse a ber con my padre; y por presto que lo quiso
lebantar, no dexaron de benir sobre el yndios como llovidos, porque vn
yndio capitan general de Ataguallpa llamado Challcochima y otro llamado
Quisquis, su conpañero, anbos de gran balor y poderio, juntaron gran
suma de gente para bengar la muerte de su señor, de tal manera que le ffue
forçado al Marques y a toda su jente benir con gran abisso por su camino
porque hera tanta la gente que los perseguia que benian por el camino con
gran trabaxo y detrimento, rresçibiendo sienpre grandes guaçabaras[11] de
los perseguidores.

Lo qual, sauido por my padre que asi benia con tanto aprieto, determino de hazer gente para yrle a ayudar; y ansy se salio del Cuzco con mas
de çient mill honbres y llego hasta Vilcacunga adonde encontro con el
Marques, que ya traia preso al Challcochima, el qual Marques viendolo
10v rresçibio muy gran contento; y my padre, yendo que yba en sus andas de
oro y cristal y corona rreal, se apeo dellass y abraço al Marques, que ya se
auia apeado de su cauallo; y anbos my padre y el Marques se conffede-
raron en vno y mandaron a sus jentes que naidie se desmandase saluo que
atendiesen a Quisquis que avn andaua por alli barlobenteando con mucha
gente, porque no se desmandasse a querer quitar al Challcochima.

Resçiuidos que fueron, en vno my padre y el Marques salieronse juntos
de Billcacunga y durmieron aquella noche en Xaquixaguana adonde le entrego el Marques a my padre el Challcochima, diziendo "veis aqui señor
Mango Ynga, os traigo preso a vuestro enemigo capital Challcochima; veis

---

11. Guasábara, "disturbio" (Moliner, vol. I, 1436).

he discovered it). Once the plot to kill the Spaniards had been discovered, and before Atahuallpa's people were able to eat the Spaniards, Pizarro 10 made lunch out of them.[40] First he sent spies out everywhere, to report anything out of the ordinary. Then, without any delay, he had Atahuallpa, my uncle, brought to the plaza. In the middle of the plaza, with no one trying to stop him, Pizarro garroted Atahuallpa on a wooden plank.[41] As soon as he had done this, he broke camp to go to where my father was. Though Pizarro tried to leave quickly, the Indians fell upon him like rain: one of Atahuallpa's captains general, named Challcochima, and another captain named Quisquis,[42] his companion—both of whom were valiant and powerful—had mustered a large number of people to avenge the death of their lord. The Marquis and all of his people were forced to be on alert all the way to Cusco, because there were so many Indians following them that the Spaniards were only able to travel with a great deal of difficulty and loss, owing to concerted attacks made on them by their pursuers.

When my father learned of Pizarro's difficulties, he decided to call up his men and go to Pizarro's aid. My father left Cusco with more than 100,000 men. He reached Vilcaconga, where he found out that Pizarro had already captured Challcochima. Pizarro was very relieved to see my father. My father, who was traveling as he always did on his litter of gold 10v and crystal and with the royal insignia, stepped down and embraced Pizarro, who had already dismounted from his horse. My father and the Marquis joined together in an alliance and ordered their followers to join with them and not to abandon them at that point, since they still had to take care of Quisquis, who was out there working against them and trying to keep his people from abandoning the cause of Challcochima.

Once they had joined in alliance, my father and the Marquis left Vilcaconga together. They spent that night in Jaquijaguana, where the Marquis turned Challcochima over to my father, saying: "Look here, Lord Manco Inca, I have brought you your capital enemy Challcochima. You decide

40. Here is the completion of the expression begun above (see note 39).

41. Titu Cusi is accurate in his description of Atahuallpa's death. Other authors would write that Atahuallpa's head was cut off.

42. The two generals who led Atahuallpa's campaign against Huascar, and who defeated and captured him. They also captured Cusco and punished Huascar's supporters.

lo que mandais que se haga del"; y my padre como lo vio, mando que luego fuese quemado a vista de todos porque ffuese la nueua a Quisquis, su conpañero, y fuese para este castigo, y a los demas, exenplo.

Hecho este castigo de tan mal yndio como hera aquel, se fueron de alli para el Cuzco juntos, avnque yba my padre con gran pena por ver la desberguença de aquel yndio Quisquis; y llegados que ffueron al Cuzco, mando my padre a toda su gente que rrespetasen y tubiesen en mucho al Marques y a los suyos y los proueyesen de todo lo neçesario hasta quel boluiese, diziendo que queria yr a matar a aquel vellaco de Quisquis y destruyr toda su generasçion, pues tanto se le desvergonçaua asy a el como a los españoles, que tanto por estonçes queria, a causa de auerle paresçido tan bien el Marques don Ffrançisco Piçarro.

Alcançe de Mango Ynga y el capitan Antonio de Soto contra Quisquis, traidor a la persona rreal y a su rrey Mango Ynga

Otro dia despues que my padre vbo hecho aposentar y proueer de todo lo neçesaria [neçesario] al Marques y a toda su jente, determino con pareçer del dicho Marques de dar alcançe e perseguir al traidor de Quisquis, porquestaua en gran manera enojado contra el por el amor y afiçion que auia cobrado a los españoles; y vista por el Marques la determinasçion con que my padre se determinaua a hazer aquel viaje, ofresçiose el tanbien a la jornada, diziendo que no hera cosa justa quedarse en el pueblo yendo my padre a la guerra, que mas harian dos que vno; my padre Mango Ynga, viendo el tan buen proposito del Marques, dixo que no se mobiese por estonçes sino que descan cansase [repetition in the original, owing to folio break] y que holgase hasta que boluiese, que presto daria la buelta, que si queria que ffuese con el alguna jente suya quel holgaria de lleuar consigo de los que el le diesse, mas que su persona no consentiria por estonçes que saliese del pueblo.

what you want done with him." When he saw Challcochima, my father ordered that he should be burned alive in front of all of them so that news of this act would reach Quisquis, Challcochima's associate. It would be fit punishment for Challcochima and serve as an example for the rest [of Atahuallpa's men].

Once this very bad Indian had been punished, Pizarro and my father went together to Cusco. But my father left Jaquijaguana feeling deeply upset by the shameful behavior of that Indian Quisquis. After arriving in Cusco, my father ordered all of his people to respect and treat the Marquis and the other Spaniards as honored guests and to supply them with everything they needed until his return. My father told his people that he had to go kill that evil Quisquis and destroy all of his kin, since he had brought such shame upon himself, Manco, and the Spaniards (of whom my father was very fond at the time since the Marquis Don Francisco Pizarro had greatly impressed him).

Pursuit by Manco Inca and the captain Antonio de Soto[43] of Quisquis, traitor to the royal person of his king Manco Inca

The day after my father gave lodging and everything else that was necessary to the Marquis and his people, he decided—with the Marquis' approval—to pursue and find the traitor Quisquis. Because of the great love and affection my father had developed for the Spaniards, he was extremely angry with Quisquis. When the Marquis saw how determined my father was to make that trip, he offered to go along himself, saying that it was not right that he, Pizarro, should stay in town while my father went to war, and that two could accomplish more than one. My father, Manco Inca, who appreciated the Marquis' generous proposal, told Pizarro not to trouble himself for the moment, but to rest and relax until his return, that he would be back soon. If Pizarro wanted to send some of his men along, Manco would be pleased to take some of them. But he would not allow Pizarro to leave town.

43. Titu Cusi errs in naming this captain, who was Hernando de Soto, who accompanied Pizarro to Peru and later led an expedition to Florida (Lockhart, 196–201).

El Marques don Ffrançisco Piçarro, viendo que my padre no le dexaua salir del pueblo para lo lleuar consigo, tomo pareçer con sus capitanes sobrel caso, a los quales paresçio que hera justo lo que my padre dezia; y ansy ellos entre sy con el gouernador nonbraron al capitan Antonio de Soto para que se ffuese con my padre, el qual lleuo consigo çinquenta españoles soldados; y nonbrado para el effeto al dicho capitan Antonio de Soto, se ffueron anbos el Marques y el a cassa de my padre que ya estaua de partida y le dieron quenta de lo que tenian conçertado; y my padre como lo supo obo dello mucho contento y dixo que le pareçia muy bien aquel conçierto, que se aparejasen los soldados que ya el se queria yr.

Este mesmo dia se salio my padre del Cuzco con toda su jente lleuando consigo al capitan Antonio de Soto con su conpañya, los quales todos de mancomun se fueron en vno en seguimiento de Quisquis, los quales, yendo por sus jornadas, en breue tienpo dieron sobrel traydor de Quisquis, al qual hallaron en vn pueblo llamado Capi, quinze leguas [75 km] del Cuzco adonde obieron con el vna cruda batalla, en la qual le mataron gran suma de gente y le desbarataron, el qual se salio huyendo de entre los suyos sin saberlo ellos, y se escapo; y my padre y el capitan Soto, desque acabaron de desbaratar a Quisquis y a toda su gente boluieronse al Cuzco, enbiando mucha gente en pos del Quisquis para que se lo traxiesen biuo de dondequiera que lo hallasen.

Y llegados que ffueron al Cuzco my padre y el capitan Antonio de Soto del desbarate de Quisquis, fueron muy bien rresçebidos del Marques don Françisco Piçarro y toda su jente y de los que en el pueblo auia, esto con mucho rregoçijo y alegria por la vitoria que auian auido de Quisquis y toda su gente; y acabado todo aquello y el rresçibimiento, my padre se rrecoxio a su casa y los españoles a la suya; y otro dia por la mañana, juntandose toda la gente que my padre auia traido de la batalla de Quisquis y la que en el pueblo estaua a casa de my padre, comio con ellos el dicho my padre; y desde que vbo comydo mando que so pena de la bida naidie se osase descomedir contra ninguna persona de las de aquella gente que nueuamente avian aportado a su tierra, mas que todos les rrespetasen y honrrasen como a cosa del Viracochan, que quiere dezir Dios; y mando mas que les diesen seruiçio, yndios e gente para su casa, y avn el mesmo my padre dio de sus mesmos criados que le seruian syrviçio al Marques para que le siruiesen; y hecho todo lo susodicho, torno otra bez a abperçiuir de nuebo gente para yr en seguimiento del traidor de Quisquis,

12

12v

When the Marquis Don Francisco Pizarro saw that my father would not let him leave town to go along, he consulted with his captains about the situation. They agreed that what my father had said was just, and so the captains and the Governor jointly named the captain Antonio de Soto to go along with my father. Soto was to take fifty Spanish soldiers with him. Once named for this mission, Soto went with the Marquis to the house of my father, who was about to depart. They told my father about what had been agreed upon. When he heard the plan, he was very pleased. He said that it seemed to be a good plan and that the Spanish soldiers should ready themselves as he, Manco, wanted to leave soon.

My father left for Cusco with all of his people that same day. He took the captain Antonio de Soto and his men with him. They all pursued   12 Quisquis together. Traveling the allotted distance each day, they soon found the traitor Quisquis in a town called Capi, fifteen leagues [45 mi] from Cusco. There they had a bloody battle in which they defeated Quisquis soundly. A large number of Quisquis' people were killed, and he was defeated. That traitor escaped, however, by sneaking off from amidst his own people without their realizing it. Since they had destroyed Quisquis and his people, my father and the captain Soto returned to Cusco and sent many people in pursuit of Quisquis to bring him back alive from wherever they might find him.

Upon arriving in Cusco after the defeat of Quisquis, my father and the captain Antonio de Soto were very well received by the Marquis Don Francisco Pizarro, Pizarro's men, and all of the other people of the town, and this with a great deal of general rejoicing and glee in response to their victory over Quisquis and his people. When their reception and the general rejoicing was over, my father went to his house and the Spaniards went to theirs. The next morning, all of the people who had accompanied my father on the campaign against Quisquis and the people who were in town   12v gathered at my father's house to eat with him. When they had finished eating, my father ordered that no one, on pain of death, should offend the people who had so recently come to his land. Instead, everyone should respect and honor them as something sent from the Viracochan (which means "God"). He further ordered that the Spaniards be given Indians to serve them, including people to serve them in their houses. My father even supplied some of his own servants to serve the Marquis. When it all was done, my father called up a new army to go after the traitor Quisquis. He

diziendo que, avnque fuese hasta en cabo del mundo, le auia de seguir y matar por la gran traiçion que auia hecho ansy a el como a los *viracochas*.

Refformado que se vbo el dicho my padre de las cossas neçesarias para su biaje yendo horden en el gobierno del pueblo, dexando en su lugar a Paulla [Paullu], su hermano, y Tiçoc y otros capitanes, y despidiendose del Marques con omenaje que no auia de boluer hasta que matase aquel traidor de Quisquis, se salio otro dia del Cuzco lleuando consigo al dicho 13 capitan Antonio de Soto con su conpañia arriba dicha, los quales se ffueron poco a poco por sus jornadas contadas hasta vn pueblo llamado Vinchu, çinquenta leguas [250 km] del Cuzco adonde le encontraron los mensajeros que de la batalla de Capi abian enbiado en su seguimiento de Quisquis, los quales dixieron que benian de buscar aquel traidor y que ni rrastro ni nueba avian hallado del en toda la tierra, saluo que sus capitanes daban muchos saltos y que del no auia nueua.

E mi padre, como oyo lo que los mensajeros dezian, rresçibio dello gran pena e quisiera pasar adelante sino que rrescibio alli cartas del Marques en que le signifficaua la gran soledad que padesçia por su ausençia, que le rrogaua mucho se boluiese, a lo qual my padre, por el amor que al Marques tenia, se boluio, enbiando desde alli mensajeros por toda la tierra por donde aquel traidor ouiese de pasar para que todos, dondequiera que aportasse, le diesen guerra y se lo matasen; hecho esto y enbiado los mensajeros para que por todas partes hasta Quito, quatroçientas leguas [2,000 km] de alli dondel desbenturado, como abaxo se dira, murio, no parasen, se tornaron al Cuzco adonde el dicho my padre supo que, despues de muchas guaçabaras que con aquel traidor obieron en muchas e dibersas partes le dieron, matandole y rrobando mucha gente hasta tanto que su mesma gente, viendo que se auia apocado en tanta manera que ya casy no 13v auia naidie, con grand despecho, affeandole sus vellaquerias y traiçion contra su rrey, le cortaron la cabeça.

Desque my padre estubo en el Cuzco ya algun tanto sosegado y contento con la muerte de aquel traidor de Quisquis, hizo llamamiento a toda su jente para que todos por cabeças diesen tributo a los españoles para su sustentasçion, y el dicho my padre, en tanto que se juntaba el tributo para suplir su neçesidad, les dio gran suma de tesoro

said that even if he had to go to the ends of the earth, he would follow and kill Quisquis for the great treason he had committed against both my father and the *viracochas*.

The next day, my father left Cusco after reequipping himself with the things necessary for his trip and after giving orders for the governance of the town in his absence (my father left his brother Paullu, along with Tizoc and other captains, in his place). Then, having made his farewells to the Marquis, and having pledged not to return until he had killed the traitor Quisquis, my father left Cusco, taking the captain Antonio de Soto and his company with him. They traveled slowly for a number of days until 13 they reached Vinchu, fifty leagues [150 mi] from Cusco. There they encountered the messengers they had sent after Quisquis from the battle of Capi. The messengers told my father and captain Soto that, though they had been searching for that traitor, they had found no trace or word of him in all the land. They had learned that his captains had made a number of attacks, but of Quisquis himself they had learned nothing.

When he heard what the messengers told him, my father was greatly distressed. Though he wanted to go on, he had received letters from the Marquis in which Pizarro conveyed the solitude he felt because of Manco's absence and pleaded with Manco to return. Because of his love for Pizarro, my father returned to Cusco. But first he sent messengers from Vinchu to the territory through which Quisquis would have to pass, so that the people would attack and kill that traitor wherever he might try to take shelter. After sending the messengers out so that they would cover the territory between there and Quito, some 400 leagues [1,200 mi] away (where the unfortunate Quisquis later died, as will be noted below), my father returned to Cusco. There he learned that, after many skirmishes with the traitor in many different places (in which his men had killed and captured many people), Quisquis' own people, seeing that their numbers had diminished to such an extent that there was almost no one left, cut off Quisquis' head, a sign of great disrespect for, and censure of, his evil 13v acts and treason against his king.

After spending some time in Cusco, my father—who was rested and content with the death of that traitor Quisquis—called forth his people, so that all of them individually would supply tribute to the Spaniards for their support. During the time it took the people to gather this tribute to supply the Spaniards' needs, my father gave the Spaniards a large treasure

que de sus antepasados tenia; y el gouernador y sus conpañeros lo rresçibieron con gran contento, dandole por ello las grasçias.

Como los españoles prendieron a Mango Ynga

Los españoles, como se bieron con tanta rriqueza, quisieron estonçes
boluerse a su tierra, pero my padre, biendo que heran avn muy nuebos en
la tierra, no les dexo yr por estonçes, mas antes dixo que se queria holgar
con ellos y tenellos en su tierra, que auisasen ellos a la suya por estenso el
subçeso que auia tenido en su biaje; y ellos tubieronlo por bien e hizieron
sus mensajeros, enbiando mucha parte del tesoro al enperador don Carlos; y desta manera se estubieron en el Cuzco muchos dias, holgando a su
plazer en conpañia de my padre; e pasadoss algunos años, como la cobdiçia de los honbres es tan grande, rreyno en ellos de tal suerte que, en-
gañados por el demonio, amigo de toda maldad y enemigo de birtud, que
se binieron entre sy a conçertar y tratar los vnos con los otros la manera y
el como molestarian a my padre y sacarian del mas plata y oro de la sacada;
y conçertados ansy vn dia, estando my padre en su cassa quieto y sosegado,
fueron a ella y otros mas de çient españoles con traiçion, so color que le
yban a ber; y llegados que fueron al dicho my padre, como los bio pensando que le yban a ber como otras bezes solian, rresçibiolos con mucha
alegria y contento; y ellos, como llebauan la traiçion armada, hecharon
mano del, diziendo "sabido hemos, Mango Ynga, que te quieres lebantar
contra nosotros y matarnos como lo hizo tu hermano Ataguallpa, por
tanto sabete que manda el gouernador que te prendamos y hechemos prissiones como a tu hermano Ataguallpa, porque no seas parte para hazernos mal".

My padre, como los vio de aquella manera determinados, alterose en
gran manera diziendo "¿que os he hecho yo porque me quereis tratar de
esa manera y

that had once belonged to his ancestors. The Governor and his companions received the treasure contentedly and thanked Manco for it.

How the Spaniards captured Manco Inca

When they saw how rich they had become, the Spaniards wanted to return immediately to their land. But my father, who saw that they were still very new to the land, would not let them go. He told them he wanted to celebrate with them and keep them there, and that they should inform the people in their land about their trip in detail. The Spaniards decided this was for the best and chose messengers to be sent back to Emperor Charles V[44] with a large part of the treasure. For these reasons the Spaniards stayed in Cusco for many days, enjoying themselves in the company of my father. After the Spaniards had been there for a few years (and since the greed of men is always great), greed reigned in their hearts to such an extent that, deceived by the devil (who is friend to all evil and enemy to all virtue),[45] they entered into an accord with each other about how to harass my father and get even more gold and silver from him than what they had already received. One day more than a hundred Spaniards acting in unison went with betrayal in their hearts to my father's house (where he was quietly and peacefully abiding) under the pretext that they wanted to see him. When they arrived where my father was, he received them with pleasure and contentment since he thought they had come to see him as they had on numerous other occasions. But the Spaniards had brought their weapons with them and took Manco prisoner, saying, "We know, Manco Inca, that you are plotting to rebel against us and kill us, just as your brother Atahuallpa did. For that reason, know that the Governor has ordered us to capture and restrain you just as we did your brother, so that you will be unable to do us harm."

My father, who could see their determination, was greatly disturbed. He replied, "What have I done so that you treat me in this manner and

14

44. Holy Roman Emperor (1521–1555) and king of Spain (as Charles I, 1519–1556).

45. The rhetorical flourishes used in reference to human greed and the devil suggest the influence of the Augustinian friar, Marcos García, who participated in the composition of Titu Cusi's *History*.

atarme como a perro? ¿desa manera me pagueis la buena obra que os he
hecho en meteros en mi tierra y daros de lo que en [e]lla tenia con tanta
voluntad y amor?; mal lo hazeis; ¿vosotros sois los que dezis que sois, *viracochas,* y que os enbia el Tecsi Viracochan?; no es posible que vosotros sois
sus hijos, pues pretendeis hazer mal a quien os haze y a hecho tanto bien;
¿por ventura no os enbie a Caxamarca gran suma de oro y plata? ¿no
tomastes a my hermano Atagualpa todo el tesoro que alli yo tenia de mis
antepasados? ¿no os he dado en este pueblo todo lo que aveis querido?,
que vno y otro sumado no thiene suma, porque son mas de seis millones
[de pesos]; ¿no os he dado seruiçio para vosotros y vuestros criados, y he
mandado a toda my tierra os tributen? ¿que quereis mas que haga?; juz-
galdo vosotros y bereis sy tengo rrazon de quexarme".

14v

    A esto los españoles, como çiegos de aquella malvada cobdiçia, tornaron
a rreplicar sobre lo dicho, diziendo "hea, Sapai Ynga, no cureis de dar agora
escusas, que çertificados estamos que te quieres alçar con la tierra; ¡oys
moços, dad aca vnos grillos!," los quales truxieron luego, que sin mas rres-
pecto ny mas myramiento de quien hera y del bien que les auia hecho se
los hecharon a sus pies; y hechados, my padre, como se bio de aquella manera, con mucha tristeza dixo, "verdaderamente digo que vosotros sois
dimonios y no *viracochas,* pues sin culpa me tratais desta manera; ¿que
quereis?"; rresponderon los españoles, "no queremos agora nada sino que
te estes presso"; y dexandole ansy preso y con guardas, boluieronse a sus
casas a dar parte de lo que auian hecho al gouernador, el qual no estaua muy
ynoçente del negoçio; y despues, como my padre se syntio preso de aquella
manera estaua con gran congoja, y con ella no sabia que se hazer porque no
auia quien le consolasse si no hera la jente de su tierra; y al fin, de ay a no se
quantos dias boluieron Hernando Piçarro e Joan Piçarro y Gonçalo Piçarro
con otros muchos, y dixieron a my padre: "señor Mango Ynga, ¿quereisos
todabia levantar con la tierra?"; dixo my padre "¿con tierra me tengo de
lebantar yo? ¿la tierra no es mya?, pues ¿que me dezis de lebantar?"; a esto
rrespondieron los españoles e dixieron "an nos dicho que nos quereis matar,
y por eso te hemos preso, por tanto si no es ansy, que no te quieres levantar, bueno sera que rredimas tu bexaçion y nos des algun oro y plata, que
eso es lo que benimos a buscar, porque dandola, te soltaremos"; dixo estonçes tanbien Hernando Piçarro: "avnque le solteis vosotros y de mas oro

15

tie me up as if I were a dog? Is this how you repay all the goodwill I have shown you, allowing you into my land and giving you all that it has to offer so willingly and affectionately? You behave very badly. Are you what you say you are, *viracochas* sent by the great Tecsi Viracochan? You cannot be his sons, since you do such evil to one who has only done good to you. Didn't I send a large quantity of gold and silver to Cajamarca?   14v
Didn't you take from my brother Atahuallpa all of the treasure there that belonged to my ancestors? Haven't I given you everything you wanted here in this town, so much treasure that it cannot be counted because it is worth more than six million [*pesos*]? Haven't I provided both you and your men with service and ordered everyone in my land to pay you tribute? Judge for yourselves and you will see that I have reason to complain."

To this the Spaniards, blinded by their evil greed, replied, saying, "Hey, Sapay Inca? You never stop giving us excuses! We have proof that you plan to rebel. Boys! Bring the leg irons here!" The leg irons were brought and, without any further consideration of who he was and of all the good he had done them, the Spaniards put the irons on his legs. When my father saw himself treated in this way, he said with a great deal of sadness, "Truly, I tell you that you are demons and not *viracochas,* since you do this to me without shame. What is it that you want?" The Spaniards replied, "We do not want anything now except to take you prisoner." They left him with guards and returned to their houses to tell the Governor, who was not innocent of the business, what they had done. Afterward, my father suffered such great anguish from the manner of his imprisonment that he did not   15
know what to do, and no one could console him except his own people. Finally, after I do not know how long, Hernando Pizarro, Juan Pizarro, and Gonzalo Pizarro[46] returned with many others. They said to my father, "Lord Manco Inca, are you still planning to take back your land?" My father said, "Why would I have to take back my land? Isn't the land already mine? What do you mean 'take it back'?" To this the Spaniards replied, "We have been told that you want to kill us and that is why we have taken you prisoner. So if it is not true that you want to rebel, a good way to redeem yourself would be to give us gold and silver, which is what we came for. And if we get it, we will release you." Then Hernando Pizarro said, "Even if the rest of you release him, and even if he gives you more gold

46. The three brothers of Francisco Pizarro (Lockhart, 157–89).

e plata que cabe en quatro bohios,[12] no se soltara de my parte si no me da primero a la señora *coya*, su hermana, llamada Cura Ocllo, por mi muger"; y esto dezia el porque la auia visto y enamoradose della, porque hera muy hermosa; y my padre, viendolos tan determinados en su mal proposito, dixo "pues, ¿eso manda el Viracochan, que tomeis por ffuerça la hazienda y mugeres de naidie? no se vsa tal entre nosostros, y bien digo yo que bosotros no sois hijos de Viracochan sino del *supay*"(que es el nonbre del demonio en nuestra lengua); "anda, que yo procurare de buscar alguna

15v   cossa que os dar"; y ellos rreplicaron, "no pienses que a de ser como quiera, que tanto nos as de dar como nos diste quando aqui llegamos, y mas," que hera tesoro que no cabia en vn galpon de yndios por grande que fuese; y my padre, viendolos tan ynportunos y tan determinados por no gastar mas palabras, les dixo: "anda, que yo hare lo que pudiere y os enbiare la rrespuesta"; y ellos, avnque con algun rreçelo si seria ansy o no, se fueron; y otro dia el dicho my padre mando hazer llamamiento por toda su tierra y que se junte toda la jente que en ella ay para juntar aquella can-tidad de tesoro que los españoles con tanto ahinco le pedian; y desde que los tubo juntos les hizo el parlamento siguiente:

Parlamento que Mango Ynga Yupangui hizo a sus capitanes sobre la junta del tesoro que dio a los españoles quando le prendieron la primera bez

"Hermanos e hijos mios, los dias pasados os hize juntar otra bez desta ma-nera para que biesedes vn genero de nueba gente que auia aportado a nuestra

---

12. Bohío, "Cabaña de América, hecha de ramas, Cañas, paja, etc., sin más ahertura que la puerta" (Moliner, vol. I, 391).

and silver than would fill four rooms, I will not consent to his being released unless he first gives me the Coya,[47] his sister named Cura Ocllo,[48] to be my wife." Hernando Pizarro said this because he had seen and fallen in love with the Coya, who was very beautiful. When my father saw that they were determined to carry out their evil plan, he said, "So this is what the Viracochan orders—that you take my property and my women by force? No one among us would do such a thing, and I can justly claim that you are not sons of Viracochan, but rather of the *Supay*"[49] (which is the name we use to refer to the devil in our language). "Go, and I will try to find something to give you." The Spaniards replied, "Do not think that it will be as you want it to be. You have to give us as much as you gave us when we first arrived—which was a treasure that did not fit in the largest of your great halls—and more." My father, who did not want to waste his words because he could see how unreasonable and how determined they were, told them, "Go, and I will do what I can and then send you my answer." The Spaniards left despite their concerns about whether Manco meant what he said or not. The next day my father issued a call throughout the land to gather all the people together so that they might assemble the quantity of treasure that the Spaniards had so insistently requested. When they had assembled, he gave the following speech:

The speech Manco Inca Yupanqui made to his captains about assembling the treasure that he gave the Spaniards when they took him captive the first time.

"My brothers and sons,[50] some days ago I gathered you together in this way so that you could see a new kind of people who had arrived in our

---

47. González Holguín defines *coya* as "queen, or princess in the line of succession" (*Ccoya Reyna, o princessa heredera;* 70). The term is not so easily translated, because the rules for affiliation and succession were different from Spanish rules (Julien, *Reading Inca History,* 24–27, 35–36).

48. From later references to Cura Occlo in Titu Cusi's *History,* it appears that Cura Ocllo became his father's principal wife, but only Titu Cusi mentions her.

49. González Holguín also defines *supay* as "devil" (*Çupay. El demonio;* 88).

50. Manco Inca often addresses his people as "my brothers and sons," which may be a standard form of address to members of his descent group (Julien, *Reading Inca History,* 24).

tierra, que son estos barbudos que estan aqui en este pueblo; y tanbien, porque me dezian que heran *viracochas* y lo paresçia en el traje, os mande que todos vosotros les serviesedes y acatasedes como a my persona mesma y les diesedes tributo de lo que en vuestras tierras teniades, pensando que hera gente grata e ynbiada de aquel que ellos dezian que hera el Tecse Viracochan" (que quiere dezir "Dios"); "y paresçeme que me a salido al rreues de lo que yo pensaua, porque sabed hermanos que estos, segund me an dado las muestras despues que entraron en mi tierra, no son hijos del Viracochan sino del demonio, porque me hazen y an hecho despues que en ella estan obras de tales, como podeis ver por vuestros ojos, que me pareçe que no podais dexar, si me amais verdaderamente, de rresçibir gran pena y congoja en ver a mi, vuestro rrey, aprisionado con prisiones y tratado desta manera sin mereçerlo, y esto por auer metido yo en my tierra semejante jente que esta, que yo mesmo me he degollado; por vida vuestra, que si me deseais dar contento que lo mas presto que pudieredes busqueis entre bosotros alguna cosa en rrazonable cantidad de oro y plata, pues estos tanto se mueren por ella, para que pueda rredimir mi bexaçion y salir desta prission en que por vuestros ojos me beis estar tan apassionado y congojado".

Respuesta que los yndios hizieron a Mango Ynga sobre la junta del tesoro quando estaua presso

Como toda la gente de la tierra juntada de las quatro partes della en las quales esta rrepartida, toda ella mas de mill e dozientas leguas [6,000 km] de largo y otras casy trezientas [1,500 km] de anchor rrepartida en esta manera, a la discrision [descripçion] del mundo, conbiene a a [repetition in the original] sauer, en oriente e poniente y norte y sur en nuestro uso llamamos Andesuyo, Chinchaysuyo, Condesuyo, Collasuyo, rrodeando desta manera: Andesuyo al oriente; Chinchaysuyo al norte; Condesuyo al poniente; Collasuyo al sur; esto haziamos puestos en el Cuzco, que es el çentro y cabeça de toda la tierra, y por esto y por estar en el medio se

land—these bearded men who are here in this town. Because they told me they were *viracochas*—and their clothes seemed to indicate that this was true—I ordered all of you to serve and obey them as you do my own person. Because I thought they were worthy people sent by that being that they identified as Tecsi Viracochan (which means 'God'), I asked you to give them tribute from what you have in your lands. It seems to me now that everything is just the reverse of what I believed because—hear me, brothers—they have shown by their deeds ever since they first entered my land that they are not sons of the Viracochan but of the devil. They do and have done the devil's work ever since they came, as you can see with your own eyes. I cannot imagine that, if you truly love me, you will not feel much sorrow and anguish at seeing me, your king, imprisoned and treated in this manner, without having done anything to deserve it except to allow such people as these into my land. I have slit my own throat and brought ruin on myself. By your lives, if you would wish to see me content, search among yourselves for anything in gold and silver, in good quantity and as quickly as you can—since these Spaniards will die for it—so that I can be freed from my distress and released from this imprisonment, that with your own eyes you can see has me so distraught and in such anguish."

Response that the Indians gave Manco Inca, while he was a prisoner, about assembling the treasure

All of the people from the four parts[51] of our land gathered together. Our land, which is more than 1,200 leagues [3,600 mi] long and almost 300 leagues [900 mi] wide, is divided into four parts just as the rest of the world is divided into east, west, north, and south. These parts, which we refer to as Andesuyu, Chinchaysuyu, Condesuyu, and Collasuyu, are arranged around the center as follows: Andesuyu to the east, Chinchaysuyu to the north, Condesuyu to the west, and Collasuyu to the south. This is how we order them standing in Cusco, which is the center and capital of all the land. For this reason, and because it is in the center, my

51. "Four parts" is a reference to Tahuantinsuyu (literally, "four parts"), the name given to the Inca empire. The four parts, or *suyus*, are described in the next two sentences.

nonbrauan mis antepasados puestos alli, por ser su çepa, señores de *tauan-*
tinsuyo, que quiere dezir señores de "las quatro partidas del mundo",
porque pensaban de çierto que no auia mas mundo que este; y a esta causa
ynbiauan sienpre desde aqui mensajeros a todas partes para que concu-
rriese toda la gente a la cabeça, como hizo my padre agora en esta junta
que arriba se dixo, porque por la mucha gente que auia, que a quererla
numerar seria ynposible, dezian todo esto, a tanto que, con aberse con-
sumido en Caxamarca y en lo de Quisquis arriba dicho sin numero de
gente y en otras muchas guaçabaras y rreffriegas, que por ebitar prolexidad callo, se juntaron a esta junta de solos los prençipales mas de diez mill;
y desque ansy estubieron juntos e puestos ante my padre, como le vieron
estar de aquella suerte, mouidos con gran llanto, dixieron:

"Sapai Ynga, ¿que coraçon ay en el mundo que, biendote a my [sic:
ansy] nuestro rrey que desa suerte estas tan afflexido y congoxado con dolor, no se haga pedaços y de lastima no se derrita?; por çierto, Sapay Ynga,
tu lo herraste mucho en meter en tu tierra semejante gente; mas, pues, que
ya ello esta hecho y no se puede rremediar por otra suerte, aparejados estamos estos tus vasallos a hazer de muy entera voluntad todo lo que por
17   ti nos ffuere mandado; y no dezimos nosotros tan solamente eso que tu
nos mandas que juntemos, que en conparasçion de lo que te debemos y
somos obligados no es nada; y si no bastase eso que tu dizes y fuese neçesario que para rredemir tu bexaçion nos bendiesemos a nosotros mismos
y nuestras mugeres e hijos, lo hariamos de muy entera voluntad por tu
seruiçio; mira, señor, quando mandas que se junte esto, que al punto y ora
que mandares sera junto y cunplido tu mandado sin faltar en ello vn punto
avnque sepamos arañarlo con nuestras propias manos debaxo de la tierra".

My padre Mango Ynga Yupangui, viendo la gran voluntad con que
sus vasallos se le ofresçian a hazer lo que les rrogaua, agradesçioselo

ancestors (who came from Cusco, because it was their place of origin) were
called the lords of Tahuantinsuyu, which means "the four parts of the
world." They were called this because they were certain that there was no
world outside of this one. [Since they were at the center of the world],
they would often send messengers from Cusco to the four parts of the land
to call the people to Cusco, just as my father did in the case of the assem-
bly just described. I have described it in this way because listing all of the
people who belonged [to Tahuantinsuyu] would be impossible. Since an
infinite number of people were consumed in Cajamarca and in the fighting with Quisquis, described above (and in the numerous skirmishes and
encounters I omit here for fear of extending myself too much in such
things), only the leaders of units of 10,000[52] gathered at this call. As soon
as they arrived and stood in the presence of my father—and seeing my father in such a miserable state—a great outpouring of grief took place, and
they said:

"Sapay Inca, what heart exists in this world that, on seeing our king so
afflicted and dismayed, would not break to pieces and melt in grief? Certainly, Sapay Inca, you erred in letting such people into your land. But it
is done and cannot be done differently now. We, your vassals,[53] are prepared and most willing to do all that we can and all that you would order   17
us to do. Fulfilling your order to gather here is nothing compared to what
we owe you; we are obligated to do much more for you. We would gladly
sell ourselves and our wives and children to save you from this misery—
and if you were to tell us this was still not enough, we would serve you in
whatever way we could. So believe us, Lord: the treasure you have asked
us to assemble will be delivered exactly on time and to the right place without fail, even if we have to scrape it out of the earth with our bare hands."

When my father, Manco Inca Yupanqui, understood the goodwill with
which his vassals offered to do what he had begged them to do, he thanked

52. A unit of 10,000 was called a *hunu*. The Incas used decimal groupings to organ-
ize the Andean population for the assessment of labor services of various kinds (Julien,
"Inca Decimal Administration in the Lake Titicaca Region," and "How Inca Decimal
Administration Worked").
53. Titu Cusi puts the term "vassals" in his father's mouth, a term that might have
translated a word for "subjects" in some sense, but which could not have had the same
meaning as it did in Spain.

mucho y dixo "por çierto, *apoes*" (que quiere dezir "señores"), "en gran obligasçion me aueis hechado por la gran voluntad que me mostrais de querer rredimir la bexaçion en que estoy puesto e para ello offresçer vuestras personas y haziendas; y os doy my palabra, como quien soy, que no perdais nada en el negoçio, que sy yo no muero yo os lo pagare, que pues yo me lo tome por mis manos metiendo tan mala gente en my tierra, yo me lo lleuare; gran plazer me hareis en daros la mayor priessa que pudieredes en la junta desto que os digo, porque rresçiuo grandisima pena en

17v   berme ansy presso y mal tratado; y porque no me molesten mas estos os sera neçesario que les hinchais aquel bohio questa alli", el qual hera vna casa grande, "de oro y plata, que quiça viendo esso sesaran de me molestar".

Los capitanes y gente rrespondieron a vna boz: "señor Sapai Ynga, para lo que te debemos no es nada esso; luego se hara como tu lo mandas"; y ansy se despidieron todos a buscar lo que my padre les auia mandado, los quales boluieron en breue tienpo con lo que les auia mandado que juntasen; y junto y puesto de la manera que my padre auia hordenado, otro dia el dicho my padre enbio a llamar a los españoles, los quales vinieron luego a su llamado.

De como llegaron los españoles en casa de Mango Ynga quando estaua preso y lo que alli acontesçio con su llegada

Llegado que fueron los españoles adonde mi padre estaua preso y aherrojado con grillos a sus pies, le saludaron segund otras vezes solian; y my padre, como los vio benir y llegar a su cassa, hizoles el acatamiento acostunbrado, a los quales començo a hablar en esta manera, preguntandoles lo primero por el *macho capito* que no estaua alli a la sazon, el qual dixo ansy a Hernando Piçarro "*apo, ¿adonde esta el macho capito?*"; y Hernando Piçarro rrespondio diziendo que quedaua en casa algo mal dispuesto; y mi padre, como le deseaua ver, dixo "pues, ¿no le enbiariamos a llamar?"; y Gonçalo Piçarro y los demas dixieron "norabuena,

18   Mango Ynga; bayanle a llamar, y bueno seria que le ffuesen a llamar de tu

them profusely and said with no hesitation, "It is true, *Apoes*"[54] (which means "lords"), "you have put me deeply in your debt for the goodwill you have shown me in wanting to redeem me from the misery in which I find myself, offering your persons and wealth. I give you my word, as I am who I am, that you will not lose anything; if I remain alive I will pay you back. I am to blame for letting such horrible people come into my land, and I will take responsibility for it. You will give me great pleasure if you gather together what I have told you as quickly as you can, since I am in tremendous distress because I have been imprisoned and badly treated. So that these people will stop bothering me, you will need to fill that house over there"—and he was indicating a very large house—"with gold and silver. Maybe when the Spaniards see that, they will stop bothering me." 17v

The captains and other people responded in one voice, "Lord Sapay Inca, this is nothing compared to what we owe you. We will do what you have ordered immediately." So they said their farewells and left to look for what my father had asked from them. They returned after a very brief time with what he had ordered them to gather. The day after it had been gathered and deposited in the manner he had ordered, he sent for the Spaniards, who came upon being called.

About how the Spaniards came to the house of Manco Inca when he was a prisoner and what happened there on their arrival

Once the Spaniards had arrived at the place where my father was held prisoner and shackled with leg irons, they greeted him as they had on other occasions. When he saw them arriving at his house, my father paid them the customary respects. He spoke with them, asking first for the *machu capitu*, who was not there at the time. He then said to Hernando Pizarro: "*Apo*, where is the *machu capitu*?" Hernando Pizarro answered that Francisco Pizarro had stayed home because he was not well. My father, who wanted to see Francisco Pizarro, said, "Well, aren't we going to call him?" Gonzalo Pizarro and the others said, "All in good time, Manco Inca. He will be called, and it would be good if your men went to call him on your 18

---

54. Again, "*Apoes*" is the Spanish plural of *apo* (see note 37).

parte"; y ansy my padre enbio algunos de sus capitanes a lo llamar, y el
gouernador rrespondio a los capitanes diziendo que se hallaua mal dispuesto por estonçes, que en estando algo mejor el yria a uer lo que mi
padre mandaua; y mi padre, como vio que no benia, dixo a los españoles
estas palabras:

Parlamento del Ynga a los españoles, estando en la prision, quando les dio el tesoro la primera vez

"Señores, muchos dias a que me hazeis gran desaguisado en tratarme de
la manera que me tratais, no os aviendo yo dado ocassion para ello, en espeçial aviendolo hecho tan bien con vosotros en dexaros entrar en my
tierra y traeros con tanta honrra y aparato a my pueblo y cassa y daros con
tanta voluntad de lo que en mi tierra y cassa tenia, lo qual, si vosotros
quereis juzgarlo, no ffue tan poco que no ffueron mas de dos millones [de
pesos] de oro e plata, que yo se que vuestro rrey no los thiene juntos; y bien
sabeis como estubo en mi mano el entrar vosotros en la tierra o no, porque
no queriendolo yo ¿que bastantes herades vosotros, ni otros diez tantos
mas, a poder entrar en ella?; no sabeis quanto poderio de jente yo tengo
en toda my tierra y quantas fortalezas e fuerças en ella ay; acordaros debriades con quanta boluntad yo os enbie a llamar, sin vosotros me lo hazer
18v   saber, y como, en señal de amistad por lo que me dixieron que herades
viracochas e ynbiados por el Tecsi Viracochan, os enbie al camino lo que
pude; acordaros debriades tanbien como, llegados que fuistes a este
pueblo, os hize proueer de seruiçio y mande juntar la jente de toda mi
tierra para que os tributasen; y en pago de todo esto, y de hazerlo yo con
tanta afiçion e boluntad, me abeis presso y puesto agora de la manera que
estoy so color de que me queria alçar contra vosotros y mataros, no teniendo yo dello tal pensamiento; bien entiendo que la cobdiçia os a segado
para hazer tan gran desatino, y mediante ella me aueis tratado desta suerte;
nunca yo pensaua que gente que tan buenas muestras daba al prençipio,
que se jataua de hijos del Viracochan, avian de hazer tal cosa; por vida
buestra, que me solteis y entendais que yo no os deseo dar pena sino
antes todo plazer; y para hartar vuestra cobdiçia, que tanta hanbre teneis

behalf." So my father sent some of his captains to call Francisco Pizarro. The Governor answered the captains by saying that he was indisposed at that moment, and that he would go as my father commanded when he was better. When he saw that Francisco Pizarro was not coming, my father said the following to the Spaniards:

Speech the Inca gave to the Spaniards, while he was a prisoner, when he gave them treasure for the first time

"Lords, you have greatly offended me for many days now by treating me as you have, since I have given you no reason for such treatment, and especially since I was so good to you, letting you stay in my land and bringing you to my town and house with so much honor and ceremony. I gladly gave you everything in my land and house: a treasure which, if you were to calculate its value, would be worth more than two million [*pesos*] in gold and silver. I know your king does not have that amount in one lump sum. You know very well that it was up to me to decide whether you entered this land or not. If I had not allowed you to enter, how could there have been enough of you—even if there had been ten times as many men as there were—to be able to enter? Don't you know what powerful armies I have in my land, how many fortresses and strongholds? You ought to remember the kindness I showed when I sent for you. Without your having to ask, and as a token of friendship—and because I had been told you were 18v *viracochas* sent by the Tecsi Viracochan—I sent you what I could while you were on the road. You ought to remember how, after you arrived in this town, I had you provided with service Indians and ordered the people all over my land to be gathered together so that they would pay tribute to you. In repayment of all this, and of the affection and kindness with which I did it, you took me prisoner and have kept me imprisoned in the manner in which I am now kept, under the pretext that I wanted to rebel against you and kill you, when I never even thought of such a thing. I know very well that greed has blinded you so that you could commit such blunders, and that is why you have treated me in this way. I never thought that people who made such a good initial impression as you did—and who represented themselves as sons of the Viracochan—would have done such things. On your lives, let me go and know that I do not want you to suffer, but to please you. To satisfy your greed, your overwhelming hunger

por plata, ay os daran lo que pedis; y mirad que os doy esto con aditamento que a my ni a jente ninguna de mi tierra abeis de molestar ni maltratar perpetuamente; y no penseis que os doy esto de miedo que tenga de bosotros sino de mi boluntad mera, porque ¿que miedo auia yo de auer de bosotros, estando toda la tierra debaxo de mi poderio y mando?, e sy yo quisiese, en muy breue tienpo os podrian desbaratar a todos; y estas prisiones que me aueis hechado, no penseis que las tengo en nada, que si yo ouiera querido muy ffaçilmente me obiera soltado dellas pero no lo he

19   hecho porque entendais que antes my negoçio emana de amor que de temor, y mediante este os he hecho y hago el tratamiento que os he rrelatado. De aqui adelante todos tengamos paz y biuamos de amor y conpañia; y si no la vbiere, bien sabeis que dareis pena al Viracochan" (que quiere dezir a "Dios"), "y a buestro rrey, e yo no rresçibire mucho contento".

Y como my padre acabase el parlamento ya dicho, todos los españoles que binieron con Hernando Piçarro y Gonçalo Piçarro y Joan Piçarro le agradeçieron mucho lo que les auia dicho, y mas, lo que les daua asy del tesoro como de las demas joyas; y todos juntamente le rrindieron las grasçias desta manera:

Modo y manera como rrindieron los españoles las grasçias a Mango Ynga del tesoro e joyas que les dio quando le soltaron

"Señor Mango Ynga, entendido tenemos todos los que aqui estamos, y el señor gouernador don Françisco Piçarro tiene lo mesmo, que mediante ser vuestra merçed quien es y hijo de tal padre como ffue Guaina Capac tenemos nosotros la tierra que oy poseemos y estamos de la manera que estamos con tanto contento y rregoçijo en estar en ella, que a no ser vuestra merçed quien es de sangre rreal ny tubieramos la tierra que tenemos ny poseyeramos las rriquezas que de su tan ffranca mano abemos rresçeuido

19v   y poseemoss; plega nuestro señor Dios todopoderoso, a quien vuestra merçed llama Viracochan, nuestro padre que por quien su diuina magestad es tan buena voluntad, como es la que vuestra merçed nos a mostrado y obras que nos a hecho, le pague traiendole a conosçimiento de quien su sacratissima magestad es para que conozçiendole le ame y amandole le posea y poseyendole se goze con el en su rreyno para sienpre, asi como

for silver, I will give you what you ask. But observe that I give it to you with the provision that you will not mistreat me or anyone else in my land ever again. Do not think that I give it to you because I am afraid: I give it out of goodwill. After all, what fear could I possibly have of you, since the land is under my power and command? I could defeat you in no time at all if I wanted to do so. And do not imagine that these restraints mean anything to me, since I could easily have gotten free of them if I wanted to do so. I have not done so because I want you to understand that I am moti- 19 vated more by love than by fear, and that is why I have treated you, and still treat you, in the way I have told you. Let us all have peace and live in love and unity from now on. If we do not have peace, you know very well that you will make the Viracochan" (which is to say "God"), "and your king unhappy, and I will not be very happy either."

At the end of my father's speech, all of the Spaniards who came with Hernando, Gonzalo, and Juan Pizarro thanked him very much for his words and for the treasure and other precious things he had given them. All together, they gave him thanks in this manner.

The method and manner in which the Spaniards thanked Manco Inca for the treasure and precious things he gave them when they freed him

"Lord Manco Inca, all of us present understand—as does the governor Don Francisco Pizarro—that we have the land we have today and are contented and happy here because you are who you are: the son of such a father as Huayna Capac. We understand that if Your Lordship were not of royal blood, we would neither have the land that we possess nor the riches we have so freely received from you.

May it please our Lord, all-powerful God (who Your Lordship calls 19v Viracochan), our father, who by being who his Divine Majesty is, is the source of all goodwill, like the goodwill Your Lordship has shown us and the good works you have done us, to repay you by bringing you to the knowledge of His Most Sacred Majesty, so that knowing Him you would love Him, and loving Him you would possess Him, and possessing Him you would enjoy being with Him in His kingdom forever,[55] in the same

---

55. Here is another rhetorical flourish that appears to have been supplied by the Augustinian Marcos García. Hernando Pizarro is unlikely to have spoken in this way.

nosotros nos gozamos poseyendo la merçed que vuestra merçed nos
haze"; Hernando Piçarro, dando la palabra por todos, dixo ansy: "todos
estos caualleros e yo hemos rresçiuido sumo contento con la merçed que
vuestra merçed nos a hecho en todo; quedamos en obligasçion de lo seruir
toda nuestra vida e protestamos de que agora ny en ningun tienpo, no
auiendo demasiada ocasion, estos caualleros ny yo no le daremos ninguna
pena".

    Acabado este rrazonamiento y hazimiento de grasçias de los españoles
a my padre, el dicho my padre les mando entregar el tesoro que les tenia
aparejado, los quales lo rresçibieron en sy, y no llegaron a ello hasta dar
parte de lo que les auia subçedido al gouernador; y ansy sin hazer mas, algunos dellos lo fueron luego a llamar para que lo vno diese las grasçias de
semejante tesoro a my padre y lo otro se hallase presente al rresçibir e par-
tir, porque segund despues paresçio por rruegos del gouernador auian los
españoles ydo a soltar a my padre de la carçel donde estaua, porque ellos
20   no fueran sy ellos del no fueran mandados; y ansy para que biese como estaua ya suelto my padre le fueron a llamar algunoss dellos, el qual enten-
diendo lo que pasaua y que my padre estaua ya suelto luego vino; y llegado
que ffue, saludo a my padre en esta manera:

Llegada del gouernador a cassa de Mango Ynga

"Dios guarde a vuestra merçed, señor Mango Ynga; por auer estado algo
mal dispuesto no bine juntamente con estos caualleros a besar las manos
a vuestra merçed, de que he estado con alguna pena por no auer hecho lo
que yo tanto deseaua que hera berme con vuestra merçed, pero ya que
hasta aqui a auido ffalta, que a ssido como dicho tengo por mi yndispusi-
sion, de aqui adelante no la abra; gran pena he rreçebido de la congoja que
me dizen vuestra merçed a rresçibido en su prission, en espeçial si ffue syn
culpa, lo qual, si a sido, es de rresçibir mayor, que bien creo que segund
vuestra merçed es de bueno es ansy; e teniendo esto entendido, como sienpre lo tube de su bondad, rrogue a estos caualleros que no molestasen
tanto a vuestra merçed, porque entendido tenia yo que quien con tanta
voluntad nos traxo a su tierra y tan de plano nos la entrego con los tesoros
que en ella auia, no se auia de mober tan ffaçilmente por ninguna cossa a
20v hazer cosa que no debiesse; suplico a vuestra merçed por me hazer merçed
no tenga pena, questos cavalleros e yo de aqui adelante procuraremos de

way we have enjoyed the favors Your Lordship has done us." Hernando Pizarro, speaking for all, said this: "All of these gentlemen and I have received great contentment from the favors you have done us in all things. We remain obligated to serve you for the rest of our days, and we swear that neither these men nor I will cause you any trouble now or in the future, if there is no reason for it."

Once the Spaniards concluded their exposition and expression of thanks to my father, he ordered that the collected treasure be given to them. Though the Spaniards claimed it, they did not go to where it was held until they could give word of what had happened to the Governor. So, without further ado, some of them went to call on Francisco Pizarro, in part to get him to thank my father for such a treasure, and in part so that he would be present to receive and distribute it. As it later turned out, the Spaniards had only released my father from his imprisonment as the result of the Governor's pleas; the Spaniards would not have freed my father if the Governor had not ordered them to do so.

So some of the Spaniards went to call on Francisco Pizarro to tell him　20 that my father was now free. When he understood what had happened, and that my father was now free, he came immediately. On arriving, he greeted my father in the following manner:

Arrival of Pizarro at the house of Manco Inca

"May God protect you, Lord Manco Inca. Because I was indisposed, I did not come with these gentlemen to kiss your hand. I have been troubled because I did not come see you as I deeply wanted to. I know I have been unavailable to you because of my indisposition, as I have said, but things will be different from now on. I have been particularly disturbed by the anguish they tell me you have suffered in your imprisonment; I would be especially disturbed if you were without blame, since your innocence would have compounded your suffering. I truly believe that you were well-intentioned if you say you were. Because I understood this—it was always evident from your kindness to us—I begged these gentlemen not to bother you. I knew that someone who had welcomed us into this land so willingly, and had so openly given it to us with all its treasures, would not have been so easily inclined to do what he should not do. I ask you,　20v as a favor, not to be upset. From now on these gentlemen and I will try

no se la dar, mas antes tener el rrespeto que a semejante persona como vuestra merçed conviene.

"Pareçeme que todabia haze vuestra merçed con estos caualleros y comigo lo que suele hazer, como pareçe por la merçed de tan gran rriqueza y tesoro como oy les a dado; por la parte que a mi me toca de ser su gouernador y por la que de su Magestad del quinto le a de caber beso las manos a vuestra merçed, que yo se que a de rresçibir tanto contento como con lo demas que hasta aqui dado por vuestra merçed le he enbiado, quedo por esta merçed en tanta obligasçion, que por palabra no lo sabre significar".

Respuesta de Mango Ynga al gouernador

"*Apo*" (que quiere dezir "señor"), "vengas norabuena; muchos dias a que te e deseado beer y no se que a sido la causa porque no me as querido dar este contento pues tanto yo lo he deseado y te he enbiado a llamar no se quantan [quantas] vezes para quexarme a ti destos tus soldados; y por les aplazer a ellos no me as querido dar a mi contento, pues por çierto que te lo he deseado yo dar y avn procurado, mal me pagais vosotros my tan buen deseo y obras; estos tus soldados me an molestado y ffatigado sin yo meresçerlo, teniendome aqui aherrojado con hierros como si yo ffuera su criado o como sy yo fuera su llama" (que quiere dezir "carnero"), "mas me pareçe esta molestia e cobdiçiosa que hazaña poderosa porque a la clara se bee que me an tenido antes preso por su hanbrienta cobdiçia que por poderio que sobre mi pudiesen tener; y como tu as visto y de todo heres testigo no me vençistes vosotros a my por fuerça de armas sino por hermosas palabras, que sy no me dixierades que herades hijos del Viracochan y que los enbiaua e yo por buestras ynsignias de tantos enlauiamientos como comigo vsastes no lo pensara, no se yo como lo ouierades en la entrada de mi tierra y por lo auer yo hecho con vosotros de la manera que lo hec [he] hecho me tratais desta manera; gentil pago me dais por tan buena obra como yo os he hecho; aqui he dado a estos tus soldados no se que oro e plata por

not to upset you, but will treat you instead with the respect that a person like yourself deserves.

"It seems to me that you are still treating me and these gentlemen as you always have: this much is apparent from the gift of great riches and treasure you have given us today. I kiss your hand for the share that belongs to me as Governor, and for the share that corresponds to His Majesty for the *quinto*.[56] I know the King will be as contented with this gift as he has been with everything else I have sent to him on your behalf. I cannot express how deeply I am obligated to you for this favor."

Response of Manco Inca to Pizarro

"*Apo*"[57] (which means "lord"), "you have come just in time. For many days I have wanted to see you. I do not know why you have not wanted to give me this satisfaction, since I wanted very much to see you and sent for you I do not know how many times to complain to you about these men, your soldiers. In order to please them, you have denied me satisfaction. I certainly wanted to satisfy you, and have even tried to do so. You have repaid my good intentions and deeds very badly. These, your soldiers, have troubled and distressed me without my having deserved it.   21 They chained me here in irons as if I were your servant, or as if I were your *llama*" (which means "sheep"). "Moreover, it seems that greed, not a desire for power, is the cause of all this harassment. It is now clear that you have held me prisoner more because of your insatiable greed rather than because of any power over me you might have. As you have seen and witnessed yourself, you never defeated me by force of arms, but rather by beautiful words. If you had not said that you were sons of the Viracochan and sent by him—and if I hadn't believed you because of the signs you gave and the deceitful promises you made—I do not know how you would have been able to enter my land. And you would treat me in this way for having done what I did for you, in the manner I did it! Polite payment you give me for such good deeds as I have done for you! Here . . . I have given these your soldiers I do not know how much gold and silver because

---

56. A reference to the royal tax of one-fifth.

57. Here, Manco Inca is using an Inca term of address (*apo*) to speak with Pizarro (see note 37).

sus ynportunasçiones; hazlo rrepartir alla como a ti te paresçiere y mira que pues heres tan buen *apo* que mandes que de aqui adelante no me den mas enojo, pues yo no se lo dexes dar a ellos, que te hago saber de çierto que sy ellos me lo dan que yo procurare de dareselo de tal suerte que quiça les pese".

El gouernador, oyda la rrespuesta que mi padre le dio, holgose mucho con ella y mando rresçibir aquel tesoro a los españoles diziendo "rres-çiuase eso que con tan buena voluntad nos haze merçed el señor Mango Ynga Yupangui, el qual no lo a de agora el hazernos semejantes merçedes sino de muy atras; e miren buestras merçedes señores, los que aqui estan presentes, que tenemos ya mucho rresçibido del señor Mango Ynga des-pues que estamos en su tierra, y que se lo pagamos muy mal segund la voluntad con que nos lo da; de aqui en adelante, por su bida que le rres-peten y tengan en mucho, pues lo merece".

Todos los soldados, con el contento que rresçibieron con el don del tesoro que mi padre les auia dado, rrespondieron con gran gozo al gouer-nador estas palabras:

Respuesta de Hernando Piçarro y Gonçalo Piçarro y Joan Piçarro y de los demas soldados al gouernador

"Por çierto vuestra Señoria thiene muy gran rrazon en rreprehendernos y affearnos semejante cosa que esa porque sy ouiera miramiento en nosotros no lo auiamos de auer hecho desta suerte sino agradeçer el bien a quien nos lo haze; de aqui adelante se hara como vuestra Señoria lo manda". Acabadas todas estas rrazones de vna parte y de otra todos los españoles rrepartieron aquel tesoro por cabeças, dando a cada vno segund su cali-dad, lo qual rrepartio Hernando Piçarro como prençipal autor en aquel caso porquel auia sido el que auia preso a mi padre, el qual tesoro rrepartieron a costales porque segund hera la cantidad tardaronse mucho en rrepartirlo por peso; y desque vbieron ya rrepartido el tesoro entre sy, my padre en señal de agradesçimiento al gouernador dixole estas palabras:

"*Apo,* pareçeme que tu as sido parte para questos tus soldados me ayan soltado de la prision en que estaua, la qual paresçio ser sin culpa; rruegote que no te bayas tan presto sino que en señal de la conffede-rasçion de nuestra amistad hagamos juntos colasçion, que yo espero que de mi parte no a de quebrar lo por mi prometido"; y el gouernador por le dar contento a mi padre e porque la demanda hera justa y no dañosa

of their importunily. Divide it up as it seems best to you and take care, since you are such a good *apo*, that you order them not to make me angry again. I have no desire to anger them. But I tell you now in no uncertain terms that if they anger me, I will manage to return their anger in such a way that it could go badly for them."

The Governor was pleased with my father's response. He ordered the Spaniards to receive the treasure with the following words: "Take this treasure, that with so much goodwill the lord Manco Inca Yupanqui has given us. He will not do us such favors again, except perhaps in some distant future. Be mindful, all of you who are present, that we have already received a great deal from the lord Manco Inca since arriving in his land and have repaid his goodwill badly. From now on—for the rest of his life— you are to treat him as a great lord, since he deserves your respect." 21v

The soldiers, content with the gift of treasure that my father had given them, all responded with great pleasure to the Governor in the following words:

Response of Hernando Pizarro, Gonzalo Pizarro, Juan Pizarro and of the other soldiers to Pizarro

"Your lordship is certainly correct to reprimand us and make us look bad for such a thing as this. We would not have done things in this way if we had been prudent. Instead, we should have given thanks to the person who was so good to us. From here on we will do as Your Lordship orders." Once these words were spoken, the Spaniards all distributed the treasure to each other, giving to each individual what he should receive according to his station. Hernando Pizarro, who was responsible for the imprisonment of my father, did the distributing. They distributed the treasure by sacks, because there was such a large quantity that it would have taken a long time to divide it up by weight. After the Spaniards had divided up the treasure among themselves, my father said these words as a token of his thanks: 22

"*Apo,* it appears that you are not to blame for my imprisonment and that your soldiers have released me on your orders. I beg you not to depart now. Instead, let us take a meal together as a sign of our friendly alliance, since I intend not to break that which I have promised." Because what my father asked was reasonable and not harmful, the Governor

obolo por bien, e sentandose todos en la sala donde mi padre estaua rresçibieron colasçion con gran rregoçijo y chacota.

Reçiuida la colasçion y confederados my padre y los españoles fueronse a sus casas cada vno con la rrasçion que le cupo de la enpressa del tesoro; de creer es que yrian aconpañando al gouernador y que alla se rregoçijarian entre si cada vno con lo que lleuauan, el qual rregoçijo segund adelante se bera no les duro mucho porque como el demonio sea tan malo como es y amigo de disçensiones e diferençias nunca para.

Rebuelta de Gonçalo Piçarro contra el Ynga

22v   No pasaron (segund my padre me dixo) tres meses quando la ynbidia, ques enemiga de toda bondad, rreyno en Gonçalo Piçarro lo vno por ver que a su hermano le auian dado tanta cantidad de oro y plata por no mas de que auia preso a mi padre con cobdiçia quando hera corregidor y lo otro porque como se bio con bara y mando por la ausençia del Marques don Françisco Piçarro, gouernador, [que] a la sazon se auia partido para Lima, despidiendose de my padre con gran amor y amistad estando sienpre confformes, quiso mostrar fausto y autoridad con la bara a costa de mi padre, achacandolo que se queria alçar diziendo que vna noche auia de dar sobre ellos estando durmiendo, y con este achaque also el dicho Gonçalo Piçarro; se procuro de armar y tomar consigo a su hermano Juan Piçarro y a otros para yr a prender a my padre, los quales todos se fueron a la casa donde mi padre estaua holgandose con toda su gente en vna fiesta que a la sazon hazia; e llegados que fueron mi padre no sospechando la traiçion

agreed to my father's request in order to please him. Seated in the hall where my father was, the two men took a meal together with great rejoicing and pleasure.

Having entered into an alliance, my father and the Spaniards returned to their houses as soon as the meal was over; the Spaniards went to their houses, each carrying the share they had been given from the business of the treasure. It can be imagined that they would have kept the Governor company [at his house], and that there they would have all rejoiced together, each one about what he had gotten. But that rejoicing, as will be seen below, did not last long because the devil—being evil and a friend to dissent and conflict—never rests.

Revolt of Gonzalo Pizarro against the Inca

According to my father, not even three months had passed when envy— the enemy of all kindness—ruled in the heart of Gonzalo Pizarro. This happened, in part, because Gonzalo saw that the people had given his brother [when he was *corregidor*]⁵⁸ a large quantity of gold and silver for having imprisoned my father out of greed; it also happened, in part, because Gonzalo then held the *vara*⁵⁹ and authority in the Marquis Don Francisco Pizarro's absence. After saying goodbye to my father with great affection and friendship (since the two were of the same mind), Francisco Pizarro departed for Lima. Gonzalo Pizarro wanted to demonstrate the splendor and authority of his office at my father's expense, so he accused my father of wanting to rebel, and then he claimed that one night my father would attack the Spaniards while they were sleeping. With this false accusation, Gonzalo Pizarro managed to persuade his brother Juan and others to arm themselves and go with him to capture my father. They all went to the house where my father, along with all of his people, was enjoying himself in a fiesta they were celebrating. When the Spaniards arrived, my father received them with great benevolence and

22v

58. A royal magistrate, appointed by the Crown. The first *corregidores* were introduced in Peru in urban areas in the 1540s, and did not yet exist at the time represented in the text. Juan and Hernando Pizarro were named as their brother Francisco's lieutenants while he was away from Cusco, but Gonzalo never was.
59. The *vara* was the insignia of Spanish office, particularly of the office of mayor. It was usually made of wood.

que tenia armada lo rresçibio con gran benebolençia y afabilidad; y ellos
como llebauan la traiçion a su casa y luego ffueron tras del y en ella al
tienpo que quiso salir le prendieron, diziendo el Gonçalo Piçarro estas
palabras.

Segunda prission de Mango Ynga por Gonçalo Piçarro

23 "Señor Mango Ynga, el otro dia quedastes con mi hermano Hernando
Piçarro en no vrdir ni tratar mas negoçios y pareçeme que no aueis
guardado lo que prometistes que ynfformadoss estamos como teneis
conçertado de dar sobre nosotros esta noche e para eso teneis junta tanta
gente, por tanto sea preso por el rrey; y no penseis que a de ser agora como
el otro dia que dexistes que no teniades en nada todas nuestras prisiones,
agora lo esperimentareis si se quibran [quiebran] o no"; y luego de manos
a boca mando traer Gonçalo Piçarro vnos grillos y vna cadena con que
aherrojasen a su sabor a mi padre, los quales grillos y cadena mando que
luego se le hechasen; y mi padre, biendo que con tanto vitoperio le querian parar de aquella suerte, quisose deffender diziendo.

Requesta [Respuesta] de Mango Ynga

"Asi que andais aqui comigo cada triquete, haziendome beffas; vosotros
no sabeis que yo soy hijo del sol e hijo del Viracochan como vosotros os
jatais; ¿soy quiera quiera [sic: qualquiera] o algun yndio de baxa suerte?
¿quereis escandalizar toda la tierra y que os hagan pedaços a todos?; no me
maltrataeis, que no os he hecho; ¿por que pensais que se me dañara por
vuestras prisiones?; no las tengo en lo que huello".

Gonçalo Piçarro y sus aferazes [alferezes], como vieron a mi padre con
23v tanta furia, rremetieron [arremetieron] todos contra el para le hechar la
cadena al pescuesso diziendo

graciousness, without suspecting the betrayal that had been planned. The Spaniards, who had brought their treachery with them into the house where my father was, later followed him to his house. When my father wanted to leave his house, they captured him. Gonzalo Pizarro said these words:

Second imprisonment of Manco Inca by Gonzalo Pizarro

"Lord Manco Inca, the other day you agreed with my brother Hernando 23 Pizarro not to plot or attempt any more such business. It seems to me that you have not kept your promise, as we are informed how you have conspired with others to attack us tonight and have gathered together many people to carry out this plan. For this reason, I imprison you in the name of the King. Do not think that this time it will be as it was the other day when you said that you considered all our restraints as if they were nothing. Now you will learn whether you can break them or not." Later, Gonzalo Pizarro carried out his words by ordering [his men to bring] some leg irons and a chain with which my father could be shackled in this new fashion. Then he ordered my father shackled with the leg irons and chain. In response to the vituperative motives behind the Spaniards' effort to restrain him, my father felt the need to defend himself and said:

Response of Manco Inca

"So this is how you treat me, grossly insulting me every time I turn around? Don't you know that I am son of the Sun,[60] and son of the Viracochan, as you have claimed to be? Do you think I am just some common person? Do you want to scandalize the whole land so that the people will cut you to pieces? Do not mistreat me. I have given you no reason to do so. Do you think that you will harm me with your restraints? They mean nothing to me."

When they saw my father in such a fury, Gonzalo Pizarro and his officials threw themselves on him to wrap the chain around his body, saying: 23v

---

60. Titu Cusi probably used the term *intipchurin,* which can be translated as "son of the sun," but which also means "member of the son's descent group" (Julien, *Reading Inca History,* 24, 103, 115). Someone who could claim descent from the sun may also have been claiming both a status that was more than human and a demonstrated right to govern.

"no os deffendais Mango Ynga; mira que os ataremos pies y manos de arte que no sea bastante quantos ay en el mundo a desataros porque sy os prendimos es en nonbre y boz del Enperador y no de nuestra autoridad, y que lo ffuera, nos abeis de dar agora mucho mas oro y plata que el otro dia, y mas me aueis de dar a la señora *coya* Cura Ocllo, vuestra hermana, para my muger"; y luego yncontinente todos de mancomun como alli estauan le hecharon la cadena al pescueso e los grillos a los pies.

Parlamento de Mango Ynga, segunda bez estando en la prision

Mi padre, como se bio asy atado y preso de aquella manera con tanta ynominia y deshonrra, dixo con mucha lastima estas palabras: "¿por ventura soy yo perro o carnero o algun *oyua* vuestro que porque no me huya me atais desta manera? ¿soy ladron o he hecho alguna traiçion al Viracochan o a vuestro rrey?; si que no, pues si no soy perro ni ninguna cossa de las que dicho tengo, ¿que es la causa porque de tal manera me tratais?; verdaderamente agora digo, y me afirmo en [e]llo, que vosotros sois antes hijos de *supai* que criados del Viracochan, quanto y mas hijos, porque, si como arriua dicho tengo vosotros ffuerades, no digo yo hijos verdaderos sino criados del Viracochan, lo vno no me trataredes de la manera que me tratais, mas antes mirades a quien yo soy y cuyo hijo y el poderio que he tenido y tengo, el qual por vuestro rrespeto he dexado, y lo otro miraredes que no a auido en toda mi tierra despues que entrastes en ella cosa ninguna, alta y baxa, pequeña ni grande que se os aya negado, mas antes, si rriquezas yo tenia, vosotros las poseis, si gente, a bosotros siruen, asy honbres como mugeres, chicos y grandes y menores, sy tierras, las mejores que en mi tierra ay debaxo de vuestro poderio estan, pues, ¿que cosa ay en el mundo de que ayais tenido neçesidad que yo no la aya probeydo a bosotros?; yngratos çierto sois y dignos de toda confussion".

Gonçalo Piçarro y Joan Piçarro y los demas que con ellos vinieron, no haziendo caso de lo que mi padre les dezia, con vn genero de desden dixieron "sosiegue, sosiegue, señor Sapai Ynga, y rreposse vn poco, que esta

"You can't defend yourself, Manco Inca. Look how we have tied your hands and feet in such a way so that there aren't enough people in the world to untie them, because, if we capture you, we do so in the name and voice of the Emperor, not on our own authority. And since we do it in his name, you must now give us a great deal more gold and silver than you did the other day. You must also give me the lady Coya Cura Ocllo, your sister, as my wife." As soon as Gonzalo Pizarro had finished saying this, all of the Spaniards chained my father's body and cuffed his legs.

Speech by Manco Inca the second time he was imprisoned

When he saw himself so ignominiously and dishonorably tied and bound in that way, my father spoke the following words sorrowfully: "Do you think it is possible that I am a dog or a sheep, or some mare of yours, that you have to tie me in this manner so I do not flee? Am I a thief or have I done some traitorous act to the Viracochan or your king? Of course not! So, if I am not a dog nor any of the things I mentioned, what is the reason for treating me in this manner? Truly I say and affirm that you are more like sons of the *Supay* than servants of the Viracochan, much less his sons. If I said before that you were, I did not mean real sons but servants of the Viracochan. I say this because [if you were sons of the Viracochan] you would not have treated me in this manner; you would have taken note instead of who I am and whose son, and the power I had and still have (and which I have not used because of the respect I have for you). You would also have noticed that after you arrived in my land, there has not been anything high or low, small or large, in all my land that has been denied you. If I had riches, you have possessed them; if people, they have served you—men and women, young and old, and children; if I had lands, the best there are in my kingdom have been given to you. What in the world could you need that I have not provided you? You are certainly ungrateful and should be ashamed of yourselves."

Gonzalo Pizarro and Juan Pizarro and all the others who came with them, paid no attention to what my father told them and said with disdain: "Calm down, calm down,[61] Lord Sapay Inca. Rest a little. You are

---

61. Note the repetition. Here and afterward, repetition seems to indicate an emotional charge.

agora con mucha colera; mañana hablaremos largo; en todo procure de dar horden como se junte mucha plata y oro." "Y acuerde de darnos la *coya*, que la deseo mucho auer", dixo Gonçalo Piçarro. Acabadas de dezir estas buenas rrazones los españoles a mi padre, fueronse a sus casas a comer, porque este prendimiento auia sido a la mañana. Ydos que fueron los españoles a sus posadas y dexando buenas guardas que guardasen a mi padre, luego toda la gente questaua en vna plaça llamada Pumaqurco, de adonde my padre se lebanto aquella mañana de comer con todos ellos para yr a su cassa a algo que le conbenia quando le prendieron los españoles, vino con gran sobresalto a la casa donde my padre estaua a uer por que causa no auia venido a la *panpa* en tanta distançia de tienpo; y como llegaron a la puerta, hallaron todos los criados de mi padre alborotados y como llorando por ber a su amo preso de aquella suerte; los capitanes y gente que anssi benian a saber lo que pasaua todos enmudeçieron, haziendo entre sy grandes esclamaçiones; y vnos a otros como marauillandosse se preguntaban "¿que es esto, ques esto?"; y estando ansy alborotados, entraron adentro los capitanes mass prençipales de toda la tierra a çertificarsse de veras como pasaua el caso y a ber que hazia mi padre; y entrando mas adentro que les fue dado para ello liçençia, sin la qual naidie podia entrar, llegaron adonde mi padre estaua preso, y de la manera arriua dicho, y biendolo todos de aquella manera hizieron vn gran llanto, que fue çierto cosa de beer, adonde, llamando todos a alta boz, vno de ellos llamado Vila Oma, persona que governaba la tierra por my padre como general de toda ella, dixo como conquestandosse e yncrepando a mi padre desta manera:

"Sapai Ynga, ¿ques esto en que andan estoss *viracochas*?; oy te prenden, mañana te sueltan; pareçe que andan contigo jugando a juego de niños,

24v

25

too angry right now. Tomorrow we will speak at length." Gonzalo Pizarro said: "Give some thought to how you are going to gather a great deal of gold and silver, and do not forget to give us the Coya, whom I desire very much." Since the capture occurred in the morning, the Spaniards went to their houses to eat after making their point. When the Spaniards had gone to their lodgings—leaving sufficient guards to watch my father—all of the people who had been eating with my father in the plaza called Pumacurco[62] when he had gotten up to go to his house to take care of 24v some matter and had been captured by the Spaniards, came in one group to the house where my father was; they wanted to know why he had not returned to the *pampa*[63] after being gone so long. When they came to the door, they found my father's servants in a state of great agitation and weeping at seeing their master imprisoned in such a way. The captains and other people who had come to find out what had happened to my father were astonished. Some made exclamations to each other and others marveled, asking themselves, "What is this? What is going on?" In the middle of this emotional outpouring, the most senior captains in the entire land went inside to find out for themselves what had happened and to see my father. After receiving the permission necessary to go inside (without which no one was able to enter), the captains came to the place where my father was imprisoned in the manner described above. There was another outpouring of grief when they saw him tied up in that way, which was certainly something to see. At that point, Vila Oma,[64] a person who had governed as general over all the land in my father's name, called out to the captains in a loud voice, and trying to control himself, he rebuked my father with the following words:

"Sapay Inca, what are the *viracochas* up to? Today they capture you, to- 25 morrow they release you. It seems that they are playing a childish game.

---

62. Pumacurco, meaning "puma's back," is the name of a street in Cusco. It defines the back of a puma figure that can be identified in the layout of the Inca city (Rowe, "What Kind of City Was Inca Cuzco?" 60, 77).

63. This Inca word, now common in English, was defined by González Holguín as a "plaza, flat or flattened place, pasture, savannah, or open country" (*Pampa. Plaça, suelo llano o llanada pasto, çauana, o campo;* 275).

64. Vila Oma, another son of Huayna Capac, was the majordomo of the Sun's estates, which included land, retainers, women, herds, and valuable objects (Betanzos, *Narrative of the Incas,* pt. 2, ch. 29: 280–81; Julien, *Reading Inca History,* 265).

pero no me marauillo que te traten desta suerte, pues tu te lo quisiste, metiendo en tu tierra de tu voluntad sin nuestro pareçer gente tan mala; yo te digo que si tu me dexaras a my quando ellos llegaron a Caxamarca que nunca ellos llegaran donde tu estas agora, porque yo e Challcochima, avnque ellos no quisieran, con la gente de nuestro bando les estoruaramoss la entrada; y no creo yo que nos ouiera ydo tan mal como nos a ydo por ser tu tan bueno, porque sy tu no nos dixieras que heran *viracochas* y enbiados por el Atun Biracochan," (que quiere dezir "gran dios"), "y no no mandaras que les obedeçiesemos y rrespetaramos por tales, porque ansy lo hazias tu, poca neçesidad teniamos nosotros ser vexados y molestados de la suerte que agora estamos, desposeydos de nuestras haziendas, de nuestras mugeres, de nuestros hijos e hijas y de nuestras *chacarras* y bernos vasallos de quien no conosçemos, tan opressos, tan ffatigados que hasta con nuestras capas nos hazen linpiar la suziedad de los cauallos; mira señor, ¿hasta quanta baxeza nos as hecho benir por quererlo tu?, e pues tu lo as querido, no te marauilles que te traten desa manera; bien sabes que avn quando tu saliste a Villcacunga a rresçibirlos te lo estoruaua yo, y te fuy a

25v la mano muchas vezes sobre que no les metieses en tu tierra, y avn, sy se te acuerda, te dixe quando tubimos nueua que auian llegado a la tierra que yo yria por la posta con diez o doze mill yndios y los haria pedaços a todos, y tu nunca me dexaste syno antes 'calla, calla, que son *viracochas* o sus hijos', como si no barruntaramos nosotros que gente desta manera que benia de tan lexos tierra, que antes venia a mandar que a obedeçer; yo e toda tu gente tenemos de lo pasado gran pena, y de berte de la manera que estas, gran conpassion; sy te pareçe, porque entiendas que soy el que ser solia, dame liçençia que yo te soltare y a estos barbudos los acabare bien breue, porque gente tienes tu en tu tierra que me ayudara, que bien sabes tu que en toda la tierra arriba y abaxo ni al traues, despues de ti no ay a quien mas

I do not wonder that they treat you in this fashion, though you asked for it by allowing such terrible people into this land on your own and without consulting us. I tell you that, if you had left it up to me when they first arrived in Cajamarca, they would never have gotten where they are now. Challcochima and I, with the people on our side, would have made it impossible for the Spaniards to enter our land, no matter how much they wanted to do so. I do not think it would have gone as badly as it has as a result of your good treatment of them. If you had not told us that they were *viracochas* and sent by the Hatun Viracochan[65] (which means 'Great God'), and if you had not ordered us to obey them and respect them as such (because that is what you did), we would not now have reason to be as vexed and bothered as we are. We are dispossessed of our property, our women, our sons and daughters, and our *chacaras*,[66] and have become the vassals of someone we do not even know. We are so oppressed and mistreated that we have even been made to clean the filth from their horses with our own capes. See for yourself, lord, how low we have come because of your wishes. And you did wish it, so do not marvel that they treat you in this manner. You well know that even when you went out to Vilcaconga to receive them, I tried to prevent you and to keep you from allowing them into your land. Do you recall that when we first received   25v
the news of their arrival in the land, I even told you that I would travel up the main road with ten or twelve thousand Indians and make pieces out of them? But you would not let me; you said, 'No, no, they are *viracochas* or his sons,' as if we did not suspect that people who came from such a distant land had come to command rather than to obey. We—all of your people and I—are very sad about what has happened and feel great compassion when we see you in this state. You know that I am who I have always been. If it seems like a good idea to you, give me license to free you and finish with these bearded people in short order. The people in your land will help me. You know very well that all over the land, from top to bottom and across it, after you there is no one who commands more

65. *Hatun* is defined by González Holguín as "The largest or best or superior; the most principal and best-known (*Hatun. Lo mayor, o mejor, o superior mas principal y mas conocido;* 154).
66. *Chacara* is a hispanization of "*chacra*," defined by González Holguín as "cultivated field or orchard" (*Chhacra. Heredad de lauor tierras o huertas;* 91).

rrespeten que a my, pues sobre todos soy general". Acabado que vbo de rrelatar a mi padre lo arriba dicho, este capitan Vila Oma juntamente con otro llamado Tiçoc, su conpañero, se boluieron a los españoles que a la sazon alli estaban presentes, y con rrostros alterados y seberos dixieron estas palabras:

Yncrepaçion hecha por los capitanes del Ynga
a los españoles sobre el mal tratamiento
que hazian a su rrey e señor

"¿Que andais vosotros aqui con nuestro Ynga daca por alla cada dia, oy prendiendole, mañana molestandole y esotro dia haziendole beffas? ¿que os a hecho este honbre? ¿asy le pagais la buena obra que os hizo en meteros a su tierra contra nuestra voluntad? ¿que quereis del? ¿que mas os puede hazer de lo que a hecho? ¿no os dexo entrar en su tierra con toda paz y sosiego y con mucha honrra? ¿no os enbio a llamar a Caxamarca a los mensajeros que le enbiastes? ¿no os los enbio muy honrrados con mucha plata y oro y con mucha gente? ¿no ffueron e binieron en hamacas, traiendolos su gente a questas en Caxamarca? ¿no tomastes dos casas grandes de oro y plata que le pertenesçian, y mas lo que os dio Ataguallpa, que todo hera de mi Ynga, y lo que el os enbio de aqui a Caxamarca, que fue gran cantidad de oro e plata?; de Caxamarca a este pueblo, en çiento y treinta leguas [650 km] que ay de camino de alla aca, ¿no os hizieron todo buen tratamiento, dandoos muchos rreffrescos y gente que os traxiesen el mesmo? ¿no os salio a rresçibir al camino seis leguas [30 km] de aqui en Xaquixaguana por vuestro rrespeto? ¿no quemo la persona mas prençipal que tenia en toda su tierra, que fue Challcochima?; llegados que fuistes aqui, ¿no os dio casas y asientos y criados y mugeres y sementeras? ¿no mando llamar a toda su gente para que os tributasen? ¿no os an tributado?; sy que sy; el otro dia quando le prendisteis por rredimir su bexasçion, ¿no os dio vna casa llena

respect than I do, since I am general over all." Once he had finished telling my father everything noted above, this captain Vila Oma joined with another captain, his companion named Tizoc, and returned to speak to the Spaniards who were there at the time. With disturbed and severe faces Vila Oma and Tizoc said these words:

Rebuke made by the captains of the Inca to the Spaniards because of the bad treatment they had given their king and lord

"What are you doing with our Inca,[67] playing back-and-forth with him every day, capturing him one day, disturbing him the next, and grossly insulting him on the following day? What has this man done to you? Is this 26 how you repay him for allowing you into his land against our will? What do you want from him? What more can he do for you than what he has done? Didn't he let you enter his land in complete peace and calm, and with honor? Didn't he send for you in Cajamarca via the messengers you sent him? Didn't he send your messengers back to you in honorable fashion, with a great deal of silver and gold and many people? Didn't your messengers travel in hammocks carried by his people on their own backs? Didn't you receive two large houses full of his gold and silver, along with the great quantity of gold and silver Atahuallpa gave you, all of which belonged to my Inca and which was sent by him from here to Cajamarca (and it was a very large quantity)? And, as you traveled along the entire 130 leagues [390 mi] of road from Cajamarca to this town, didn't my Inca see to your every need, supplying you himself with refreshments and the people who would bring you here? Out of respect for you, didn't Manco Inca go out to meet you on the road himself, six leagues [18 mi] from here in Jaquijaguana? Didn't he burn Challcochima, the most important person in all the land, alive? Once you had arrived here, didn't he give you houses and places to stay, servants, women, and fields? Didn't he call all the people together and order them to pay tribute to you? Haven't they paid tribute to you? They absolutely have. The other day when you captured him, and in order to free himself of such vexation, didn't he give you a house full

---

67. Here begins a long series of questions. This rhetorical device expresses displeasure, without making outright accusations.

26v   de oro y plata?; a nosotros los prençipales y a toda la gente, ¿no nos aueis
quitado las mugeres nuestras e hijos e hijas, y a todo callamos porque el
lo quiere por bien?; y por no le dar pena, ¿nuestra gente no os syrue hasta
linpiar con sus capas la suziedad de los cauallos y de buestras casas? ¿que
mas quereis?; todas quantas vezes aueis dicho 'daca oro, daca plata, daca
oro, daca plata, junta esto, junta estotro', ¿no lo a hecho sienpre hasta
daros sus mesmos criados que os syruan? ¿que mas pedis a este honbre?
¿vosotros no le engañastes, diziendo que beniades por el biento por mandado del Viracochan, que hera del sus hijos, y deziades que beniades a
seruir al Ynga, a quererle mucho, a tratarle como a vuestras personas mes-
mas a el y a toda su gente?; bien sabeis vosotros, y lo beis sy lo quereis mirar atentamente, que en todo aveis ffaltado y que en lugar de tratarle como
publicastes al prençipio le aueis molestado y molestais cada credo syn
mereçerlo ni aberos dado la menor ocasion del mundo; ¿de donde pensais
que a de sacar tanto oro e plata como vosotros le pedis?, pues os a dado
hasta quitarnos a nosotros nuestras joyas, todo quanto en su tierra tenia;
¿que pensais que os a de dar agora por la prision en que le teneis preso?
¿de donde a de sacar esto que le pedis?; ni avn nada sy no lo thiene ni tiene
que daros.

27   "Toda la gente desta tierra esta muy escandalizada y amedrentada de tal
manera de ber vuestras cossas, que no saben ya que se dezir ni adonde se
puedan yr; porque lo vno bense desposeydos de su rrey, lo otro de sus
mugeres, de sus hijos, de sus casas, de sus haziendas, de sus tierras, fynal-
mente de todo quanto poseyan, que çierto estan en tanta tribulasçion que
no les rresta syno ahorcarse o dar al trabes con todo, y avn me lo an dicho
a my muchas vezes; por tanto, señores, lo mas açertado que a mi me
paresçe seria que dexasedes ya descansar a my Sapai Ynga, pues por vuestra causa esta con tanta neçesidad e trauajo, e le soltaredes de la prission
en que esta, porquestos sus yndios no esten con tanta congoxa".

Respuesta de los españoles a Vila Oma

"¿Quien te manda a ti hablar con tanta autoridad al corregidor del rrey?
¿sabes tu que gente somos nosotros los españoles?; calla,

of gold and silver? Haven't you taken our women, sons, and daughters 26v
from us, the principal lords and all the people, and haven't we kept quiet
about it all because he thought we should and we did not want to upset
him? Haven't our people served you, to the point of cleaning the filth from
your horses and your houses with their own capes? What more do you
want? Every time you have told us: 'over here, gold'; 'over here, silver';
'over here, gold'; 'over here, silver'; 'near this'; 'near that'; hasn't he done
what you wanted, even giving you his own servants to serve you? What
more would you ask from this man? Didn't you deceive him, saying that
you came on the wind by order of the Viracochan, that you were the Viracochan's sons, and that you came to serve the Inca, to love him and treat
him and his people the same way you treat yourselves? You know well and
would see, if you were willing to look carefully, that you have proved to
be lacking in every way, and that, instead of treating him as you first an-
nounced you would, you have disturbed him and continue to disturb him
at the drop of a hat without his having deserved such treatment or given
you the slightest occasion in the world for it. Where do you think he can
get as much gold and silver as you have asked him for, since he has already
given you all he had in the land, to the point of taking our own valuables?
What do you think he should give you now to free himself from imprisonment? Where is he supposed to get what you ask him for, if he does not
have it nor anything else to give you?

"All of the people of this land are so scandalized and terrorized by what 27
you have done that they do not know what to say anymore nor where they
can go to escape. They see themselves dispossessed of their king, and also
of their women, their children, houses, property, and land—that is, of
everything they own. They suffer such tribulation that there is nothing left
for them but to hang themselves or hand everything over to you, and they
have said as much to me many times. For all these reasons, lords, I think
it would be prudent for you to leave my Sapay Inca alone—since it is you
who have caused him such need and travail—and release him from imprisonment so that these, his Indians, are not so troubled."

Response of the Spaniards to Vila Oma

"Who orders you to speak in such a commanding tone to the *corregidor*
of the king? Do you know what kind of people we Spaniards are? Keep

si no, por vida de su Magestad, que si te arrebato, que os haga vn juego a
ti y a tus conpañeros que se os acuerde para toda vuestra bida; juro a tal
sy no callas que te abrase biuo y te haga pedaços; mira ¿quien te manda a
el parlar con tanta autoridad delante de mi?"; esto dixo Gonçalo Piçarro
27v   por meter miedo ansy a Vila Oma como a los demas que estaban presentes,
el qual torno luego a rreplicar sobre lo dicho, diziendo "acaba, dados
priesa a juntar esa plata y oro que os he mandado; si no, yo os juro a tal
que de la prission no me salga vuestro rrey hasta que se junte avnque sea
de aqui a vn año; por eso no me rrepliqueis mas ni me rrepresenteis haza-
ñas de aca ffue de aqulla vino". Acabadas todas estas cosas entre los españoles y aquel capitan Vila Oma, los españoles le dixieron [sic: dexaron],
yendose a sus casas; y el se bino a mi padre a dezirle por estenço todo que
les auia dicho y la rrespuesta que ellos le dieron tanbien; y my padre, como
los vio de aquella manera y que con tanta lastima se condolian de su
trauajo, les dixo de la manera syguiente:

"Hijos y hermanos myos, bien entiendo que yo me tengo my meresçido
por auer consentido a esta gente entrar en esta tierra, y tanbien vio la
rrazon que de quexaros de mi teneis; mas pues, ya no ay otro rremedio,
por vida buestra, que con la mas breuedad que podais, junteis algo
con que esta tan agrauada veexaçion [vexaçion] rredima, y doleos de
ber a vuestro rrey atado como a perro con cadena al pescueso y como
esclauo y cosa fuxitiua, grillos a los pies". Los capitanes y gente, con la
28   gran conpassion que les dio de ber a mi padre de aquella manera tan mal-
tratado, no tubieron que rresponder sino con todo silençio y amorti-
guamiento de ojos, vnos en pos de otros, se salieron a buscar, qual mas
podria, lo que mi padre les mandaua por sy pudiesen con mucha breuedad
soltarle, pero no pudieron tan presto que no pasaron mas de dos meses
primero que pudiesen juntar lo que juntaron, lo qual ffue quitandose los
vnos a los otros sus dixes y trajes que traian en sus personas, de los
quales, segund que fue la cantidad de la gente que lo junto, hinchieron
de todo ello vn bohio muy grande, abiendo entrello algunas baxillas que
a mi padre le auian quedado en su casa para seruiçio de su persona;

still! Otherwise, on the life of His Majesty, if I wanted to get you hot, I would play a game with you and your companions that you would remember all your lives. I swear that, if you do not keep still, I will grill you alive and cut you into pieces![68] Look, who is it that orders you to speak with such authority before me?" Gonzalo Pizarro said this to scare Vila Oma and the others who were present. Then Gonzalo returned to his subject, saying, "Hurry up and be done with gathering that silver and gold I ordered you to collect. I swear that otherwise I will not let your king out of prison until it is done, even if it takes a year. So do not spend time replying or giving me your version of events." When all of these dealings between the Spaniards and that captain Vila Oma were done, the Spaniards left to return to their houses. Vila Oma went to tell my father in detail everything that had been said to the Spaniards, as well as the answers the Spaniards had given him. When he saw his people in such pain, my father shared their burden and told them, in the following way:

    "My sons and brothers, I truly understand that I have gotten what I deserved for having allowed these people into this land. I also see that you have a right to complain about me. But there is nothing else to be done now, on your lives, than to gather something up that will redeem me from this grievous vexation as soon as possible. I know it pains you to see your king tied up in chains like a dog and shackled with leg irons like a slave or fugitive." The captains and people, with the great compassion they felt on seeing my father treated so badly, had nothing to say in response. So, silently and with their eyes cast down, one after another, they left to look, as best they could, for what my father had ordered them to find so that they might free him quickly. But they were not able to do it so quickly, and more than two months passed before they could gather what they did. They did it by taking ornaments and clothing from the people wearing them. So many people did this that they were able to fill up a very large building. Among the things gathered were the serving vessels that had been in my father's house for his own personal use.[69] The Spaniards

27v

28

68. The Spaniards sometimes burned people alive. For example, Francisco Pizarro had the general Chalcochima burned alive in the square of Jaquijaguana in 1533 (Hemming, 109).

69. There was a finely decorated polychrome ceramic service, used to serve food, although the Inca ruler and other important people ate on dishes of gold and silver (Julien, "Las tumbas de Sacsahuaman," 44).

e ya junto todo, por el acosamiento tan grande que aquellos honbres le acosaban cada vez, diziendo "¿no se junta?, sy, se junta esta plata"; "¿no acabais? ¿hasta quando nos abeis de hazer esperar?; acaba ya"; con estas y otras palabras, que fatigaban a mi padre de contino, les enbio a llamar, diziendo que, para que acabasen aquellos ya de molestarle, les llamasen porque les queria dar aquello que tenia junto; y ansy los ffueron a llamar, los quales vinieron luego, y llegados que fueron adonde mi padre estaua

28v preso, le saludaron, diziendo "Dios os guarde, señor Sapay Ynga; ¿ques lo que nos mandais, o por que nos aueis enbiado a llamar?"; my padre, como los vio asy benir, porque entendia que ya se llegaua la ora en que le auian de soltar de las prisiones en questaua, dixo a los españoles estas palabras:

Parlamento del Ynga a los españoles

"*Apocona*" (que quiere dezir "señores"), "los dias pasados, quando me prendistes la otra bez, os dixe que no hera posible que fuesedes hijos del Viracochan, pues tan mal tratauades a quien tanto bien os a deseado hazer y a hecho y haze, y os di las rrazones bien equibalentes para ello; y agora questa segunda bez tan pesadamente e tan syn piedad abeis agrauado mi molestia, doblandome las prissiones e tienpo, pues aya mas de dos meses questoy preso y aherrojado como perro, no dexare de deziros que lo aueis hecho no como cristianos e hijos que dezis que sois del Viracochan sino como sieruos del *supay*, cuyas pisadas vosotros seguis, haziendo mal a quien os haze bien; y avn peores sois vosotros que el, quel no busca plata ni oro porque no la a menester, y bosotros buscaisla e quereisla sacar por ffuerça de donde no la ay; peores sois que los *yungas*, los quales por vn poquillo de plata mataran a su madre y a su padre y negaran

29   todo lo del mundo, y ansy vosotros, no se os acordando de tanto bien que de mi abeis rresçiuido, amandoos yo con tanta voluntad y deseando vuestra amistad, me aueis negado por vn poco de plata e tratadome por causa della peor que tratais a vuestros perros, por donde paresçe que teneis en mas vn poco de plata que la amistad de todos los honbres del mundo, pues por amor della abeis perdido la mia y la de todos de mi tierra, pues por vuestra ynportunasçion y demasiada cobdiçia yo y

persecuted my father continuously. As soon as something was gathered, those men would taunt him, saying "Are you or aren't you gathering silver? Aren't you done yet? How long are you going to make us wait? Finish up!" With these and other words they wore my father down. He called for the Spaniards saying that he wanted to give what he had collected to them so they would stop bothering him immediately. And so his men called [the Spaniards], who came quickly. When the Spaniards arrived at the place where my father was imprisoned, they greeted him, saying, "God keep you, Lord Sapay Inca. What is it that you order us to do?" Or, "Why have you sent for us?" When he saw them come, my father knew that the hour had come for his release and said these words to the Spaniards:

Speech of the Inca to the Spaniards

"*Apocona*" (which means "lords"),[70] "some days ago, when you captured me the last time, I told you that it was not possible for you to be sons of the Viracochan, since you had treated someone so badly who had only wished to do you, has done you, and still does you, such good. And I gave you solid reasons in support of what I said. Now you have aggravated my suffering a second time, harshly and pitilessly doubling the restraints you have used and the time of my imprisonment. I have now been imprisoned and chained like a dog for more than two months. I must tell you that you have done this not like Christians and the sons of the Viracochan, as you said you were, but as servants of the devil, in whose steps you follow by doing evil to those who do you good. You are even worse than the devil, who does not seek gold or silver because he has no use for it. But you look for it and try to take it by force even when there is none to be had. You are worse than the *yungas* who would kill their own mothers and fathers for a little silver and then deny they had done so before all the world. And so you, forgetting all the good treatment I gave you out of my sincere affection and desire for your friendship, have rejected me for a little silver, and have treated me worse than you treat your own dogs to get it. It seems you value a little silver above the friendship of all the men in the world, since for love of it, you have lost my friendship and that of everyone in my land. Because of your demands and your excessive greed, my people and

70. An Inca plural of the word *apo*.

ellos nos abemos desposeydo de nuestras joyas e rriquezas, las quales
vosotros nos aueis tomado a puras ffuerças y molestias y agras ynportunasçiones; yo os digo que a lo que yo entiendo, no os a de luzir mucho esto
que a mi e a mi jente nos tomais tan syn justiçia y rrazon; ayan juntado esos
pobres yndios con harto trauajo, no se que; mandaldo rresçibir y acaba ya
de quitarme desta prission". Todo esto dezia my padre con mucha lastima
y avn con lagrimas de sus ojos por verse tratado de aquella suerte.

La manera de como los españoles quisieron
soltar a Mango Ynga de la segunda prision
y de como les dio la *coya*

Pues como los españoles oyeron lo que mi padre les dixo con alguna alegria e plazer por la plata questaua junta, dixieron que se holgauan mucho
dello; y haziendo algun ademan de quererlo yr a soltar, lo qual todo hera
fengido, salio muy de presto Gonçalo Piçarro y dixo, "¿ques?; boto a tal
no suelte, que primero nos a de dar a la señora *coya*, su hermana, que el
otro dia bimos; ¿que priessa teneis vosotros de quererlo soltar sin que os
lo manden? Ea, señor Mango Ynga; venga la señora *coya*, que lo de la plata
bueno esta, que eso es lo que prençipalmente deseauamos".

La manera del dar de la *coya*

My padre, como los vio que con tanta ynportunidad le pedian la *coya* y que
no se podia ebadir dellos de otra suerte, mando sacar vna yndia muy hermosa, peinada y muy bien adereçada, para darsela en lugar de la *coya* que
ellos pedian; y ellos, como la vieron, desconosçiendo la *coya*, dixieron que
no les paresçia a ellos, que [no] hera aquella la *coya* que ellos pedian syno

I have been dispossessed of our valuables and wealth, which you have taken from us through pure force, aggravation, and bitter demands. From what I understand, I tell you that the treasure you gathered so unjustly and without reason from me and my people will not look like much to you. I don't know what these poor Indians, with all their effort, could possibly have gathered. Order it to be received and let me out of this prison." My father said all this with great sorrow and even tears in his eyes because of the way he had been treated.

The manner in which the Spaniards wished to release Manco Inca from the second imprisonment and how he gave them the Coya

When the Spaniards heard what my father said, they replied with joy and 29v pleasure in their voices, because of the silver that had been gathered there, how pleased they were. Gonzalo Pizarro pretended to come out very quickly as if he wanted to go to release my father. He said: "What is this? I vote that he not be released, that first he must give us the lady Coya, his sister,[71] whom we saw the other day. Why are you in such a hurry to have him released before I have even given the orders? Well then, Lord Manco Inca, the lady Coya may come. The silver you have gathered is fine, and it is what we desire most."

How the Coya was given

When he realized that the Spaniards were firm in their demands for the Coya and that he could not avoid the matter, my father ordered that a beautiful young Indian woman, exquisitely dressed and groomed,[72] be brought out and given to the Spaniards in place of the Coya for whom they had asked. Though the Spaniards did not know the Coya, when they saw the young woman [that had been brought out] they said that it did not seem to them that this was the Coya they had asked for, but rather

71. Marriage to a full sister or to a woman closely linked to the dynastic line of descent was practiced from the time of the tenth Inca onward (Julien, *Reading Inca History*, 29–30, 32). This incident indicates how the Spaniards were trying to take women who were important in the reproduction of the dynastic line.

72. Rich or elaborate dress and headdress was apparently an indicator of Coya status.

otra yndia por ay, que les diese la *coya* y que acabase de negoçios; y mi
padre, por tentarlos hizo sacar otras mas de beynte, casy de aquella suerte,
vnas buenas y otras mejores, y ninguna les contentaua; ya que le paresçio
a my padre que hera tienpo, mando que saliesa vna, la mas prençipal muger
que en su casa tenia, conpañera de su hermana la *coya,* la qual le paresçia
casy en todo, en espeçial sy se bestia como ella, la qual se llamaua Ynguill
(que quiere dezir "fflor"), y que aquella les diesen, la qual salio alli en pre-
sençia de todos, vestida y adereçada ni mas ni menos que *coya* (que quiere
dezir "rreyna"); y como los españoles la viesen salir de aquella suerte, tan
bien adereçada y tan hermosa, dixieron con mucho rregoçijo y contento
"esta sy, esta sy; pese tal es la señora *coya,* que no las otras"; Gonçalo
Piçarro, como hera el que mas la deseaua que todos, pues particularmente
la auia pretendido, dixo a mi padre estas palabras: "señor Mango Ynga,
si ella es para mi, deseme luego porque ya no lo puedo suffrir"; y mi padre,
como la tenia bien catetizada, dixo "mucho de norabuena, haze lo que
quisierdes"; y el, ansy delante de todos syn mas mirar a cossa, se fue para
ella a la bessar y abraçar como sy fuera su muger ligitima, de lo qual se
rrio mucho my padre, y los demas puso en admirasçion, y a la Yunguill
[Ynguill], en espanto y pabor; como se bio abraçar de gente que no
conosçia daua gritos como vna loca, diziendo que no queria arrostrar a
semejante gente, mas antes se huya y ni por pensamiento los queria ver;
y mi padre, como la vio tan zahareña y que tanto rrehusaua la yda con
los españoles, por ver que en aquella estaua el ser el suelto o no, la
mando con mucha furia que se fuese con ellos; y ella, viendo a mi padre

some kind of common Indian.[73] They said that Manco should give them the Coya and get the business over with. To tempt the Spaniards, my father had almost twenty other young women, some good and others better, brought out—but none of them satisfied the Spaniards. Then, when it seemed to my father to be the right time, he ordered the most important woman in his household to come out and said that she should be given to the Spaniards. This woman was the companion of his sister the Coya and looked like the Coya in almost every detail, especially when she dressed as the Coya did. Her name was Ynguill,[74] which means "flower." 30 She came out in front of everyone there, dressed and groomed in exactly the same way as the Coya (which means "queen"). When the Spaniards saw her, dressed so well and looking so beautiful, they exclaimed with rejoicing and contentment, "Yes, this one. Yes, this one. She is so important that she, and not one of the others, has to be the Coya." Since he desired her more than anyone else, Gonzalo Pizarro said these words to my father: "Lord Manco Inca, if she is for me, give her to me right now, because I can't stand it any longer." My father, who had trained Ynguill well, said: "My felicitations, do with her what you like." Then, right there in front of everyone and without any hesitation, Gonzalo Pizarro kissed and embraced Ynguill as if she was his legitimate wife. My father had a good laugh about this while the others looked on with admiration. Because she was being embraced by a stranger, Ynguill screamed like a madwoman. She said that she would have nothing to do with such people, that she would sooner flee to where she would never see them again, not even in her dreams. My father saw her wild look and understood that she emphatically refused to go with the Spaniards. But since he knew that he must give her to the Spaniards in order to earn his freedom, he ordered her in great fury to go with them. Ynguill was afraid when she saw my father 30v

73. Again, the word "Indian" is being used to refer to someone native to the Andes. González Holguín translates the word "Indian" as "runa" (*Yndio. Runa. Yndia. Runa huarmi;* 555), which he translates elsewhere as "person" (*Runa. Persona, hombre, o muger y el baron. Huc runa;* 320).

74. The same Ynguill was mentioned in later documents as having produced a daughter with Juan Pizarro, named Francisca Pizarro (Julien, "Francisca Pizarro, la cuzqueña, y su madre, la *coya* Ynguill," 53). Titu Cusi has misidentified the Pizarro brother, perhaps because Gonzalo eclipsed Juan in fame and Juan died much sooner (1536 as opposed to 1548).

tan enojado, mas de miedo que de otra cossa hizo lo que le mandaua y fuese con ellos.

Como Gonçalo Piçarro rreçibio el tesoro y la *coya* de mano de Mango Ynga y de como en señal de amistad se fue a comer con el

El Gonçalo Piçarro la rresçibio en sy y mando que quitasen a my padre de prisiones; y suelto, rresçibieron el tesoro y rrepartieronlo entre sy, el qual rrepartido rrogo Gonçalo Piçarro a mi padre, diziendo que pues les auia dado tantas cossas asy de oro como de plata y sobre todo a la señora *coya* para sy tanto deseada, que le rrogaua mucho para señal de que la amistad auia de durar mucho entre los dos por causa del quñadazgo les hiziese merçed de yrse con el y con aquellos caualleros a su casa a rresçiuir seruiçio en ella, la qual se ofresçia desde estonçes por suya; y my padre, lo vno por el deseo que tenia ya de salir ffuera e ber el canpo y lo otro por darle aquel contento, pensando que por aquella via auia de durar mucho tienpo la amistad con los españoles, hizo lo que Gonçalo Piçarro le rrogo y fuese con el y con sus conpañeros a comer aquel dia en su casa adonde vbo gran ffiesta y gran rregoçijo; y desde que vbieron comido los vnos con los otros, el dicho mi padre dixo que se queria boluer a su casa porque hera ya tarde; y los españoles le aconpañaron hasta alla, en la qual, dexandole con mucho contento, ellos se boluieron a las suyas. Entienda el que esto leyere que, quando estos negoçios pasaron del dar de la *coya* e la prission de las cadenas y grillos, el Marques don Françisco Piçarro ya hera ydo a Lima y a la sazon no estaua en el Cuzco, y por eso no piense naidie que en todo se hallo.

     Pasadas todas aquellas cosas de la prission segunda y el dar de la Ynguill en lugar de la *coya* a Gonçalo Piçarro, no pasaron muchos dias que Gonçalo Piçarro, digo que mi padre Mango Ynga, hizo una fiesta muy prençipal,

so angry. She did what she had been told and went with the Spaniards more out of fear than for any other reason.

How Gonzalo Pizarro received the treasure and the Coya from the hand of Manco Inca and how my father went to eat with him as a token of his friendship

Gonzalo Pizarro received the Coya personally and ordered that the restraints be removed from my father. Once my father had been freed, the Spaniards took the treasure and distributed it among themselves. Afterward, Gonzalo Pizarro entreated my father to accompany him, since my father had given them so many things of gold and silver and, most importantly, the Coya he so desired. Gonzalo pleaded with my father to do him the favor of accompanying him and the other Spanish gentlemen to Gonzalo's house where they would be served; Gonzalo said that my father was to consider Gonzalo's house his own from now on. He asked my father to do all of this as a sign of the friendship that would endure between them since they would now be brothers-in-law. My father, who wanted to get out into the countryside, thought that doing as Gonzalo asked would satisfy Gonzalo and ensure that his friendship with the Spaniards would last. So my father went with Gonzalo and his companions to eat at Gonzalo's house that day. There was a great fiesta and general rejoicing. After they had eaten together, my father said he wanted to return to his own house because it was late. The Spaniards accompanied him and left him there, happy to be home; they then returned to their own houses. Those who read this should know that at this time—while this business of giving the Coya and restraining my father with chains and leg irons took place—the Marquis Don Francisco Pizarro had already gone to Lima; he was not in Cusco. No one should misunderstand and think that he was present.[75]

Soon after all of the events surrounding my father's second imprisonment and the giving of Ynguill in place of the Coya to Gonzalo Pizarro were over, Gonzalo Pizarro, I mean my father Manco Inca, held an

31

---

75. Titu Cusi is careful to let the king know that his father was abused by Francisco Pizarro's brothers and not by Pizarro himself. Imbedded in his account is a story about Manco's affection and reliance on Francisco Pizarro and his eventual disillusionment.

en la qual se horadaua las orejas; y en esta fiesta nosotros los yngas solemos hazer la mayor ffiesta que hazemos en todo el año porque entonçes
nos dan mucho nonbre y nuebo nonbre del que teniamos antes, que
tira casy esta çerimonia a lo que los cristianos hazen quando se confirman,
en la qual ffiesta my padre salio con toda la autoridad rreal confforme a
nuestro vso, lleuando delante sus setros rreales, y el vno dellos como mas
prençipal hera de oro masisso y con sus borlas de lo mesmo, llevando todos los demas que con el yban juntamente cada vno el suyo, las quales
31v heran la mytad de plata y la mitad de cobre, que serian mas de mill, todos vnos y otros los que yban a rrebautizar, que en nuestro vso llamamos
vacaroc [*varayoc*]; y estando questubieron todos nuestros yndios y los
españoles questaban en vn llano de vn çerro que se llama Anauarque
adonde se hazia la çerimonia, acabada de hazer (el como se haze se dira
delante), al tienpo que se yban a labar los que ansy abian sydo rrebauti-
zados en el bautizmo, los tresquilar y horadar las orejas, los españoles, no
se sy por cobdiçia de la plata que yba en los çetros o de algun rreçelo

important fiesta in which the piercing of ears took place.[76] That fiesta was the most important fiesta that we the Incas celebrated in the entire year. At that fiesta we were given an important name and a different name from the one we had before.[77] This ceremony is almost like what the Christians do when they are confirmed.[78] My father arrived at this fiesta with all the customary royal pomp, in conformance with our practice. His royal scepters[79] were carried before him. One of the scepters, the most important of all, was solid gold and had golden tassels. All the other people who came with my father carried their own scepters, each of which was half silver and half copper. All together, there were more than a thousand of these scepters which, in our usage, we call *vacaroc* [sic: *varayoc*].[80] Both Indians and Spaniards stood on a flat place on the hill called Anahuarqui[81] where this ceremony was held. Once the ceremony was finished (and how it was performed will be explained below), those who had been rebaptized went to wash. During the baptism, the cutting of hair, and ear piercing, the Spaniards took up arms and began to harass the people. Perhaps they did this out of greed for the silver in the scepters; perhaps they were afraid

31v

76. This is the rite of *capac raymi,* which took place at the time of the December solstice (Molina, 98–110). It involved the initiation of young men of the dynastic line whose ears were pierced in the ceremony so that they could wear golden ear spools. These individuals were called *orejones,* or "big ears" by the Spaniards.

77. We know some of the initial names of the Inca rulers. Huascar was the initial name of Titu Cusi Huallpa (Sarmiento de Gamboa, ch. 63: 112). Inca Yupanqui appears to have been the initial name of Pachacuti (Sarmiento de Gamboa, ch. 27: 63).

78. The similarity between Inca initiation and Christian confirmation is that they were both performed at the time of adolescence. As in the case of equating an Andean supernatural to the Christian God, the establishment of equivalences between the two cultures was well underway.

79. The "royal scepters" are called *yauris* later in the paragraph (see note 78).

80. I have corrected *vacaroc* to *varayoc.* If I am right, what was intended was *huarayoc,* derived from the word *huara,* meaning "diapers or narrow breechcloth" (*Huara. Pañetes o çaragueles estrechos*). *Huarayoc* was the person who wore them (*Huarayoc. El que los atrae* [sic: *trae*]; González Holguín, 182). This is the logical meaning, given that *capac raymi* was when males were initiated to adult male status and first wore items of adult dress, like the breechcloth. Since they are carrying what seem to be staffs, there seems to be confusion with the Spanish word *vara* (see note 59). The Spanish word for "staff" is the phonological equivalent of *huara.*

81. The hill of Anahuarqui was one of three mountains near Cusco that were important during *capac raymi* (Molina, 104).

que de ber tanta gente les debio de caer, pusieronse en arma y començaron
a alborotar a toda la gente, hechando mano a sus espadas con este apellido, los quales dezian "o bellacos, ¿vosotros levantaros quereis?; pues no
a de ser ansy; esperad, esperad"; y ansy desta manera arremetieron a los
setros para los quitar, a los quales lleuauan con deseo de llegar a quitar el
de mi padre; y como tenia tanta guarda al derredor de sy por sus mangas
no pudieron llegar syno quitaron de los otros los que pudieron, que fueron
muchos. Mi padre, que ansy oyo tanto rroydo y mormullo entre la gente,
atendio a uer lo que pasaua; y desque supo que los españoles se auian des-
32   bergonçado de aquella manera, alço la boz, diziendo "¿ques esto?"; y los
yndios, todos como llorandose, le quexaron desta suerte, los quales dixieron: "Sapai Ynga, ¿que gente es esta que tienes en tu tierra que no se con-
tentan con tanto oro y plata como les as dado y por fuerça nos an quitado
nuestros *yauris* de plata?" (que quiere dezir "çetros"); "nos an quitado
con amenazas, de lo qual rresçebimos gran pena; diles que nos los bueluan
y que les basta ya la plata y oro que les avemos dado"; y mi padre, viendo
que con tanta ansya se le quexaban aquellos yndios, rresçivio dello pena;
e hablando hazia los españoles dixo ansy:

Razonamiento del Ynga a los españoles quando la terçera bez hizieron ademan a prenderles

"A, señores, pareçeme que todavia estais en darme pena a mi y a mi jente,
no queriendo yo darosla ni teniendo tal pensamiento; el otro dia, ¿no me
prometistes a mi e a mi gente, diziendo que no me dariades mas pena?; no
teneis rrazon, porque yo no os he hecho por donde me la ayais de dar; ¿no
estais hartos de plata que me benis a quitar avn vna meaja que traigo en
32v   mis ffiestas?; si lo hazeis por ynçitarme para que me lebante contra vosotros
yo o la gente de my tierra, dezidmelo, porque andare aperçebido, y lo

when they saw so many Indians gathered together. The Spaniards grabbed their swords with this call to arms: "Vile people, do you want to rebel? It is not going to turn out like you think. Just you wait, just you wait." Then they attacked the scepter-bearers and tried to take the scepters, hoping to take the scepter my father held. But they could not reach my father, because he had such a large number of guards close by him. Since they could not get near my father, they took the scepters they could from the rest of the people, and there were a lot of them. When he heard the noise and commotion among his people, my father tried to find out what had happened. When he found out that the Spaniards had humiliated themselves in such a fashion, he raised his voice, saying, "What is this?" The Indians 32 complained to him in what seemed like crying: "Sapay Inca, who are these people that you have allowed into your land? They are not content with all the gold and silver you have given them! They have taken our silver *yauris*[82] (which means "scepters") "by force! They have taken them from us with threats, which gives us great sorrow. Tell them to return them and that all the silver and gold we have given them is enough." When he saw how those Indians complained to him in their anxiety, my father was very upset. Speaking to the Spaniards, he said:

Reasoning of the Inca to the Spaniards when they took him prisoner for the third time

"Oh lords, it seems that you are still trying to trouble me and my people, even though I have not wanted to trouble you nor have I given any thought to it. Just the other day, didn't you promise me and my people not to bring us any more grief? You have no reason to, because I have not given you any reason. Is your hunger for silver so insatiable that you have to take even the trivial amount I use in my fiestas? If you are doing this to provoke me,[83] so that I or my people will rise and rebel against you, then 32v tell me so, because then my people and I will be forewarned and will not

---

82. González Holguín does not define *yauri*, but *yaurina* is "hook" (*Yaurina. El anzuelo*; 365), and in Cusco today, the word refers to any kind of needle.

83. It may well have been that the Pizarro brothers were trying to provoke Manco to rebel and abandon Cusco. That argument was made in the years following the siege of Cusco by Pizarro's enemies (Medina, vol. 6: 321).

mesmo mi gente no andare tan descuydado como agora benia; y si no, pues nos dimos vnos a otros nuestras palabras el otro dia en casa del *apo* y en la mia de conseruarnos en paz e amor los vnos con los otros, guardemosnosla; y ansy ni vosotros terneis rreçelo ni nosotros temor"; y los españoles, oyendo lo que mi padre les dezia, dixieron "señor Mango Ynga, no deseamos dar aqui pena a vuestra merçed; algunos soldados por pasar tienpo harian por ay algun aspabiento; no rresçiva vuestra merçed pena, que no es nada"; y mi padre, viendo la gente ya quieta y sosegada, callo y acabo de hazer sus ffiestas, yendose los españoles a sus casas, porque ya hera tarde y ora de rrecoxerse a dormir.

Muerte de Pascac, hermano del Ynga

Acabadas todas las ffiestas y lo que arriba se a dicho, estando vn dia mi padre quieto y sosegado en su cassa, le acontesçio vna braua hazaña; y fue que vn hermano suyo que alli tenia, llamado Pascac, algo argullosso [orgulloso], no se saue por ynu [crossed out] du [inserted above the line] çion [yn-duçion] de quien, le vino pensamiento de matar a my padre, diziendo que, muerto, el seria alçado por rrey; y no se sy por la persona o personas que a ello le ynsistieron o no se por quien le fue dado vn puñal, con el qual, yendo que fue a uer a my padre debaxo de que le yba a *mochar* como a señor, le diese de puñaladas con aquel puñal, y que luego, muerto que fuese, seria alçado por rrey e podria dar mucha plata a los españoles, que ansy le dieron aquel puñal para aquel effeto. Y como ninguna cosa ay secreta que no sea tarde o tenplano [temprano] maniffiesta, vn çierto español cuyo nonbre

33

appear before you as carelessly as we have until now. If not, then remember that we spoke words to each other the other day—in the house of the *Apo*[84] and in my house—about keeping the peace between us. So let us keep it! Thus you will not have reason to be vigilant nor we to be afraid." The Spaniards, who heard what my father told them, said: "Lord Manco Inca, we do not want to trouble you. Some soldiers may have been playing around just to pass the time. Do not be upset, because there is nothing to be upset about." When my father saw that the people were quiet and calm, he said no more and finished his fiestas. The Spaniards went home to their houses because it was late and time to sleep.

Death of Pascac, brother of the Inca

Soon after the fiestas (and the events described above) were over, a frightful thing happened to my father one day while he was minding his own business quietly and calmly at home. His brother Pascac[85]—who was a proud man and who may have been provoked by someone—began to think about killing my father. Pascac said that when my father was dead he, Pascac, would be proclaimed king. Someone—and I do not know if it was the person or persons who provoked him or someone else—gave Pascac a dagger with which he could stab my father when he went to visit my father under the pretext of worshipping him[86] as his lord. Pascac would do this so he would be named king after my father was dead, and would then be in a position to supply the Spaniards with much more silver. That is why they gave him the dagger. But there are no secrets that are not revealed sooner or later—and so, a certain Spaniard (whose name

33

84. Again, the term *apo* is used to refer to Francisco Pizarro (see note 57).

85. Pascac was another son of Huayna Capac (Medina, vol. 7: 459).

86. There was a particular kind of obeisance made to the Inca ruler and other sacred objects, known as *mocha*. The term itself is used later in the paragraph, but here it means "worshipping him as his lord." It was constructed from an Inca verb, defined by González Holguín as "to adore, beg, reverence, honor, venerate or kiss the hands" (*Muchhani, muchhaycuni, o vpaycuni. Adorar, rogar, reuerenciar, honrar, venerar, o bessar las manos;* 246). In Spain and Spanish America at the time, the formal greeting paid to the king or an important royal official was to kiss the hand, so here an equivalent might be suggested, rather than the actual act.

no se sabe, el qual hera criado de my padre y estaua sienpre en su casa, le
auiso "sabete, señor Mango Ynga, que tu hermano Pascac te anda por
matar y trae para el efeto, debaxo de la manta escondido, vn puñal, el qual
te a de matar quando te benga a hazer la *mocha;* por eso, quando le vieres
venir, esta sobre auiso, que sy tu me mandares que yo le mate a el, yo le
matare"; y my padre, como fue avisado desta manera por aquel su criado
español, agradesçioselo mucho e tubo quenta para quando biese benir
a su hermano como otras vezes solia hazerle la *mocha;* y quando le vio,
dexole hazer la *mocha,* y con vn puñal que para el effeto tenia le dio de
puñaladas, y el español que asy auia dado el auiso le acabo de matar; visto
todo esto por los sircustantes que alli estavan presentes, cayoles a todos
gran admiraçion de ber vn hecho tan estraño y tan supito, y no vbo naidie
que osase a hablar palabra.

33v

　　Pasadas todas estas cosas y otras muchas mas, que a auerlas de contar
por estenso hera alargarnos mucho, por lo qual e por ebitar prolexidad
pasare con mi yntento, ques dar a entender que fue de mi padre y en que
pararon los españoles despues de todo esto, para lo qual, sabran que como
Gonçalo Piçarro, siendo corregidor del Cuzco en nonbre del gouernador
don Françisco Piçarro, estubiese en el con Hernando Piçarro y Juan Piçarro
y otros muchos, acaesçio que Joan Piçarro, hermano de Hernando Piçarro
y Gonçalo Piçarro, como viese que a sus hermanos entranbos a dos mi
padre les auia dado tanta cantidad de moneda, cobro dello gran ynbidia,
diziendo "pues, ¿a mis hermanos solamente an de dar plata y a mi no?;
boto a tal que no a de pasar desta manera, sino que me an de dar a mi tanbien oro e plata como a ellos, y si no, que les tengo de hazer vn juego que
se les acuerde"; y con estos ffieros andaua muuiendo [moviendo] toda la
gente, y dezia "¡prendamos, prendamos a Mango Ynga!"; y mi padre,
como oyo que en el pueblo se trataua la traiçion questaua armada contra

34　　el, mando juntar a todos los prençipales de la tierra, que mucha parte dellos estaua en el Cuzco haziendole cuerpo de guardia; y desque los tubo

is unknown but who was my father's servant[87] and someone who was always present in my father's house), told my father about the plan. This Spaniard said, "Know, Lord Manco Inca, that your brother Pascac is coming to kill you. He has hidden a dagger under his cloak for that purpose. He will try to kill you when he comes to worship you, so be alert when you see him coming. I will kill him if you order me to." Having been advised in this manner by his Spanish servant, my father thanked him greatly and took this advice into account when he next saw his brother (who had come to worship my father just as he had on previous occasions). When my father saw Pascac, he let him make the *mocha*.[88] Then, with a dagger Manco brought for the purpose, he stabbed Pascac a number of times; he also finished off the Spaniard who had given him the news. Witnesses who happened to observe this strange and sudden   33v
event were filled with a deep admiration for my father. No one dared to say a word.

After all these events took place (and so many more that to relate everything in detail would make our story very long, so—in order to avoid being prolific—I will return to my original purpose, which is to convey some understanding of what happened to my father and what the Spaniards were up to), you [my audience] will know that when Gonzalo Pizarro was *corregidor* in Cusco in the name of the governor Don Francisco Pizarro, he was accompanied by Hernando Pizarro, Juan Pizarro, and many others. When Juan Pizarro, brother of Hernando and Gonzalo Pizarro, saw that my father had given a great deal of money to each of his brothers, he was envious and said: "So you give silver to my brothers, but nothing to me? I swear that it should not turn out like this. You have to give me gold and silver like my brothers. If you do not, I will have to play a game with you that you will long remember." With these fierce words Juan Pizarro went about rallying all the people, saying, "We must capture, we must capture Manco Inca." When he heard betrayal was being plotted against him, my   34
father ordered all the important lords in the land, many of whom were in Cusco serving as his guard, to gather together. Then, when he had these

87. Betanzos told of a Marticote who murdered a brother of Manco's (*Narrative of the Incas,* pt. 2, ch. 28: 279).
88. See note 86.

juntos les hizo el parlamento, auisado por el capitan general Villa Oma, arriba dicho.

Parlamento del Ynga a sus capitanes
sobre lo del çerco del Cuzco

"Muy amados hijos y hermanos mios, nunca pensse que me fuera neçesario aberos de hazer lo que agora pienso, porque pense y tube sienpre por muy çierto que esta gente barbuda, que vosotros llamais *viracochas* por aueroslo yo dicho antiguamente, por pensar que hera ansy que benian del Biracochan, [no] me auian de ser auiessos ni darme pena en ninguna cossa, pero agora que beo, como he hallado sienpre por esperiençia y vosotros tanbien abeis visto, quan mal me an tratado y quan mal me an agradesçido lo que por ellos he hecho, haziendome mill beffas y prendiendome y atandome como a perro los pies y el pescueso, y que sobre todo, despues de me auer dado su palabra que ellos comigo e yo con ellos abernos conffederado en amor y amistad, diziendo que perpetuamente abriamos de lo pasado, andan agora otra bez vrdiendo como me podrian prender y matar; no dexare de rrogaros como a hijos, que mireis quantas vezes vosotros me aueis ynportunado a que yo haga esto que agora quiero hazer, diziendo que me levante contra estos y que para que los consiento en mi tierra, e yo no he querido por pensar que no subçediera lo que agora beo; y pues, ansy es, y ellos no quieren sino porffiar en darme enojo, fforçado me sera darselo yo tanbien y no consentir mas negoçios; por vida buestra, que pues sienpre me aueis mostrado tanto amor y deseado darme contento, en este me lo deis, y sea que, todos juntos asy como estais, os conçerteis en vno y enbieis vuestros mensajeros a toda la tierra para que de aqui a beinte dias esten todos en este pueblo sin que dello entiendan nada estos barbudos; e yo enbiare a Lima a Queso Yupangui, mi capitan que gouierna aquella tierra, a auisarle que para el dia que aqui dieremos sobre los españoles, de el alla con su gente sobre los que alla ouiere, y haziendonos a vna, el alla y nosotros aca, luego los acabaremos syn que quede ninguno, y quitaremos esta

34v

men together, he gave a speech, having first been advised by the captain general Vila Oma (mentioned above).

Speech of the Inca to his captains about the surrounding of Cusco

"Beloved sons and brothers of mine, I never thought that it would be necessary to have you do what I now ask. I thought and was always certain that these bearded people who you call *viracochas* (I told you they were *viracochas* because I originally thought they had come from the Viracochan) would not be inclined to do evil nor cause me any sort of grief. But now I realize, as I have learned from my experiences with them (and as you have also seen) how badly they have treated me and how ungrateful they have been for what I have done for them: they have insulted me a thousand times, captured me and tied up my feet and body like I was a dog. What is worse, after we aligned ourselves with them in love and friendship, and after we said that we would perpetually keep the accord between us, they are now weaving yet another plot to capture and kill me. I will not stop begging you like sons (and look how many times you begged me) to do what I now want to do, and how you told me to rise   34v
up against them and asked why I allowed them into my land. I have not wanted to do anything because I never thought that what has happened would happen. But since it has, and since the Spaniards seem to like nothing better than to make me angry, I am forced to make them angry and not put up with any more of this business. By your lives, since you have always shown me so much love and desired my happiness, I ask that you grant me a request, and that would be that all of you together, just as you are, act in unison and send your messengers out to all the land so that, twenty days from now, all the people will come to this town without giving any indication to these bearded people. I will send to Lima for Quizu Yupanqui,[89] my captain who governs that land, and advise him to attack the Spaniards there with his people on the same day we attack the Spaniards here. Acting in unison, he there and we here, we will finish them off so that not one Spaniard remains. We will rid ourselves of the

---

89. Quizu Yupanqui attacked the Spaniards at a number of points along the main highland road west of Cusco, including Jauja, before attacking Lima in August 1536.

pesadilla de sobre nosotros y holgarnos hemos". Acabado este rrazonamiento que mi padre hizo a sus capitanes para lo que auian de hazer en
el aperçibimiento de su gente para la batalla que con los españoles se es-
peraua, todos en vno, y a vna boz, rrespondieron que rresçiuian de aquello mucho contento y estaban prestos y aparejados de hazer lo que por mi
padre les hera mandado; y ansy sin ningun dilasçion, luego lo pusieron por
la obra y enbiaron por sus parçialidades, cada vno como le cauia: la vez de
los Chinchaisuyo, enbio Vila Oma a Coyllas y a Ozca y a Cori Atao y a
Taipi que truxiesen la gente de aquella parçialidad; de los Cullasuyos ffue
Lliclli y otros muchos capitanes para que traxiesen la gente de aquella
parçialidad; a Condesuyo, Suran Vaman, Quiçana y Suri Vallpa y otros muchos capitanes; y los de Andesuyo, Ronpa Yupangui y otros muchos capitanes, para que todos estos, cada *suyo* por si, juntasen la gente neçesaria
para el effeto; nota questos quatro *suyos* que aqui son nonbrados, conbiene a saber como arriua tengo dicho son las quatro partes en que toda esta
tierra esta deuisa y rrepartida, como mas por estenso arriba esta declarado.
Despues que se obieron enbiado a las partes arriua dichas, andando como
andaua el dicho Joan Piçarro de mala manera y con malos yntentos, vn yndio lengua de los españoles llamado Antonico llego donde estaua mi padre
y le dio auiso, diziendo que Joan Piçarro y los demas le querian prender
otro dia y avn matarle si no les daua mucho oro y plata; y mi padre, como
oyo lo quel yndio le dezia, creyolo e finjio luego que queria yr a Callca a
caçar; y los españoles, no cayendo en lo que mi padre pensaua hazer,
tubieronlo por bien, pensando que a la buelta, porque creyan seria breue,
abria effeto su mal proposito.

Desque mi padre estubo en Callca algunos dias, en tanto que se jun-
taua alguna jente de la que avian enbiado a llamar, despacho desde alli
por la posta a Quiso Yupangui questaua en Lima para que estubiese
auisado del dia y la ora en que el aca auia de dar sobre los españoles, que

nightmare hanging over us and will celebrate." Once my father had told his captains what they had to do to prepare his people for the upcoming battle with the Spaniards, all of them—together and in one voice—responded that they were greatly contented with the plan and were ready and able to do what my father ordered. So, without any delay, they put the plan into effect. They sent messages to their provinces, requesting a certain number of men be sent [to Cusco]. My father sent Vila Oma to Coyllas and to Orca and to Cori Atao and to Taypi, so that they would bring people from Chinchaysuyu; Lliclli and many other captains went out to bring people from Collasuyu; Suran Huaman, Quizana and Suri Huallpa, and many other captains went out to Condesuyu; and Ranpa Yupanqui and many other captains, to Andesuyu. In this way all of the captains—and each *suyu*[90] for itself—were to gather the necessary people. (Note that the four *suyus* named here, as I have noted above, are the four parts into which this land is distinguished and divided, as I have explained in some detail above.) After the messages had been sent to the areas mentioned (and while Juan Pizarro was acting badly and with evil intentions), a native interpreter named Antonico[91] who worked for the Spaniards came to my father and told him that Juan Pizarro and the rest [of the Spaniards] wanted to capture him the following day. They were even planning to kill my father if he did not give them a great deal of gold and silver. When my father heard what that Indian had to say, my father believed him. He then pretended that he wanted to go to Calca to hunt.[92] The Spaniards, unaware of what my father was planning, decided his trip was a good idea. Since they imagined my father's trip would be brief, they thought they could put their evil plan into effect upon his return.

35

35v

After my father had been in Calca for a few days—and while waiting for some of the people for whom he had sent to gather—he sent word by post to Quizu Yupanqui in Lima so that he would be advised of the day and time Manco Inca planned to attack the Spaniards. His purpose was to have

90. The word *suyu* meant "division" or "part" (*Suyu. Parcialidad;* González Holguín, 333).

91. No other account of Manco's departure from Cusco mentions Antonico or his warning.

92. Huascar had built palaces in Calca (Niles, "The Provinces in the Heartland," 333). Whether Manco Inca had palaces of his own there seems unlikely.

juntamente el diese y fuese todo a vna, el Quiso Yupangui en Lima y el dicho mi padre en el Cuzco; y al tienpo que esto hizo mi padre, los españoles le enbiaron muchas cartas diziendo que se diese priesa a boluerse a su cassa, que no se hallauan vn punto syn el, el qual dicho mi padre les torno a rresponder, diziendo que avn no auia acabado de caçar, quel bolueria lo mas presto que pudiese; y los españoles, viendo que de quantas vezes le enbiauan a llamar no queria benir ninguna, mas antes, mas antes de día en día se alargaua mas y les enbiaua peores rrespuestas, determinaron de yr sobre el para o le traer por fuerça o matarle, los quales hizieron sus capitanes en el Cuzcu [Cuzco]; y ordenando su canpo vn capitan dellos con su gente, se ffue la via de Callca con su gente para el effeto dicho, quedando los demas en el Cuzco a punto de guerra para yr en su seguimiento si fuese menester, los quales llegaron hasta la puente del rrio de Callca, en la qual sobrel pasajere ouieron çierta rrefriega con las guardas della, las quales les defendieron el paso; y alli se desafiaron los españoles a la gente de mi padre, y hecho el desaffio, se boluieron al Cuzco, biniendo en su seguimiento dando muchos alaridos y gran grita mucha jente de la questaua con mi padre; llegados que fueron al Cuzco, los españoles, algo escandalizados de la guaçabara pasada y de la gente que benia en su seguimiento, desde Carmenga, ques parte donde se señorea el Cuzco, dieron bozes a ssus conpañeros pidiendo socorro, y los conpañeros que no estaban descuydados acurrieron [ocurrieron] con su ffabor a los que con neçesidad estaban; y alli en la dicha Carmenga ouieron otra gran rrefriega con la gente que le seguia y en [sic: con] mucha otra que al apellido acudio; y acabada la rrefriega, los acorralaron al Cuzco syn matar ninguno; y essa mesma noche los tubieron muy açoçados con gran griteria çercados de todas partes; y no dieron sobre ellos porque esperauan la [sic: las] gentes que otro dia llego e tanbien porque my padre les auia dicho que no diesen sobre ellos, lo vno hasta que llegase la jente porque les pudiesen tomar

Quizu Yupanqui attack then so that they would attack in unison, Quizo Yupanqui in Lima and my father in Cusco. While my father was doing this, the Spaniards sent him many letters, telling him to hurry úp and return home since they were lost without him. My father replied that he was not yet done hunting and would return just as soon as he could. The Spaniards began to realize that my father never responded affirmatively to any of their entreaties, regardless of how many times they called for him; and instead, that his absence grew longer and longer and he sent the Spanish captains poorer and poorer excuses. So they decided to go after him and either take him by force or kill him. They chose their captains in Cusco. One of them organized the men of his company and headed toward Calca with some of his men to carry out the capture. He left the rest of his men in Cusco on high alert so that they could follow if necessary. The com- 36
pany that set out got as far as the bridge over the Calca river, where the Spaniards had a skirmish over passage with the guards. The guards prevented the Spaniards from crossing. Then the Spaniards provoked my father's men at the bridge, and once they had provoked them headed back to Cusco with many of my father's men in hot pursuit, yelling and shouting. When the Spaniards returned to Cusco—and while they were still in a state of shock from the recent skirmish and from being followed—they yelled down from Cusco to their companions in Carmenca,[93] a place that overlooks the town, and asked them for help. Their companions, who were on the alert, came to the rescue of those in need. There, in Carmenca, a major encounter took place between the people who had chased the Spaniards [and those they were chasing], together with many other Spaniards who turned out in response to the Spanish call to arms. When the battle was over, my father's men had corralled the Spaniards in Cusco without killing any of them. That night, my father's men surrounded the Spaniards on all sides and persecuted them with a great deal of shouting. But they did not attack because they were waiting for all of my father's men who were to arrive the next day and because my father had told them not to attack. One reason he waited was that he wanted to wait until the rest of the people had come, so that they could take the Spaniards

93. Carmenca was an Inca settlement on a hill just northeast of Cusco itself. The parish of Santa Ana was founded there in 1560 (Julien, "La organización parroquial del Cuzco," 85).

a manos, y lo otro porque dezia quel se queria ber con ellos.

Çerco del Cuzco

Otro dia, despues que ffueron desta manera rretraidos al Cuzco, abiendoles puesto la misma noche muchas guardas y bien aperçebidos por todos los passos, esa tarde llego a uista del Cuzco el tomulto de la gente, los quales no entraron estonçes, porque les paresçia que hera muy noche y no se podrian aprouechar siendo noche de sus enemigos por la escuridad [oscuridad] grande que hazia, y a esta causa hizieron alto por todos los visos y çerros de donde pudiese señorearse el pueblo, poniendo grandes guardas e çentinelas a sus canpos; otro dia de mañana a ora de las nueue, estando todos los españoles en esquadron en la plaça del Cuzco bien aperçebidos, cuyo numero no se saue saluo que dizen que hera mucha gente y que tenian muchos negros consigo, asomaron por todas las vistas del Cuzco, a la rredonda del en el çerco, gran suma de gente con muchos chifflos y bozinas e tronpetas e gran griteria de bozes que asonbrauan a todo el mundo, que en numero serian mas de quatroçientos mill yndios, los quales entrarorn rrepartidos en esta manera:

Entrada de la gente al çerco

Por la parte de Carmenga, que es hazia Chinchaisuyo, entraron Cori Atau y Cuyllac y Taipi y otros muchos que çerraron aquel postigo con la gente que trayan; por la parte del Condesuyo, que es hazia Caocachi, entraron Vaman Quicana y Curi Guallpa y otros muchas

prisoners. Another reason was that he said he wanted to deal with the Spaniards himself.

The siege of Cusco

The next day, in the afternoon, after Manco Inca's men had kept the Spaniards in Cusco all night by surrounding them with many guards and keeping the passes well-guarded, a great mass of people arrived within sight of Cusco. But no one entered the city then, because it seemed that it was too late in the day and that the Indians would not be able to fight their enemies effectively in the dark of night. So, for this reason, those arriving stopped at all the vantage points and hills from which they could dominate the town and placed large numbers of guards and sentinels in their camps. All of the Spaniards' squadrons were on alert the next morning in the plaza. (Though the exact number of Spanish men is not known, they say there were a lot of them and that they had many black men with them.) Then at nine, a great number of people appeared in view all the way around Cusco in a ring surrounding the city, to the sound of much whistling and horns and trumpets and a great deal of shouting, astonishing the whole world. There were more than 400,000 Indians in all, divided up in the following manner:

Forming the ring

Cari Atau, Cuyllas, Taypi,[94] and many other captains entered from the direction of Carmenca (which is toward Chinchaysuyu) and closed that entrance with the people they brought. From the direction of Condesuyu, 37 toward Cayocache,[95] Huamani, Cuicaña, and Curi Huallpa[96] and many

94. Cari Atau and Cuyllas are alternate spellings of the names Cori Atao and Coyllas, mentioned earlier (see f. 35).

95. Cayocache was an Inca settlement on a low hill southeast of Inca Cusco, probably the hill known as Qoripata, where the parish of Belén was first founded. The parish church was probably rebuilt on its present site after the 1650 earthquake, which entirely destroyed some Cusco parishes, including Belén (Julien, "La organización parroquial del Cuzco," 94; Rowe, "El barrio de Cayau Cachi").

96. These three captains appear to be the same three named above as Suran Huaman, Quizana, and Suri Huallpa. All three are later mentioned in contexts that make it clear that they are Incas and not provincials.

que çerraron vna gran mella [malla?] de mas de media legua [2.5 km] de
box todos muy bien adereçados en orden de guerra; por la parte de Collasuyo entraron Llicllic y otros muchos capitanes con grandisyma suma
de gente, la mayor cantidad que se hallo en este çerco; por la parte de
Andesuyo entraron a Anta Allca y Ranpa Yupangui y otros muchos, los
quales acabaron de çercar el çerco que a los españoles pusieron este dia;
y despues de puesto este çerco, el qual estaua tan çerrado que hera cosa
de beer, y luego quisieron dar sobre los españoles pero no osaron hasta
que por mi padre les ffuese mandado lo que auian de hazer, el qual como
arriua dixe auia mandado que so pena de la bida naidie se mudase del lugar adonde estaua; y Vila Oma, capitan general de aquella gente, bien-
dola ya toda aperçebida y a punto hizolo luego saber a mi padre, el qual
estaua a la sazon en Callca diziendo que ya los tenia çercados y en gran
aprieto, que sy los matarian o ¿que harian dellos?; e mi padre le enbio a
dezir que los dexase estar ansy en aquel aprieto con aquella congoxa
37v   quellos tanbien le abian a el congoxado, que padesçiesen que tanbien
abia el padesçido, quel llegaria otro dia y los acabaria, la qual rrespuesta
bino al Vila Oma; y el dicho Vila Oma, como vio lo que mi padre le enbiaua a mandar, rresçiuio gran pena porque quisiera el luego acabarlos
asi como estaban, que tenia harto aparejo para ello, mas no oso por lo
que mi padre le enbio a a [repetition in the original] mandar, el qual
mando luego a pregonar por todo el exerçito que so pena de la vida naidie se menease del lugar dondestaua hasta quel se lo mandasse, y mando
tanbien soltar todas las açequias de agua que avia en el pueblo para que
anegasen todos los canpos y caminos que a la rredonda y dentro del estaua, y esto porque si acaso los españoles se quisiesen huyr, que hallasen
toda la tierra anegada y asi atollando los cauallos pudiesen ser señores de
sus enemigos a pie y en el lodaçal, porque gente bestida amañaese mal
en el lodo, lo qual todo ffue cunplido ni mas ni menos quel general Vila
Oma lo mando; los españoles, como se bieron ansy çercados en tanto
aprieto y que tanta gente les çercaua, sospechando entre sy que alli seria
los postrimeros dias de sus vidas no biendo de ninguna parte ningun
rremedio, no sabian que se hazer porque de vna parte beyanse çercados
38   de aquella manera, por otra beian los escarnios y las beffas que los yndios les hazian, tirandoles muchas piedras a los toldos y alçandoles la per-
neta por el poco casso que dellos hazian; començabanles a quemar las
casas; acometieron a ponerles ffuego a la yglessia sino que los negros que

other captains formed a great net of more than half a league [1.5 mi] around. All of them were well equipped and in fighting formation. From the direction of Collasuyu, Lliclli and many other captains came with a huge number of people, the greatest number in the ring surrounding the city. From Andesuyu, Anta Allca, Ranpa Yupanqui, and many others came; they closed the ring placed around the Spaniards that day. Once the ring was in place—and it was so well-closed that it was a sight to see—the captains wanted to attack the Spaniards. But they did not dare to attack until my father gave them orders about what they were to do. As mentioned above, my father had ordered that no one should move from the place where he was, on pain of death. So when Vila Oma, the captain general of the people assembled, saw that the Indians were entirely alert and ready to attack, he sent word to my father, who was then in Calca. Vila Oma said that now that he had the Spaniards very tightly surrounded, should he kill them or what should he do with them? My father sent word that Vila Oma should leave the Spaniards there in that fix so that they would feel the same anxiety that they had made him feel. Another day would come and he would finish them off then. When Vila Oma received that message and saw what my father had sent him, he was deeply troubled because he wanted to finish the Spaniards off just as they were and was well equipped to do it. Still, he didn't dare to, because of the message my father had sent him. Vila Oma then ordered that the entire army be advised that, on pain of death, no one should move the slightest bit from where they were until he ordered them to do so. He also ordered that the water should be released from all the canals in the town so that if the Spaniards tried to flee they would find all the fields flooded. Then, when the Spanish horses were stuck in the mire, Vila Oma's men could overcome them on foot and in the mud because people who dressed as the Spaniards could not maneuver very well in the mud. This was done in exactly the way Vila Oma had ordered. Upon seeing themselves surrounded so tightly and by so many people, the Spaniards imagined that they would spend the last days of their lives there. They could not find any solution to their problem and had no idea what to do. On the one hand, they were surrounded. On the other, the Indians were humiliating and grossly insulting them, throwing many stones at their awnings and lifting their legs toward them, and the Spaniards could do nothing about it. The Indians began to burn the houses in the city. They tried to set the church on fire. But the black men

37v

38

ençima della estauan se lo estoruavan avnque con hartos fflechazos que los yndios Satis y Andes les tiraron, a los quales no hizo daño ninguna [sic: ninguno] por guardarles Dios y ellos escudarse, pues como estubiesen desta manera desconfiados, de rremedio tubieron por prençipal socorro en acudirse a Dios, los quales estubieron toda aquella noche en la yglessia llamando a Dios que les ayudase, puestos de rrodillas y las manos junto a la boca, que lo bieron muchos yndios, y avn los questaban en la plaça en la bela hazian lo mesmo y muchos yndios de los que heran de su banda, los quales auian venido con ellos desde Caxamarca.

Batalla de los españoles contra los yndios en la ffortaleza

Otro dia de mañana, bien de mañana, todos salieron de la yglesia y se pusieron ençima de sus cauallos a guisa de pelear, y començaron a mirar a vna parte y a otra; y ansy mirando, pusieron piernas a sus cauallos y a mas correr, a pesar de sus enemigos, rronpieron aquel portillo que como muro estaua çerrado y hecharon a huyr por la cuesta arriua a matacavallo; los yndios que en el çerco del Cuzco estaban, como los bieron ansy huyr, començaron a gritar, diziendo "¡a que se ban a Castilla! ¡ha que se ban a Castilla! ¡ataxaldos!"; y ansy todo el çerco questaua hecho se deshizo, los vnos en su seguimiento, los otros ataxarlos, algunos a dar auiso a las guardas de las puentes porque no se pudiese escapar ninguno por ninguna parte; y los españoles, como bieron que les seguia tanta gente, boluieron la rrienda a sus cauallos y hizieron vna buelta por vn çerro llamado Queancalla, y llegaron a tomarles las espaldas de la parte por donde estaua Vila Oma, el qual se auia subido con toda su gente a hazerse ffuerte en la ffortaleza del

38v

who were on top of it managed to prevent them from doing so,[97] in spite of being bombarded by arrows shot by the Satis and Andes Indians.[98] No damage was done to the black men because God protected them, and they were able to shield themselves. Since the Spaniards were so disheartened, their principal aid was to seek out their God. Many Indians saw that the Spaniards spent that night in the church calling on God to help them, kneeling and clasping their hands to their mouths. The Spaniards keeping watch in the plaza did the same, as did many of the Indians who had joined them, who had come with them from Cajamarca.

Battle between the Spaniards and the Indians in the fortress

The next day, very early in the morning, all of the Spaniards emerged from the church and mounted their horses as if they were going to fight. They began to look first in one direction and then the other. Still looking, they kicked their horses and, at top speed, in the face of their enemies, they opened a door in the wall that enclosed them and fled uphill at breakneck   38v speed. When they saw the Spaniards fleeing, the Indians who were surrounding Cusco began to shout, saying: "They are heading for Castille, they are heading for Castille![99] Intercept them!" And so the ring that the Indians had made was undone. Some of the Indians followed the Spaniards, others tried to keep the Spaniards from passing, and some warned the guards at the bridges so that no Spaniards could escape anywhere. When they saw so many people coming after them, the Spaniards gave rein again to their horses and turned toward a hill called Quiancalla.[100] They managed to take the rear of the position held by Vila Oma who had climbed the hill with all of his people to make himself secure in the fortress of

97. The anonymous author of the other major account of the siege of Cusco, the *Sitio del Cuzco,* says nothing about what happened to the church during the siege. Later authors would say that the Virgin appeared and extinguished the flames with cloth mantles (Hemming, 194).

98. Both are peoples whose homeland was in the lowland region north and east of Cusco.

99. It is interesting to note that Castille, in Spain, was where the Incas thought the Spaniards were going.

100. A hill near the road leading out of Cusco to Yucay.

Cuzco llamada Sacsaguaman; y alli pelearon ffuertemente y les coxieron las quatro puertas de la ffortaleza, desde los muros de la qual, que son muy fuertes, arrojauan muchas galgas, tirauan muchas fflechas, muchos dardos, muchas lanças que ffatigaban grauemente a los españoles, con las quales galgas mataron a Joan Piçarro y a dos negros y muchos yndios de los que les ayudaban; y como a los de Vila Oma se les acabase la muniçion de gal-

39   gas y de lo demas, mediante el ffauor diuino tubieron lugar los españoles de entrar en la ffortaleza e tomarla por ffuerça, matando y destroçando muchos yndios de los que dentro estauan; otros se arrojaban de los muros abaxo, y como son altos, todos los que primero cayeron murieron, y los que despues, como ya abia gran rrimero de gente muerta, cayan sobre ellos; escapauanse algunos; ffue esta batalla de vna parte y de otra muy ensangrentada por la mucha gente de yndios que ffaboresçian a los espa-ñoles, entre los quales estavan dos hermanos de mi padre, llamados el vno Ynguill y el otro Vaypar, con mucha gente de su vando y chachapoyas e cañares.

Duro esta batalla, de vna parte y de otra, tres dias despues de la toma desta ffortaleza, porque otro dia despues se rretornaron a rrefformar los yndios para beer si podrian tornar a rrecobrar el ffuerte que auian perdido; y con gran animo acometieron a los españoles que estauan en el ffuerte, mas no pudie-ron hazerles ninguna cossa por las muchas guardas que de todas partes ten-ian, asi de cañares que les ayudauan como de los mesmos españoles, y lo otro porque dizen estos yndios que vn cauallo blanco que alli andaua, el qual ffue

39v   el primero que entro en la ffortaleza al tienpo que se tomo, les hazia mucho

Cusco, called Sacsahuaman.[101] There the Spaniards fought fiercely and took the four gates of the fortress. From the fortress walls—which are very strong—Vila Oma's men threw many boulders and shot many arrows, darts, and lances, that greatly harassed the Spaniards. With the stones Vila Oma's men killed Juan Pizarro[102] and two black men, along with many of the Indians who were helping the Spaniards. After the supplies of stones and other projectiles had run out and owing to divine favor, the Spaniards were able to enter the fortress and take it by force, killing and destroying   39 many of the Indians inside. Other Indians threw themselves over the walls, and since these walls were very high, those who fell first died. Some of those Indians who fell afterward fell on top of the dead and, since there was a great pile of dead people, they escaped. The battle was very bloody everywhere it was fought because of the many Indians who sided with the Spaniards. Among these were my father's brothers, one named Ynguill[103] and another, Huaypar, along with many Incas of their faction and the Chachapoyas and Cañares.[104]

   This battle, fought here and there, lasted three days after the fortress was taken. After the first day, the Indians regrouped to see if they could retake the fortress they had lost. Though they vigorously attacked the Spaniards inside, they couldn't do anything to them because of the resistance of the many guards the Spaniards had put in place (like the Cañares who were helping them, as well as the Spaniards themselves). They also couldn't do anything because, as the Indians say, a white horse,[105] the first horse to enter the fortress at the time it was taken, did them a lot of   39v

101. The fortress above the city of Cusco with massive stone walls of polygonal basalt masonry.

102. Juan Pizarro led the attack on the fortress (Hemming, 197–8). He received a fatal head wound but lived another two weeks.

103. Titu Cusi has already glossed *ynguill* as "flower" and used it to refer to an important Inca woman. Here it is the name of a man.

104. The Chachapoyas and Cañares were the local inhabitants of the region east of the main trunk of the Andes in northern Peru and southern Ecuador. They were quick to side with the Spaniards. A number of them had been brought to the Cusco area by the Incas before the Spanish arrival and settled as *mitimaes,* or colonists, but they played a more prominent role after the Spanish arrival, when they were settled in the parish of Santa Ana (on the site of Carmenca, see note 93) by the Spaniards.

105. If Juan Pizarro led the attack (Hemming, 197), this was his horse. It is interesting to note that here the horse itself plays an important role in the siege.

daño; y duro todo el dia este rrebate, e ya que la noche le sobreuenia, por la mucha escuridad que en ella hazia no se pudiendo aprouechar de sus enemigos, se rretraxieron a sus sytios; y los españoles, por no dexar el ffuerte que tenian y desanpararlo, dexaronlos yr y otro dia de mañana tornaron a la batalla començada, la qual rriñieron muy fuertemente los vnos con los otros; y al fin, biniendo con gran animo los yndios contra los españoles, los españoles salieron todos de tropel del fuerte y fueronse contra ellos con gran esffuerço y arremetiendose; los yndios se rratraxeron [rretruxeron] hazia donde mi padre estauan [sic: estaua], que hera en Callca, y fueron tras dellos matando y desbaratando gran parte de la gente hasta el rrio de Yucay, en el qual los yndios dieron lado a los españoles, los quales españoles pasaron adelante derecho a Callca adonde mi padre estaua, el qual no le hallaron alli porque estaua haziendo vna fiesta en el pueblo llamado Sacsasiray; y como no le hallassen alli, dieron la buelta hazia el Cuzco por otro camino con harta perdida de ffardaje que los yn-
40 dios coxieron en la rretaguarda, saliendo del lado que les auian dado, con el qual despojo se ffueron derechos adonde mi padre estaua haziendo la fiesta.

Hecha mi padre esta ffiesta en aquel pueblo Sacsasiray, sa [sic: se] salio de alli para el pueblo de Tanbo, pasando de camino por Yucay; adormio sola vna noche, y llegado que fue a Tanbo mando que se juntase alli toda la tierra porque queria hazer vna fortaleza muy fuerte para en ella defenderse de todos los españoles que le quisiesen acometer, la qual jente fue junta muy breue; y desque la tubo junta, les hizo el parlamiento siguiente:

Parlamento que hizo el Ynga a todos sus capitanes y gente en el pueblo de Tanbo luego como se rrecojio a el despues del desbarate del Cuzco

"Muy amados hijos y hermanos mios, en las platicas pasadas que os he hecho antes de agora, abreis entendido como yo sienpre os estorue que no hiziesedes mal a aquella gente tan mala que debaxo de engaño y por dezir que heran hijos del Viracochan y enbiados por su mandado auian entrado en mi tierra, a lo qual yo les di consentimiento; y por esto y por otras muchas y muy buenas obras que les hize,
40v dandoles lo que yo tenia en ella, plata y oro, rropa y maiz, ganados,

damage. This rematch lasted the whole day. When night came the darkness prevented Vila Oma's men from gaining an advantage over their enemies, so they retreated to their positions. The Spaniards let them go because they could not leave the fortress undefended. The battle began again the next day. Both sides shouted bitter accusations at each other. Finally, when the Indians made a spirited attack on the fortress, the Spaniards left it in a single force and came out to meet them with great energy, throwing everything they had into the fight. The Indians withdrew to Calca, where my father was staying. The Spaniards came after them, killing and vanquishing a large number of them until they reached the Yucay river where the Indians allowed the Spaniards to pass them by staying to one side. The Spaniards went on ahead, straight to Calca where my father had been. They did not find him there, however, because he was involved in a fiesta in a town called Sacsasiray. When the Spaniards did not find him, they went back to Cusco, following another route. They suffered great losses to their baggage that the Indians took from the Spanish rear 40 guard, attacking from the side position they had taken. With these spoils, the Indians went straight to where my father was celebrating the fiesta.

When he had finished with the fiesta in the town of Sacsasiray, my father left for the town of Tambo. He passed through Yucay on the way but slept only one night there. Once he had arrived at Tambo, he ordered a gathering of all the people of the land because he wanted to build a strong fortress from which they could defend themselves against all the Spaniards who might want to attack him. The people came together very quickly. After they were together, my father made the following speech:

Speech made by the Inca to all of his captains and people in the town of Tambo after they arrived there, following the defeat of Cusco

"Beloved children and brothers of mine, you will understand from past conversations I have had with you how I have always tried to prevent you from doing any harm to those people whom I know are so evil that—through deceit and by saying they were sons of the Viracochan and sent on his orders—entered my land. I gave my consent for them to enter. To repay this and the many other good deeds I did for them, giving them what I had—including silver and gold, clothing and maize, livestock, 40v

basallos, mugeres, criados e otras muchas cossas sin numero, me prendieron, vltraxaron y maltrataron syn yo se lo meresçer; y despues me
trataron la muerte, la qual entendi por auiso de Antonico, su lengua, el
qual esta aqui pressente, que se huyo dellos por no los poder sufrir; y como
entendistes por el parlamento que sobre el çerco del Cuzco os hize para
la junta del, me rrecoxi yo a Callca para que desde alli sin entendellos
ellos les diesemos en la caueça, lo qual me pareçe que ansy se hizo como
yo lo mande avnque no me halle pressente como pensava, de lo qual
rreçiuistes detrimento en la toma de Sacsaguaman, que por descuydo os
tomaron y despues os desbarataron, syguiendoos hasta Yucay sin poderles
hazer nada; pena me aueis dado de que, siendo tanta gente vosotros y
ellos tan pocos, se os saliesen de las manos; quiça el Viracochan les ayudo por lo que me aveis dicho de questubieron de rrodillas toda la noche
mochandole, porque sy no les ayudara, ¿como se podrian escapar de buestras manos syendo vosotros syn numero?; ya esta hecho, por vuestra vida que
de aqui adelante mireis como abeis con ellos porque sabed que son nue-
41   stros enemigos capitales y nosotros lo abemos de ser suyos perpetuamente,
pues ellos lo an querido. Yo me quiero hazer ffuerte en este pueblo y hazer
aqui vna ffortaleza para que naidie me puede entrar en el, por vida buestra
que me hagais este plazer, que algun dia podia ser que nos aproueche".

Respuesta que los capitanes hizieron al Ynga

"Sapai Ynga, estos tus pobres criados te besamoss las manos y con muy gran
conffusion y berguença venimos ante ti por auersenos escapado de entre las
manos tan gran enpressa como hera la de aquella gente malina [maligna],
auiendote hecho tantos y tan malos tratamientos y auiendote sido tan yngratos a lo mucho que por ellos hezistes; [h]a nos caydo tanta confussion
que no te osamos mirar a la cara, pero en alguna manera nos da algun aliuio
el poderte hechar a ti alguna culpa, y es porque te enbiamos a preguntar que
hariamos dellos quando los teniamos çerrados e syn ninguna esperança de
rremedio y nos enbiaste a dezir que los dexasemos padesçer como ellos avian
hecho a ti, que tu bernias y los acabarias; y nosotros, por no yr contra lo que
tu mandabas, dexamoslos vn dia e vna noche aguardandote, y quando pen-
41v   samos questauamos seguros y que mas çiertos los teniamos en las manos,

vassals, women, servants, and other things in infinite quantity—they took me prisoner and gravely offended and mistreated me, although I had done nothing to deserve [such treatment]. Afterward, they tried to kill me, as I learned from the report of Antonico, their interpreter, who is here now and who fled from them because he could not stand them (as you know from the speech I made when I called you together to surround Cusco). I retired to Calca, so that from there, and without their knowing it, we could attack the Spaniards head on. Though I was not present at the time as I thought I would be, this plan seems to have been carried out in the manner I ordered. You received the worst of it in the taking of Sacsahuaman. Because of your carelessness the Spaniards took it from you and then defeated you; they pursued you to Yucay, and you were unable to do anything to stop them. You have given me great sorrow. You have so many people and the Spaniards are so few—yet they slipped through your grasp. Perhaps the Viracochan helped them, since, as you told me, they kneeled all night worshipping him. In fact, how could they have escaped from your grasp, since there were so many of you, if he hadn't helped them? Now it's done. By your lives, be careful how you get along with them from now on, because you know that they are our capital enemies and we will be theirs perpetually, since that is what they wanted. I want to fortify myself in this town and build a fortress here so that no one can enter it. By your lives, grant me this pleasure, because some day we may need it." 41

Response that the captains made to the Inca

"Sapay Inca, we your poor servants, kiss your hands. We come before you in great distress and shame because the enterprise related to those evil people—who did so many and such evil things to you and were so ungrateful in spite of all that you did for them—slipped through our hands. We are so overcome by our distress that we do not dare look you in the face. But we take some comfort in being able to blame you in part, since we sent to ask you what we should do with the Spaniards when we had them trapped with no way out, and you sent word that we should leave them there suffering like they had made you suffer and that you would come and finish them off. Since we could not disobey your orders, we left the Spaniards alone for a day and a night while we waited for you. Then, when we thought we were secure and that we had them in our hands for 41v

se noss escabullieron sin ser señores de hazerles nada; no sabemos que fue
la causa ni que te digamos desto syno que fue nuestra desdicha en no
acudir con tienpo y la tuya en no nos dar lisçençia para ello; aparejados estamos para rresçibir el castigo que por esta culpa nos quisieres dar; y lo
que dizes que te hagamos aqui fuerte en este pueblo para poderte defender
de aquella gente y de todos los que te quisieren acometer, dezimos que lo
haremos de muy entera voluntad, que mas que esto te debemos"; y ansy
la hizieron vna de las mas ffuertes que ay en el Peru en año y medio ques-
tubo en Tanbo.

En este medio tienpo, ya que auia hablado a los yndios y dadoles a entender la desgrasçia que les auia acontesçido, llegaron al dicho pueblo de
Tanbo los mensajeros del desbarate que auia auido en Lima y Cullcomayo,
ques en Xauxa donde ouieron vna rrefriega los españoles con los yndios en
que los yndios ouieron la vitoria, y truxieron a mi padre muchas cabeças de
los capitanes y dos españoles biuos y vn negro y quatro cauallos, los quales
llegaron con gran rregoçijo de la bitoria auida; y mi padre los rresçiuio muy
honrradamente y animo a todos los demas a pelear de aquella suerte; y alli
mesmo llego al dicho pueblo de Tanbo el capitan Diego Ordoñez con vna
42   quadrilla de soldados a pelear con mi padre, y sauido por el, le salieron al
enquentro muchos yndios antes que llegasen al fuerte de Tanbo, ya pasado
el rrio, y en vn llano llamado Pascapanba y Pachar ouieron gran rrefriega
los vnos con los otros; y al fyn no se conçedio de ninguna parte la vitoria
porque los mesmos españoles, por causa de vnas espinas que alli estauan,
se desbarataron, y avn murio el vno dellos en la rrebuelta y tres negros

certain, they slipped through our fingers without our being able to do any-thing about it. We do not know why this happened, nor what to tell you about this, except that it was our misfortune not to have attacked sooner and yours for not giving us permission to attack.[106] We are ready to receive any punishment you might want to give us for our failure. As to what you say about strengthening the defenses of this town in order to defend your-self from those people and any others who might want to attack you, we will do it willingly, for we owe you far more than that." So they built one of the strongest places of all those in Peru during the year and a half they were in Tambo.[107]

Then, after my father had spoken to the Indians and let them know what a disgrace had befallen them, messengers arrived in the town of Tambo to tell them about the events of Lima and Cullcomayu, which is in Jauja. A battle had been fought there between the Spaniards and the Indians in which the Indians were victorious. The messengers brought my father the heads of many Spaniards, as well as two live Spaniards, two black men, and four horses.[108] These Indians arrived rejoicing over their victory. My father received them very honorably and tried to inspire the rest [of his men] to fight as well as they had. The captain Diego Ordoñez[109] also came to the town of Tambo with a squadron of soldiers to fight my father. When my father learned of Ordoñez's arrival, he took many Indians to meet Ordoñez on a plain called Pascabamba and Pachar, which is reached before arriving at the fortress of Tambo but after crossing the river. There my father and Ordoñez fought a great skirmish with each other. In the end, no one could claim victory. The thorny plants there had defeated the Spaniards. One of the Spaniards and three black men died in the action.

42

106. Here is Titu Cusi's explanation for how the Incas lost the battle that cost them Peru.

107. Tambo is Ollantaytambo, where the remains of fortifications on both sides of the Urubamba river, facing Cusco, can still be seen.

108. Taking prisoners and bringing them back to Cusco was part of the ritual of Inca warfare. They were dressed in long red tunics covered with tassels and marched ahead of the victorious captain, to the singing of songs about their defeat (Betanzos, *Narrative of the Incas,* pt. 1, ch. 19: 87–89).

109. Elsewhere (see note 122) Titu Cusi confuses "Diego Ordoñez" with Rodrigo Orgóñez. In this case, it was Hernando Pizarro who attacked Ollantaytambo in this period (Hemming, 213–14).

y los yndios coxieron otra [sic: otro] alla en su fuerte porque se quiso aben-
turar; e ya que la noche los despartio, rrecoxieronse todos, cada vno a su
fuerte, y los españoles asentaron su toldo a prima noche e hizieron sus lun-
bradas; a la madrugada a guissa de que querian pelear, y antes que ama-
nesçiesse boluieron las espaldas [sic: los españoles] hazia el Cuzco, y
quando los yndios pensaron que estaban alli a la mañana, no hallaron
ninguno, de que les dio muy gran rrisa, diziendo que se auian huydo de
miedo. Despues que paso todo esto y los españoles se fueron a sus casas,
quedose my padre en Tanbo dando priessa a su ffortaleza; y estando ansy
en el mesmo Tanbo, dos españoles, presos rrendidos que alli tenia consigo,
a los quales hazia muy buen tratamiento, dandolos de comer junto a ssi,
se le huyeron por auisos que del Cuzco les vino; y no se sabiendo dar maña,
42v   los tornaron desde vn pueblo llamado Maras, dos leguas [10 km] del dicho pueblo de Tanbo, a los quales, como my padre preguntase la caussa
porque se huyan, no supieron dar rrazon de sy; e uisto por mi padre que
avn estos les [sic: le] pagaban tan mal el bien que les hazia, y avn al vno
dellos que hera Antonico arriba dicho que auia auisado a my padre en el
Cuzco de lo que los españoles tratauan contra el, no sabiendo conoçer
el tratamiento que my padre le auia hecho y hazia, traiendole hen hamaca
y haziendole el tratamiento de hijo, le acontesçio lo que a los demas, que
ffue que los mando entregar a vnos yndios moyomoyos andes para que,
despedaçados, los comiesen.

Acabado todo esto y acabada tanbien la ffortaleza, determino mi padre de
quererse entrar a los Andes y dexar aquella tierra dalla fuera, porque le daban mucha pena los españoles; y los Andes le ynportunavan mucho a que se
fuese a su tierra, que ellos le guardarian alla y le seruirian como a su señor y

The Indians captured another Spaniard in their fort who had risked entering it. When darkness had divided the Indians and Spaniards, each side returned to their stronghold. The Spaniards made their camp and bonfires when night had fully fallen. At dawn and before it was light, the Spaniards returned to Cusco, making it appear that they were still there and planning to fight on the morrow. The Indians, who thought the Spaniards were still there in the morning, found no one. This gave them a good laugh, and they told each other the Spaniards had fled out of fear. When all this was finished and the Spaniards had gone to their houses, my father stayed in Tambo and stepped up the pace of work on the fortress. While he was there in Tambo, two Spaniards who had been taken prisoner fled because of some news they received from Cusco. My father had treated these prisoners very well and had even let them take their meals with him. Since the prisoners made no effort to cover their tracks, they were captured in a town called Maras, two leagues [6 mi] from the town of Tambo. When my father asked the prisoners why they had fled, they did not even know how to answer. My father saw that even these Spaniards repaid the good he had done them badly. One of these prisoners was the Antonico mentioned above who had told my father in Cusco that the Spaniards were plotting against him, and even he did not know enough to recognize the good treatment that he had been given (and was still being given). He had been carried around in a hammock[110] and treated like a son. Antonico was given the same treatment as the other prisoners: he was turned over to some Moyomoyo Andes[111] so that they would eat the prisoners, after first cutting them into pieces.

42v

When this business was over, and when the fortress was finished, my father decided he wanted to go to the Andes and leave the outside world. He said this because the Spaniards had given him so much grief and because the people of the Andes had pleaded with him to come to their lands; these people had offered to guard him and serve him as their lord and

110. Carrying hammocks were used to transport individuals.

111. The name Moyomoyo (or Moyosmoyos), also used to refer to a province in the Andean foothills northeast of what is now Sucre (Bolivia), seems to be a generic term for some kind of lowland people. It is interesting to note that "Moyosmoyos" and not "Andes" is the generic term. The Andes or Antis were a specific group who inhabited the lowlands north of Cusco.

rrey; e ya determinado que estubo en la dicha entrada, hizo juntar a su gente para les dar a entender la manera que auian de tener en la biuienda con los españoles, el qual les dixo asy:

Documento que Mango Ynga dio a los yndios quando se quiso rrecoger a los andes en [sic: e] la manera que auian de tener con los españoles

"Muy amados hijos y hermanos mios, los que aqui estais presentes y me aueis seguido en todos mis trauajos e tribulasçiones, bien creo no sabeis la caussa porque en vno os he mandado juntar agora ante my; yo os la dire en breue, por vida buestra que no os altereis de lo que os dixiere porque bien sabeis que la neçesidad muchas vezes conpela a los honbres a hazer aquello que no querrian, y por esso, por serme fforçado dar contento a estos andes, que tanto tienpo a que me ynportunan que los vaya a ber, abre de darles este contento por algunos dias; rruegoos mucho que dello no rreçibais pena porque yo no os la deseo dar, pues os amo como a hijos; lo que aqui os rrogare me dareis mucho contento haziendolo [inserted above the line of text].

"Bien sabeis como muchas vezes, syn esta, os lo he dicho la manera como aquella gente barbuda entro en mi tierra so color que dezian que heran *viracochas,* lo qual por sus trajes e diuissas tan diferentes de las nuestras vosotros e avn yo lo pensamos, por el qual pensamiento y çertifficasçion de los tallanas *yungas,* que de cossas que les vieron hazer en su tierra me hizieron, como aveis visto, los traxiese a my tierra e pueblo y les hize el tratamiento ya notorio a toda la tierra y les di las cossas que sabeis, por lo qual e por ellas me trataron de la manera que aueis visto; y no solamente ellos sino mis hermanos Pascac e Ynguill y Guaipar me desposeyeron de mi tierra y avn me trataron la muerte, de la qual yo me libre por el auisso que os dixe de Antonico, como el otro dia aqui os dixe, al qual comieron los andes por no se sauer valer; y biendo todas aquellas cosas y otras muchas, que por la prolexidad dexo, os mande juntar al Cuzco para que les diesemos algun tartago

king. Now, determined to make the trip, my father collected his people together to tell them how they were to live with the Spaniards. He told them in the following way:

Document[112] that Manco Inca gave to the Indians when he wanted to retire to the Andes and the manner they should use in dealing with the Spaniards

"Very beloved sons and brothers of mine, I can well believe that those of you who are present and who have followed me in all my trials and tribu-   43
lations do not know why I have called all of you to gather together before me. I will tell you right now. By your lives, I hope that you will not be dissuaded from doing what I now tell you to; you know very well that necessity compels men to do what they do not want to do. For that reason, and because I have to satisfy these Andes who have begged me for some time to visit them, I will give them that pleasure for a few days. I beg you not to be upset by my decision. Since I love you like sons, I do not want to cause you any anguish. You will give me great contentment if you do what I ask you to do here.

"You know very well how many times, not counting this one, I have told you how those bearded people entered my land under the guise that they were *viracochas*. Their clothes and other customs so different from our own persuaded us all—including me—that they really were *viracochas*. Because of this idea, and because the Tallanas *yungas* presented me with testimony of what they had seen the Spaniards do in their land (as you know), I brought the Spaniards to my land and town and gave them the treatment that everyone in the land knows about. I gave them the things that you know about. The Spaniards then treated me in the manner you have seen. And the Spaniards were not the only ones [to have treated me   43v
this way]: my brothers Pascac, Ynguill, and Huaypar also took the land from me and even tried to kill me, as I learned because of the warning from Antonico that I told you about (who was eaten by the Andes because he did not know how to value himself). Having witnessed all these things—and much more that I omit to avoid being prolific—I ordered you to gather in Cusco so that we could bring disgrace upon the Spaniards just

112. Here the term "document" is used to refer to a speech.

de los muchos que nos auian dado; y pareçeme que, o porque su Dios les ayudo o porque no me halle yo pressente, no salistes con vuestro yntento, de lo qual yo he rresçiuido gran pena, pero como a los honbres no les sub-çedan todas las cossas como desean syenpre, no nos emos de marauillar ni congoxarnos demasyada, por lo qual os rruego que vosotros no tengais congoxa, que en ffin no nos a ydo tan mal que no les ayamos coxido algo porque, como sabeis, en Lima y en Chullcomayo y Xauxa les coximos algunas cossas que no dexan de dar algun aliuio avnque no equibalente a la pena que ellos nos an dado.

"Ya me pareçe se ba haziendo tienpo de partirme a la tierra de los an-des, como arriua os dixe, y que me sera forçado detenerme alla algunos dias; mirad que os mando que no se os oluide lo que os he dicho y pienso dezir agora, ques que mireis quanto tienpo a que mis aguelos e visaguelos e yo os hemos sustentado y guardado, ffauoresçido y gouernado todas vuestras casas, probeyendolas de la manera que abeis abido menester, por lo qual teneis todos obligasçion de no nos olvidar en toda vuestra vida, vosotros y vuestros deçendientes, ansy a mi como a mis aguelos y visague-los, y tener mucho rrespeto y hazer mucho casso de mi hijo y hermano Titu Cusy Yupangui y de todos los demas mis hijos que dellos deçendieren, pues en ello me dareis a mi mucho contento y ellos os lo agradeçeran, como yo se lo dexo mandado; por tanto, basteos esto açerca de lo dicho".

Respuesta de los yndios al Ynga

"Sapai Ynga, ¿con que coraçon quieres dexar a estoss tus hijos solos, que con tanta voluntad te an deseado y desean syenpre seruir, y que sy neçesario fuese pornian mill vezes la vida por ti, sy ffuese menester? ¿a que rrey, a que señor, a quien los dexas encomendados? ¿que deseruiçios, que traiçiones,

as they had so often brought it upon us. It seems to me that you were unsuccessful in your efforts, either because their God helped them or because I was not present. The failure has me deeply troubled. But things don't always work out the way men want them to, and so we should not wonder or feel too anxious. For that reason I beg you not to feel any anguish. It didn't go so badly for us that we weren't able to take something from them: as you know, we took some things from them in Lima and Chullcomayu and Jauja,[113] and that is a source of some relief—although it does not begin to make up for the grief they have caused us.

"Now it appears that it is time for me to leave for the lands of the Andes, as I told you above, and that I will be forced to remain there for a few days. Look to what I have ordered. Do not forget what I have told you and what I say now, which is that you consider how long my grandparents, great-grandparents, and I sustained and preserved you, favored and governed all of your houses, and supplied you as was necessary. For all of this you are obligated never to forget us for the rest of your lives, neither me nor my grandparents or great-grandparents, and to respect and continue to give your allegiance to my son and brother[114] Titu Cusi Yupanqui and the rest of the children who descend from me, my grandparents, and my great-grandparents. In doing so you will give me much contentment, and my descendants will thank you for doing as I have ordered you to do in the way that I have ordered it done. Let this be enough for you, with regard to what has been said."

The Indians' response to the Inca

"Sapay Inca, what kind of heart permits you to abandon these, your children? They have desired and will always desire to serve you. If it were necessary, they would give their lives a thousand times for you. What king, what lord have you left in charge of us? What disservice, what betrayals,

---

113. Taking booty after winning a battle was an Inca practice, and certain items became trophies of war.

114. A man cannot be both a son and a brother to another man. In the Inca language, these terms also referred to lineage membership: "son" was a member of a man's lineage younger than himself, and "brother" a member the same age or older (Julien, *Reading Inca History*, 24). Manco appears to be saying that Titu Cusi has the maturity and wisdom of someone his equal in status.

que maldades te hemos hecho para que nos quieres dexar ansy desanparados e syn señor ni rrey a quien rrespetar?, pues jamas hemos conosçido otro
señor ni padre syno a ti y a Guaina Capac, tu padre, y a sus antepasados;
no nos dexes señor desa manera desanparados, desconsolados, mas antes
nos da este contento, si fueres seruido, de lleuarnos contigo adondequiera
que fueres, que chicos y grandes e biejos y biejas aparejados estamos para
no te dexar de seguirte avnque tu nos dexes"; y luego el dicho mi padre,
biendo que con tanta ansya le deseauan seruir toda su gente, les boluio a
dezir lo que aqui paresçera:

"Yo os agradesco hijos la buena voluntad y deseo que mostrais de quererme seguir dondequiera que vaya; no perdereis la paga de mi, que yo os
lo agradesçere e pagare antes que vosotros pensais; y agora, por vida buestra que os rreporteis y no tengais tanta pena, que muy breue os bolvere a
ver; y de aqui a que buelua o hasta que os enbie mis mensajeros para lo que
ayais de hazer terneis este modo en vuestra biuienda. Lo primero que hareis
sera que a estos barbudos, que tantas beffas a mi me an hecho por me fyar
yo dellos tanto, no les creais cosa que os dixieren, porque mienten mucho,
como a mi en todo lo que comigo an tratado me an mentido, y ansy haran
a vosotros; lo que podreis hazer sera dar muestras por de fuera de que con-
sentis a lo que os mandan y dar algun camarico y lo que pudieredes que en
vuestras tierras ouiere, porque como esta gente es tan braua y de diferente
condiçion de la nuestra, podria ser que no se lo dando vosotros os lo
tomasen por fuerça o vos maltratasen por ello, y por evitar esto os sera buen
rremedio hazer lo que os digo, lo otro, que esteis sienpre con abisso
para quando os enbiare a llamar o auisar de lo que con esta gente abeis de
hazer, y si acaso ellos os acometieren o quisieren tomar vuestras tierras, no
dexeis de defenderos y sobre ello perder la vida sy ffuere menester; y si tanbien se os offresçiere neçesidad estrema de que ayais neçesidad de my persona, darmeeis avisso por la posta adondequiera que yo estubiere. Y mirar
que estos engañan por buenas palabras y despues no cunplen lo que dizen,
que ansy como abeis visto hizieron a mi, que me dixieron que heran hijos

what evil deeds have we done so that you want to leave us without anyone to protect us and without a lord or king to respect? We have never
known any other lord or father except you and Huayna Capac, your father, and his ancestors.

"Do not leave us unprotected and disconsolate, our lord. Instead give   44v
us the pleasure, if you would be served by it, to take us with you wherever
you might go. Small and large, young and old—we will all follow you
whether you want us to or not." When my father saw how anxious his
people were to serve him, he responded with the following:

"I thank you, children, for your goodwill and the desire you have shown
to follow me wherever I would go. You will not go without my repayment,
and I will thank you and pay you sooner than you think. And now—by
your lives—put a stop to your passions. Do not be troubled, since I will
see you again very shortly. From now to the time I return or send you my
messengers to tell you what to do, live your lives in the following manner.
First, you must not believe a thing these bearded people—who have offended me so deeply because I placed so much faith in them—tell you, because they lie a great deal as they have in all my dealings with them. They
will lie to you, too. What you can do is act as if you consent to what they
order and give them some *camarico*[115] and whatever you can from what
can be found in your lands. Because these people are so fierce, and so dif-   45
ferent from our own people, they might try to take what they want from
you by force if you do not give them what they ask. They might mistreat
you to get what they want. To prevent this from happening, you can do
what I have told you. The other thing I would tell you is to always be on
alert for a message or summons from me regarding what you have to do
with these people. If they attack you or want to take your lands, do not
fail to defend yourselves. In such cases, you must give your lives if necessary. If you should find yourselves in extreme need, such that you need
me, send word by post to me wherever I might be. Remember that these
men will deceive you with their good words and afterward will not do what
they have said, as you have seen in my case. They told me they were sons

---

115. The term *camarico* was in common use to refer to the material support given to
priests or other outsiders by members of Andean communities. González Holguín defines it as "he who makes something ready, or likewise, something available or
equipped" (*Camaricuk. El que apareja algo o asi mesmo se dispone o apareja;* 48).

del Viracochan y me mostraron al prençipio gran afablidad [afabilidad] y mucho amor y despues hizieron conmigo lo que bistes; sy ellos fueron hijos del Viracochan como se jataban no ouieran hecho lo que an hecho, porquel Viracocha puede allanar los çerros, sacar las aguas, hazer çerros donde no las ay, no haze mal a naidie; y estos, no vemos que an hecho esto, mas antes en lugar de hazer bien nos an hecho mal, tomandonos nuestras haziendas, nuestras mugeres, nuestros hijos, nuestras hijas, nuestras chacaras, nuestras comidas y otras muchas cosas que en nuestra tierra teniamos por ffuerça y con engaños y contra nuestra voluntad; y a jente que esto haze no les podemos llamar hijos del Viracochan syno, como otras vezes os he dicho, del *Supay* peores, porque en sus obras le an emitado [imitado], pues an hecho obras de tal, que por ser tan bergonçosas no las quiero dezir.

"Lo que mas aveis de hazer es que, por ventura estos os diran que adoreis a lo que ellos adoran que son vnos paños pintados, los quales dizen ques Viracochan y que le adoreis como a *guaca*, el qual no es sino paño, no lo hagais sino lo que nosotros tenemos; eso tened porque, como beis, las *villcas* hablan con nosotros, y al sol y a la luna beemoslos por nuestros ojos, y lo que esos dizen no lo veemos; bien creo que alguna bez por ffuerça o con engaño os an de hazer adorar lo que ellos adoran quando mas no pudieredes, hazeldo delante dellos y por otra parte no oluideis nuestras çerimonias; y si os dixieren que quebranteis vuestras *guacas*, y esto por ffuerça, mostraldes lo que no pudieredes hazer menos y lo demas guardaldo, que en ello me dareis a mi mucho contento".

45v

of the Viracochan and showed me great friendship and love at first but later did what you saw. If they were the sons of the Viracochan that they pretended to be, they would not have done what they did, because the Viracochan can flatten hills, bring forth streams, and make hills where there were none before—but he does no harm to anyone. We have not seen these people behave in this way; instead of doing good, they have done us evil. They have taken our property, our women, our sons, our daughters, our fields, our food, and many other things in our lands through force, deceit, and against our will. People who would do such things cannot be called sons of the Viracochan. Instead, as I have said other times, they must be called sons of the *Supay,* or worse, because they have imitated him in their deeds and have done his work. They have committed deeds so shameful that I do not want to speak of them.

45v

"Most importantly, if by chance they tell you that you should worship what they worship—that is, some painted sheets that they say are the Viracochan but are only sheets—and tell you to adore them like a *huaca,*[116] do not worship them but worship what is ours instead. Keep what is ours. As you see, the *villcas*[117] speak with us, and we can see the sun and the moon[118] with our own eyes. We cannot see what those [papers] say. I can well imagine that at some point they will get you to worship what they worship through force or deceit. When you can't avoid it any longer, do it in front of them but do not forget our ceremonies. If the Spaniards tell you that you must break your *huacas,* and if they try to force you to do so, show them that you would do no less than that, but keep your other practices, for in so doing you will give me great contentment."

116. González Holguín defines *huaca* as "idols, figures of men and animals that they carry with them" (*Huacca. Ydolos, figurillas de hombres y animales que trayan consigo;* 45).
117. Here the term *villca* is used like *huaca,* in this case to refer to something with the power of speech. González Holguín defines *villca* as a kind of tree (*Villca. Vn arbol que su fruta como chochos es purga;* 352), not seemingly akin to the usage by Titu Cusi. In *The Huarochirí Manuscript,* an early-seventeenth-century collection of stories about the deeds of *huacas* and others from Huarochirí, the word *vilca* can be understood from the context of its use as "a person who has entered into the society of *huacas* by achievement or marriage" (Salomon and Urioste, 46, n. 44). *Vilca* and *villca* are not linguistic equivalents, so perhaps there is an error in transcription.
118. Both the sun and moon were beings that could be represented, like living beings, as images or objects. They had a material existence and were ritually fed.

46   Acabadas todas estas cosas arriba dichas y otras muchas, despidiose mi
padre de los yndios, trayendome a mi alli delante para les dezir como yo
hera su hijo y como despues de sus dias me avian de tener en su lugar por
señor de todos ellos, el qual lo hizo; e se leuanto en pie para partirse de su
gente, la qual quando lo vio en pie ffueron tales y tan grandes los alaridos
que todos començaron a dar que paresçia que se horadaban los çerros; y
la gente con la ansya que tenia todavia le queria seguir, pero nunca mi
padre les dexo sino ffue a qual a qual [repetition in the original] que no
tenian ynpedimiento que les estoruasen, porque dezia a aquellos que con
tanta ansya le querian seguir que ¿como auian de dexar sus sementeras, sus
casas, sus mugeres y sus hijos, sus *oybas* o crias, para seguirle?, que se rre-
portasen y que muy breue bolueria a berlos o les enbiaria a dezir lo que
auian de hazer; e ansy se partio de todos ellos para el pueblo de Vitcos.

Llegada del Ynga a Vitcos

Llegados que fuymos a Vitcos, ques pueblo treynta leguas [150 km] del
Cuzco, con la gente que a mi padre seguia, asentamos nuestro pueblo y
asiento con yntençion de biuir alli algunos dias y descansar; hizo hazer mi
46v   padre vna cassa para dormir porque las que antiguamente auia heran de
mis aguelos Pachacuti Ynga, Topa Ynga Yupangui y Guaina Capac y los
demas, cuyos cuerpos pussimos alli porque no los osamos dexar en el Cuzco ni en Tanbo; y despues, ya que mi padre estaua quieto y sosegado,
descuydados de que naidie auia de entrar en esta tierra, quiso hazer vna ffiesta muy solenne, conbidado por los andes y gente desta tierra; y al mejor
tienpo questaban en ella, desacordados de lo que les subçedio, hallaronse

Once all of the things above and many other things had been said, my   46
father took his leave from all the Indians. He had me brought forward in
order to tell the people that I was his son and that when his days were over
they had to treat me as lord over all of them in his place, which he did.
Then he stood up to leave his people. When they saw him, his people began to cry out with such volume that it seemed the hills themselves would
be pierced. Because they still felt very anxious, his people wanted to follow my father. But he would not let them, unless it was someone who had
no impediment to prevent him from going. He asked the people who were
anxious to follow him, how could they leave their fields, their houses, their
women and children, their *oybas*,[119] or babies, in order to follow him? They
should keep in contact with him; he would come to them without delay
or send word about what they should do. And so he left them for the town
of Vitcos.

Arrival of the Inca at Vitcos

After arriving in Vitcos (a town thirty leagues [90 mi] from Cusco), with
my father's followers, we settled into our town and headquarters with the   46v
intention of staying there a few days and resting. My father had a house built
to sleep in,[120] because the houses that were already there belonged to my
grandfathers Pachacuti Inca, Tupa Inca Yupanqui, and Huayna Capac and
the rest, whose bodies[121] we put there because we did not dare to leave
them in Cusco or Tambo. Afterward, once my father was calm and at ease—
taking no precautions to prevent people from entering the region in which
he was staying—he decided to hold a very solemn fiesta, having been in-
vited to do so by the Andes and the people there. And, right when everyone was most involved in the fiesta, they found themselves surrounded

119. González Holguín defines *huyhuaccuna* (*huyhua*, a linguistic equivalent of *oyba*,
plus the suffix *cuna*, denoting a plural or class) as "all manner of things that are raised,
birds, animals, groves of trees" (*Huyhuaccuna. Todas maneras de crias, de aues, de animales, y arboleda criada;* 205).

120. There are various structures at Vitcos, including residential architecture (Lee,
figs. 17–30, 464–77).

121. Manco had the physical remains of a number of important Inca men and women
with him. He names some of them later in the paragraph where he mentions that he
and others were captured by the Spaniards and taken to Cusco.

çercados de españoles; y como estaban pesados los yndios por lo mucho que auian beuido y tenian las armas en sus casas y no tubieron lugar
de poderse deffender porque los tomaron de sobresalto don Diego de
Almagro y el capitan Diego Ordoñez e Gonçalo Piçarro y otros muchos,
que nonbrarlos seria muy largo, los quales lleuaron por delante todos quantos yndios e yndias pudieron antecoxer y los cuerpos de mis antepasados,
los quales se llamauan Vanacauri, Viracochan Ynga, Pachacuti Ynga, Topa
Ynga Yupangui y Guaina Capac, y otros muchos cuerpos de mugeres con
muchas joyas e rriquezas, que auia en la ffiesta mas de çinquenta mill
cabeças de ganado, y estos escoxidos, los mejores que aca auia que ffue de
47   mis antepasados y de mi padre; y lleuaronme a mi y otras muchas *coyas;* e
mi padre escabullose lo mejor que pudo con algunos; y los españoles se
tornaron al Cuzco con la presa que lleuauan y comigo, muy contentos; y
aportados que fuymos al Cuzco, vn ffulano Oñate me rrecoxio a mi en su
cassa y me hizo mucho rregalo y buen tratamiento, y sabido por mi padre,
le enbio a llamar y se lo agradesçio mucho y me encomendo de nueuo a el
a mi y a otras hermanas suyas, diziendo que mirase por mi e por ellas, que
el se lo pagaria; despues de pasadas todas estas cosas, estando yo en el
Cuzco en casa de aquel Oñate que dixe, mi padre se salio de Bitcos porque

by Spaniards. (Later, there was disagreement over how it actually happened.) Because the Indians were impeded by all they had drunk, and had left their weapons in their houses, they were unable to defend themselves. Diego de Almagro, the captain Diego Ordoñez, and Gonzalo Pizarro[122]—and so many other Spaniards that to name them would take considerable space—took the revelers by surprise. The Spaniards left with as many men and women as they could capture; they also took the bodies of my ancestors named Huanacauri,[123] Viracochan Inca, Pachacuti Inca, Tupa Inca Yupanqui, and Huayna Capac, and many women's bodies. The Spaniards also took many valuable objects that had been brought to the fiesta, plus 50,000 head of livestock chosen from the best found here that had belonged to my ancestors and my father. The Spaniards also took me and many Coyas.[124] My father quietly escaped as best he could with some of his people. Content, the Spaniards returned to Cusco with me and the loot they had taken. Once we arrived in Cusco, someone named Oñate[125] took me into his house and gave me very good treatment. When my father found out, he sent for Oñate and thanked him. My father charged him with my care and the care of some of my father's sisters; my father said Oñate should look after me and them and that he would repay him for doing so. After all these things had happened, and while I lived in Cusco in the house of that Oñate, my father left Vitcos because some

47

122. Titu Cusi is mixing up the names of people involved in two separate attacks. He refers to events that took place in 1537, and he has probably confused "Diego Ordóñez" with Rodrigo Orgóñez, the captain Almagro sent down to Vitcos (Hemming, 231–32). The Pizarro and Almagro factions were at war with each other at this time, and Gonzalo Pizarro was not involved in any way in this campaign.

123. Huanacauri was a hill south of Cusco where one of the brothers of the first Inca, Manco Capac, had turned to stone (Sarmiento de Gamboa, *Geschichte des Inkareiches*, ch. 13: 37); it was also the name of the stone. Other accounts of what happened to it after the Spanish arrival do not mention that it was taken from Cusco by Manco and captured in Vitcos (Rowe, "An Account of the Shrines of Ancient Cusco," 47).

124. One of the Coyas was apparently Titu Cusi's mother, since she was returned to Vilcabamba at the same time that he was. Unfortunately, he never gives her name.

125. Pedro de Oñate, one of the supporters of Diego de Almagro who had negotiated with Manco on Almagro's return from Chile, and who participated in Gonzalo Pizarro's campaign in Vilcabamba in 1539. He was later executed by Vaca de Castro after the defeat of Almagro's son, Diego de Almagro, "the younger" (*el mozo*) (Hemming, 225–26, 245, 273).

le dixieron vnos capitanes chachapoyas que le lleuaron a su pueblo llamado
Rabanto y que alli estaba vn buen ffuerte donde se podian deffender de todos sus enemigos; y tomando su paresçer siguiole, y en el camino, viendo
que yvan a aquel Rabantu, en vn pueblo llamado Oroncoy descanso algunos
dias porque le hizieron ffiesta los del pueblo; y acabadas las ffiestas, estando
vn poco de asyento, enbio sus corredores a los caminos a saber si auia españoles o gente alguna que les estoruase el pasaje; y desque los vbo enbiado, essa mesma noche a la madrugada llegaron al dicho pueblo de
47v Orongoy dizen que mas de dozientos españoles armados de todas armas y
en sus cauallos en busca de mi padre, los quales tomaron las guardas de las
puentes que alli estauan y les dieron trato de cuerda para sauer donde estaua el dicho mi padre, los quales les dixieron que estaua alli arriba en el
pueblo de Orongoy; y dexadas las guardas, se ffueron vno en pos de otro a
mas correr por la cuesta arriba, pensando de coxer a mi padre durmiendo;
y acaso saliendose a proueer, mi tia Cura Ocllo, hermana de mi padre,
vio la gente que benia desde lexos y oyo el tropel de los cauallos e bino
corriendo adonde mi padre estaua en la cama e dixole con gran alboroto
que benian enemigos, que se lebantasse y fuese a ellos. Mi padre, como la vio
tan despaborida, sin hazer caso de nada leuantose con gran priesa para yr a
rreconoçer si hera ansy lo que su hermana le dezia; y desque se assomo al
viso, vio ser ansy lo que le auia dicho, y boluio a casa con gran priesa y mando
que le hechasen el ffreno al cauallo para de presto, asy como estaua, poner
cobro en su gente porque no le tomasen los enemigos de sobresalto syn estar aperçebido; e ya que lo tubo puesto a punto de guerra, mando que le
48   hechasen la sylla al cauallo, porque estauan ya çerca los enemigos, a la vista
de los quales puso en vn çerro muchas mugeres en rrengleras, todas con
lanças en las manos para que pensasen que heran honbres; y hecho esto, con
gran lijeresa ençima de su cauallo con su lança en la mano çercaua el solo

Chachapoyas captains told him they would take him to their town known as Rabanto[126] where there was a good fortress from which he could defend himself from all of his enemies. My father took their advice and followed them. On the way, he rested for a few days in a town called Oroncoy because the people of that town, when they learned he was on his way to Rabanto, held a fiesta for him. Once the fiesta was over, my father, who was somewhat settled there, sent runners along the roads to find out if there were any Spaniards or other people who might prevent his passage. In the early hours of the same evening, the runners returned to the town of Oroncoy to tell my father that more than 200 well-armed and mounted   47v Spaniards were searching for him. They had captured the guards at the bridges and whipped them so that they would reveal my father's location. The guards told the Spaniards that my father was just above them in the town of Oroncoy. Leaving the guards, the Spaniards went single file so that they could climb up the hill faster; they thought they would find my father sleeping. By chance, going out to take care of her needs, my aunt Cura Ocllo, the sister of my father,[127] saw the Spaniards coming from a distance and heard the sound of the horses. She came running to where my father was in bed and frantically told him the news that his enemies were coming and that he should get up and go out to meet them. When he saw how terrified and out of her mind she was, my father got himself up quickly to go see if things were as his sister told him. When he got to where he could look out, he saw that it was just as she had said. He went back to his house in a great hurry and ordered that his horse be bridled so that, just as he was, he could warn his people so that their enemies would not take them in a sneak attack without being noticed. Now that he had readied his people, my father ordered that his horse be saddled because the enemy was near. In plain view, my father stationed a lot of women on the   48 hill in a row and armed them all with lances so that the Spaniards would think they were men. When this was done—and they had been placed where the Spaniards could see them—my father skillfully[128] rode a circuit

126. Rabanto, also spelled Levanto, can be identified as the fortress of Cuelap in Chachapoyas (Hemming, 236–37).

127. By describing Cura Ocllo, his father's principal wife, as his aunt, Titu Cusi makes it clear that she was not his mother.

128. We learn here that Manco Inca mounted a horse, with saddle and bridle, and rode with considerable skill.

toda la gente porque no pudiese ser enpeçida de sus enemigos hasta en tanto que llegasen los corredores que auian ydo a correr el canpo, los quales, que asi llegaron a vna con los españoles al viso, a tienpo que mi padre solo los traia a malandar, y como llegaron, y vieron a su amo que andaua [su amo vio que andauan] de aquella suerte tan ffatigados, avnque cansados de la cuesta arriba, cobraron nueuo esffuerço para pelear contra sus enemigos que de la parte de abaxo estaban, con el qual esffuerço dieron de tropel sobre ellos con sus lanças y adargas de tal arte que les hizieron rretirar la cuesta abaxo, mas que de passo y desque les dieron esta rrefriega descansaron vn poco para tomar aliento; y desque los españoles vieron questauan sentados beuiendo, pensaron que ya no podian mas y con grande animo boluieron la cuesta arriba hazia los que no estauan des-
48v cuydados, mas antes mas ffortalesçidos y con mas gente que les auia so-brevenido de vna parte y de otra, los quales como vieron benir a sus ene-migos tan determinados, boluieron sobre ellos de tal suerte que de vn enbion, qual ençima, qual en baxo, los desbarataron y desbarrancaron por vnas barrancas y peñas abaxo ssin poder ser señores de sy, mas antes ellos mesmos se desbarataron asimismos por no ser señores de sy en cuesta tan aspera por la mucha fatiga que las armas les dauan y el gran calor que los ahogaban, que todo junto le causo la muerte a todos ellos sin escapar cauallo ni honbre biuo si no ffueron dos, los quales el vno paso el rrio a nado y el otro se saluo por vna crisneja de la puente.

Y ansy la gente de mi padre, alcançada aquella vitoria, rrecoxieron el despojo de los españoles; y desnudandolos a todos los que pudieron auer, les quitaron los vestidos y armass que tenian, y junto todo, lo lleuaron arriua al pueblo de Orongoy; y mi padre y ellos por la vito-ria que auian alcançado se rregocijaron mucho e hizieron ffiestas e bailes çinco dias por honrra de aquel despojo e vitoria. Acabadas estas
49   ffiestas y hecho lo arriba dicho, se partio mi padre con toda la gente, caminando por sus jornadas derecho al pueblo de Rauanto, que es

around all of his people, on horseback and carrying his lance in his hand, so that his enemies would not confront him until the runners who had gone to sound the alert had returned. The runners and the Spaniards came into view at the same time, while my father was still the only person there who might be able to do some harm to the Spaniards. When the runners, who were tired from coming uphill, arrived and saw their master in such a difficult situation, they regained their strength and fought against their enemies who were down below. With this new-found strength, they attacked the Spaniards in a single force, with their lances and shields, in such a way that they forced the Spaniards back down the hill. In the interval that followed this skirmish, my father's men could rest a bit and catch their breath. When the Spaniards saw them sitting and drinking, they thought that Manco's men could not take any more, and with great energy they came back up the hill toward them. My father's men were not at all unprepared, but had been fortified by the addition of more people who had come from different parts. When they saw how determined the Spaniards 48v were, my father's people attacked so fiercely that, with one big push (whether from above or below), they defeated the Spaniards and pushed them off the hill. The Spaniards fell, out of control, down the slopes and cliffs. In truth, the Spaniards defeated themselves, because they could not manage on such a steep slope due to the fatigue from carrying their weapons and the suffocating heat, which combined to cause the death of all the Spaniards. No man or horse escaped alive except for two men: one got across the river by swimming, the other saved himself by hanging onto a strand of the bridge.

After achieving that victory, my father's people gathered up the spoils from the Spaniards. Stripping the Spaniards of all they could, they removed their clothing and arms. Once all the spoils were gathered, they took them up to the town of Oroncoy. My father and his people celebrated a great deal because of their victory. They held fiestas and dances for five days in honor of the spoils and the victory.[129] Once the fiestas and the other events described above were over, my father left Oroncoy with 49 all his people. He traveled by day in the direction of Rabanto, which is

---

129. Titu Cusi again mentions the booty that was taken following a military victory.

hazia Quito; y en el camino en el valle de Xauxa en vn pueblo que llaman Llacxapallanga, supo como los guancas, naturales de aquella tierra, se auian avnado con los españoles, y rresçiuio dello mucho enojo e determino de hazerles vn castigo, el qual fuese sonado por toda aquella tierra diziendo que les auia de quemar a ellos y a sus casas sin dexar a ninguno a vida, y esto porque auian dado lo [sic: la] obediençia a los españoles y subjetadose a ellos y sus mugeres e hijos a su seruiçio con vna *guaca* prençipal que en el valle tenian llamada Guarivillca, ques çinco leguas [25 km] de Llacxa Pallaga [Pallanga].

Sauido todo esto por los guancas y que mi padre se auia enojado de tal manera con ellos que dezia que los auia de quemar a ellos y a Varivillca, su ydolo, por la conffederasçion que con los españoles abian hecho, siendo el su señor natural, determinaron de deffenderle la entrada, dando parte a los españoles, debaxo de cuyo anparo se auian puesto para que les viniesen a ayudar en el aprieto en que estauan; y sabido por los españoles la determinasçion de mi padre contra los guancas, vinieron con gran priesa dizen que çient españoles a los socorrer; y llegados que fueron, tubo de ello auiso mi padre y endereçio su derrota para alla, abiendo en el camino muchas rreffriegas con los guancas de vna parte y de otra del camino, matando y destroçando en ellos en gran manera, diziendoles "ayudenos vuestros amos"; y desta manera llego por sus jornadas a Xauxa la Grande, que ansy es llamada, adonde tubo vna gran rreffriega con los españoles arriua dichos y con las [sic: los] guancas, la qual rrefriega duro dos dias; y al fyn, por la mucha gente que mi padre lleuaua y por darse buena maña los vençio y mataron çinquenta españoles y los demas se escaparon a vña de cauallo; y algunos de los nuestros

toward Quito. Along the way, in a town called Llacsa Pallanga[130] in the valley of Jauja, he learned how the Huancas, who are native to that land, had allied with the Spaniards,[131] and he became very angry and decided to punish them. He proclaimed this decision throughout their territory, informing them that he was going to burn the people and houses, without leaving any of them alive. This would be done because the Huancas had sworn obedience to the Spaniards and become their subjects and given their women and children in their service, as had a principal *huaca*[132] located in that valley called Huarivilca,[133] some five leagues [15 mi] from Llacsa Pallanga.

When the Huancas heard this proclamation, and that my father was so angry with them that he was going to burn them and their idol Huarivilca because of the alliance they had made with the Spaniards, they decided to prevent his entry into their territory (despite the fact that he was their natural lord). The Huancas sent word to the Spaniards under whose protection they had placed themselves so that the Spaniards would come and help them out of the tight spot they were in. Once the Spaniards learned of my father's determination to go against the Huancas, they came very quickly to the Huancas' rescue; they say about 100 Spaniards came. My father received word as soon as the Spanish had arrived, and he set off to find them, fighting many skirmishes with the Huancas in different places along the road, killing and destroying the Huancas in a grand manner. And to them he said: "Side with us. We are your lords." In this fashion he arrived several days later at Jauja the Great[134] (which is what it is called). There he fought a major skirmish with the Spaniards who had come to assist the Huancas and their allies. The skirmish lasted two days. By the end of it, he had defeated and killed fifty Spaniards, with the assistance of the large number of people with my father and because of their skill. The rest of the Spaniards escaped by a hair. Some of our men

49v

130. A *tambo*, or road station, east of Jauja on the main highland road (D'Altroy, fig. 6.13, 100–1).

131. The Huancas were famous allies of the Spaniards (Espinoza Soriano).

132. See note 116.

133. Cieza de León, a Spaniard who traveled in the Andean highlands at the end of the 1540s, visited the site and describes it (ch. 84: 243–44).

134. This is probably a direct translation of "Hatun Jauja," the site of an important Inca provincial center located near modern Jauja (D'Altroy, fig. 6.13, 100–1).

siguieron el alcançe algun rrato, y como bieron que se daban tanta priessa se boluieron adonde mi padre estaua ençima de su cauallo, blandeando su lança, sobre el qual auia peleado fuertemente con los españoles; e ya que se vbo acabado esta batalla, mi padre, que algo cansado quedaua del pelear, se apeo de su cauallo y se ffue a descansar con los suyos, que muy cansados y heridos algunos dellos auian quedado de la rrefriega passada.

50   Otro dia despues, ya algo rreffaçinada la gente, se tino [sic: tiro] de alli por las jornadas que auia ydo a vn pueblo llamado Vayocache, que es la parte dondestaua el ydolo llamado Varivillca; y en vn dia que alli descanso lo mando sacar del lugar dondestaua enterrado hasta los honbros; y cabada la rredondez della mando sacar todo el tesoro que le tenian ofresçido; y las *yanaconass* e criadas e criados questauan diputados para el seruiçio de aquella *guaca,* en el qual la gente de aquella tierra tenia mucha confiança los mando matar a todos para que entendiesen que el hera el señor; y al ydolo, hechandolo vna soga al pescueso, le truxieron arrastrando por todo el camino con gran denuesto por çerros e piedras y çienagas y lodos, beynte leguas [100 km] de camino, deziendo "veis aqui la conffiança que tenian aquellos guancas deste ydolo, al qual tenian por Viracochan; mira en que an parado ella y ellos y sus amos los españoles"; y viniendo ansy por su camino, llegaron a vn pueblo llamado Acostanbo, y alli descansaron vn año, donde hizieron sus casas y heredades que agora poseen los españoles, lo qual llaman Viñaça porque se ve alli mucho vino de Castilla; la *guaca* o

50v   ydolo llamado Variuillca la mando mi padre hechar en vn gran rrio.

Despues desto, por ynportunasçiones de vnos capitanes andes que le ynporturaron [ynportunaron], se fue a la tierra y pueblo llamado Pillco-suni, adonde tubo otra rrefriega

followed the Spaniards for a while, but the Spaniards traveled very quickly. Our men returned to my father's camp. He was there, brandishing his lance, astride the horse with which he had fought valiantly against the Spaniards. Now that the battle was over, my father, somewhat fatigued from fighting, got down from his horse and went to rest with some of his people who had remained after the recent encounter. They were very tired and some were wounded.

The next day, after some regrouping, my father and his people traveled   50
back for several days along the route by which they had come; they were headed for the town called Huayocache, where the idol Huarivilca was located. On the day they rested there, my father ordered that the *huaca* be removed from the place where it had been buried up to its shoulders. Once the area around the *huaca* had been excavated, my father ordered that all the treasure that had been offered to it be removed. He also ordered the deaths of all the *yanaconas*[135]—men and women[136]—who had been assigned to serve that *huaca* in which the people of that land had placed their trust. He acted so that all Huancas would understand that he was their lord. My father's people then threw a rope around the idol and dragged it, with great disrespect, along the road, over hills and rocks and swamps and through mud, for twenty leagues [60 mi]. They said: "Remember the faith that those Huancas had in this idol that they took to be the Viracochan? Look at what the men and women of this province and their masters, the Spaniards, have come to!" Traveling along the road in this way, my father and his people came to a town called Acostambo.[137] There they rested a year and built the houses and fields that the Spaniards possess today. It is called Viñaza, because a great deal of wine from Castille is produced there. My father had the *huaca* or idol called Huarivilca   50v
thrown into a great river.

Afterward, my father went to the land and town called Pilcosuni[138] at the request of some Andes captains. There he fought another skirmish

135. Defined by González Holguín as a servant in either singular or plural form (*Yanacuna. Los criados, o vn criado;* 364). Under the Incas, people with this status served particular Incas, *huacas,* or other important individuals.

136. See D'Altroy, fig. 6.13, 100–1.

137. A province in the lowland region north of Cusco (Hemming, Map 4: 14).

138. Titu Cusi appears to be describing the 1539 campaign, headed by Gonzalo

con çiertos españoles que le binieron a buscar, y los bençio y desbarato el, como seria muy largo [contar], saluo se sepa que traxo de alli mucha artilleria, arcabuzes, lanças, vallestas y otras armas, y despues que en Yeñupay ubo aquella rrefriega con los españoles y descanso alli vn año; y ansy se boluio por sus jornadas e pueblos que por la brreuedad no quento al pueblo de Vitcos, y desde ay hasta Villcapanpa, adonde estubo algunos dias sosegado y descansando, haziendo sus casas y aposentos para hazer en este asiento, porques buen tenple, el asiento prençipal de su persona.

Despues de auer descansados algunos diass y que ya pensaua que le querian dexar los españoles, oyo dezir por las espias que tenia puestas en los caminos como venian sobre el Gonçalo Piçarro y el capitan Diego Maldonado y Ordoñez e otros muchos, y que venian con ellos tres hermanos suyos, conviene a sauer: don Pablo e Ynguill y Guaipar, a los quales traian antepuesto porque dezian que querian hazer con mi padre contra los españoles; y mi padre los salio a rrescibir tres leguas [15 km] de aqui a vna fortaleza que alli tenia para en ella deffenderse dellos y no se dexar ganar aquella fuerça; llegado que fue alli, se encontro con no se quantos españoles, que por ser montes espesos no se podian contar, adonde peleo ffuertemente con ellos a la orilla de vn rrio, vnos de vna parte y otros de otra, que en diez dias no se acabo la pelea porque peleauan a rremuda los españoles con la gente de mi padre y con mi padre, y sienpre

with some Spaniards who had come looking for him. He defeated and destroyed them. My story would be considerably longer were I to tell about this skirmish; I will only note here that my father took a great deal of artillery—harquebuses, lances, crossbows, and other weapons—away from this fight. Then, after my father fought the Spaniards in Yeñupay and rested there a year, he returned along the same road by which he had come. He stopped in the customary places—which, to be brief, I will not mention—before coming to the towns of Vitcos, and then Vilcabamba. There he spent some time relaxing and resting, and building his houses and other lodgings so that this place could serve as his principal place of residence, because of its good climate.

My father thought that the Spaniards were no longer interested in him. But after he had rested for a few days, my father heard, from the spies he had along the roads, that Gonzalo Pizarro, the captain Diego Maldonado, Ordoñez, and many other Spaniards were coming after him, and that with them were three of his brothers—named Don Pablo,[139] Ynguill, and Huaypar. The three brothers traveled ahead of the Spaniards, saying they wanted to join my father and help him fight the Spaniards. My father went out to receive them at a fortress he had three leagues [9 mi] from here.[140] He thought he could defend himself from there and prevent his brothers from taking the fortress. As soon as he arrived [at the fortress], he found himself besieged by I do not know how many Spaniards. (Because of the thick growth, they could not be counted.) He fought with them fiercely on the banks of a river, some men fighting on one side and some on the other. After ten days the fighting was still going on because the Spaniards took turns fighting with my father's men and with my father, and it always

51

Pizarro (Hemming, 251–55). Diego Maldonado may very well have participated; he is one of the men who arrived in Cusco with Francisco Pizarro (Lockhart, 221–23). If "Ordoñez" is Rodrigo de Orgóñez, however, he certainly could not have participated for he was already dead.

139. Don Pablo was Paullu Tupa, the son of Huayna Capac and an important woman from the northern highlands. He was named Inca at one point by Diego de Almagro, but managed to switch sides and join Pizarro after Almagro's defeat. He was baptized while Cristóbal Vaca de Castro was governor (1541–1544), but this had not yet occurred at the time of the events Titu Cusi describes here.

140. The fortress mentioned appears to be a place now called Urpipata (Lee, figs. 44–45, 107–8, 151–55, 405–7).

les yba mal por el ffuerte que nosotros teniamos; y binieron a tanto que, biniendo alli vn hermano carnal de mi tia Cura Ocllo llamado Guaipar, y mi padre se enojo tanto con el porque les venia a buscar que le bino a costar la vida el negoçio, y queriendole matar mi padre con el enojo que tenia, la Cura Ocllo se lo quiso estoruar porque le queria mucho; y mi padre, no queriendo consentir a sus rruegos, cortoles las caueças a el y a otro su hermano llamado Ynguill, diziendo estas palabras: "mas justo es que le corte yo sus cabeças que no que lleuen ellos la mya"; y mi tia, por el enojo que rresçiuio de la muerte de sus hermanos, nunca jamas se quiso mudar del lugar donde estauan muertos.

Y en estos medios, ya que esto ffue acabado, por la parte adonde mi padre estaua binieron çiertos españoles, y como los vio venir, biendo que no se podia escapar, tomo por rremedio hecharse al agua y pasar el rrio a nado; y desque se bio de la otra parte començo a dar bozes, diziendo "yo soy Mango Ynga, yo soy Mango Ynga"; los españoles, como vieron que no se podian aprouechar del, determinaron de bolverse al Cuzco, y lleuaron por delante a mi tia Cura Ocllo y a Cusi Rimache, hermano tanbien de mi padre que consigo tenia, y otras cosas, los quales llegaron con mi tia al pueblo de Panpaconac adonde yntentaron a querer fforçar a mi tia, y ella, no queriendo, se defendia fuertemente en tanto que vino a ponerse en su cuerpo cosas hediondas y de dispresçio porque los que quisiesen llegar a ella thubiesen asco; y ansy se deffendio muchas vezes en todo el camino hasta el pueblo de Tanbo donde los españoles de muy enojados con ella, lo vno porque no quiso consentir a lo que ellos querian y lo otro porque hera hermana de mi padre, la asaltearon biua, sufriendolo ella por la castidad, la qual dixo estas palabras quando la asaltearon: "¿en vna muger bengais vuestros enojos? ¿que mas hiziera otra muger como yo?; dados priesa a acabarme porque se cunpla vuestro apetito en todo"; y ansy la acabaron de presto, teniendo con vn paño tapados sus ojos ella mesma.

Vila Oma, capitan general que ffue de mi padre, e Tisoc e Taipi y Yanqui Guallpa y Orco Varanca y Atoc Suyru y otross muchos capitanes que fueron de mi padre, como vieron que auian lleuado los españoles y la *coya* e que la auian tratado de aquella manera, mostraron rresçiuir pena dello; y los españoles, como lo sintieron, prendieronlos, diziendo "vosotros tornaros debreis de querer al Ynga y hazeros con el, pues no a de ser ansy sino que aqui abeis de acabar la vida juntamente con vuestra ama";

went badly for the Spaniards because of our fortress. When Huaypar, the blood brother of my aunt Cura Ocllo, arrived, my father became so angry with him for pursuing my father that it cost Huaypar his life. When my father, in his anger, wanted to kill Huaypar, Cura Ocllo tried to prevent him from doing so because she loved her brother a great deal. My father, who did not want to give in to her pleas, cut off the heads of both Huaypar and his other brother Ynguill with these words: "It is better that I cut off their heads than that they cut off ours." My aunt was so angry about the 51v death of her brothers that she wanted to stay in the place where they had been killed and never leave.

Meanwhile, after this deed was done, some Spaniards came to where my father was. When he saw them coming he realized that he could not escape and threw himself into the water and swam across the river. As soon as he reached the other side he began to shout, saying: "I am Manco Inca, I am Manco Inca." When the Spaniards saw that they could not capture him, they decided to return to Cusco, and they took my aunt Cura Ocllo and Cusi Rimache (another of my uncles who had accompanied my father), and other things, in the lead. When they arrived in the town of Pampacona, the Spaniards tried to force themselves on my aunt. But she did not want to submit and defended herself bravely; she even rubbed her body with foul and demeaning substances so that those who might want to go to her would be disgusted. She defended herself in this way many times along the road to the town of Tambo. That is where the Spaniards— who were very angry with her, partly because she would not consent to 52 what they wanted to do and partly because she was my father's sister— roasted her alive. She paid dearly for her chastity. She said these words when they roasted her: "So you take out your anger on a woman? What more could a woman like me do? Hurry up and finish me off. The deed expresses your nature in every way." So they finished her off quickly. She had covered her eyes with a cloth.

When Vila Oma, my father's captain-general, and Tizoc and Taypi and Yanqui Huallpa and Urco Huaranca and Atoc Suyru and many others among my father's captains, learned that the Spaniards had taken the Coya Cura Ocllo and had treated her in that manner, they showed their grief. When the Spaniards detected this grief, they attacked the captains, saying: "You will return to loving the Inca and being his men. But it is not to be. Instead, your lives will end here, at the same time as your mistress." The

y ellos defendiendose dezian que no pensaban tal syno ser sienpre con los
españoles e servirlos; mas los españoles, no creyendo dellos sino pensando
que lo que dezian hera ffingido, los mandaron quemar, e todos; y que-
mados estos y muerta la *coya*, se fueron a Yucay donde quemaron a Ozcollo y a Cori Atao y a otros muchos porque no se tornasen a hazer con
mi padre y por tener las espaldas seguras. Pasadas todas estas cosas arriba
dichas y otras muchas, que por abreuiar he dexado, el dicho mi padre se
torno a Bilcabanba, cabeça de toda esta prouinçia, adonde estubo con algun sosiego algunos dias; y desdeste pueblo porque no se hallaua syn mi,
me envio a llamar al Cuzco adonde yo estube desde que me lleuaron a Bitcos en casa de Oñate arriba dicho, los quales mensajeros me hurtaron del
Cuzco a mi e a mi madre y me truxieron escondidamente hasta el pueblo
de Vitcos, al qual ya mi padre se auia salido a tomar ffrescor porque es tierra
fria; y alli estubimos mi padre e yo muchos dias, adonde aportaron siete españoles en differentes tienpos, diziendo que se benian huyendo de alla fuera
por delitos que auian hecho y que protestauan de seruir a mi padre con todas sus ffuerças toda su bida, que le rrogaban mucho que les dexase entrar
en su tierra y acabar en ella sus dias; y mi padre, biendo que benian de buena
boya, avnquestaria sentido de los españoles, mando a sus capitanes que no
les hiziesen daño porquel los queria tener en su tierra como a criados, que
les hiziesen casas en que morasen; y ansy los capitanes de mi padre, avnque
quisieron luego acabarlos, hizieron lo que mi padre les mando; y el dicho
mi padre los tubo muchos dias y años consigo, haziendolos muy buen
tratamiento y dandoles lo que auian menester hasta mandar que sus mes-
mas mugeres del dicho mi padre les hiziesen la comida y la beuida; y avn
el mismo los traia consigo y los daua de comer junto a sy, como a su persona mesma, y se holgaua con ellos como sy ffueran sus hermanos propios.

captains, defending themselves, denied that they had thought like that and said they would always serve the Spaniards. But the Spaniards, who did not believe the captains, and thought that they were lying instead, ordered all of them to be burned alive.[141] When the captains had been burned and the Coya was dead, the Spaniards went to Yucay where they burned Ozcollo and Cori Atao and many others alive so that they would not rejoin my father and so that the Spaniards could secure their rear. After all these things (and many others that I have not mentioned so that my story will be short) had happened, my father returned to Vilcabamba, the capital of this province, and remained there, calmly, for a few days. Because he was lost without me, he sent for me from there to be brought from Cusco (where I had been since the time I had been brought from Vitcos to the house of Oñate, as mentioned above). My father's messengers secreted me and my mother out of Cusco[142] and brought me to the town of Vitcos, where my father had come to refresh himself because it is cool. My father and I were there many days. Seven Spaniards also came there at different times, saying that they had fled to this place because of the crimes they had committed and that they would serve my father with all of their strength all their days. They begged my father to let them remain in his land and finish out their lives there. My father could see that these Spaniards had some breeding. Thus, though he knew the Spaniards would learn of his actions, my father ordered his captains not to harm the seven Spaniards because he wanted to have them in his land to serve him. He ordered that they be given houses to live in. My father's captains did what my father ordered them, even though they would have preferred to finish these Spaniards off immediately. My father kept the seven Spaniards with him for many days and even years. He always treated them very well and gave them everything they needed, to the point of ordering his own women to make their food and drink. He even took them along with him and gave them meals near him, in the same way he was served. My father passed his time with these Spaniards in the same way he would have if they had been his brothers.

141. The death of these men, perhaps more than anything else, put an effective end to any real possibility that the Vilcabamba Incas could remove the Spaniards by force.
142. Titu Cusi's mother is never named, and nothing is known of what became of her.

Despues ya de algunos dias y años estos españoles arriba dichos estubieron en conpañia de mi padre en el dicho pueblo de Vitcos en la
mesma casa de mi padre, estaban vn dia con mucho rregoçijo, jugando al
herron solos mi padre y ellos y yo, que estonçes hera mochacho, sin pensar my padre cosa ninguna ni aber dado credito a vna yndia del vno dellos llamada Bauba que le auian dicho muchos dias antes que aquellos
53v españoles le querian matar, sin ninguna sospecha desto ni de otra cosa se
holgaua con ellos como antes; y en este juego, como dicho tengo, yendo
el dicho mi padre a leuantar el herron para auer de jugar, cargaron todos
sobre el con puñales y quchillos y algunas espadas; y mi padre, como se
syntio herido, con la rrabia de la muerte procuraba de deffendersse de vna
parte y de otra, mas, como hera solo y ellos heran siete y mi padre no tenia
arma ninguna, al fin le derrocaron al suelo con muchas heridas; le dexaron
por muerto, e yo, como he[ra] pequeño y bi a mi padre tratar de aquella
manera, quise yr alla a guareçerle; y boluieronse contra mi muy enojados,
arrojandome vn bote de lança con la mesma lança de mi padre que a la
sazon alli estaua, que herraron poco que no me mataron a mi tanbien; e
yo de miedo, como espantado de aquello, huyme por vnos montes abaxo
porque avnque me buscasen no me pudiesen hallar; y ellos, como dexaron
a mi padre ya para espirar, salieron por la puerta con mucho rregoçijo,
diziendo "ya hemos muerto al Ynga, no ayais miedo"; y vnos andes, que
a la sazon llegaron, y el capitan Rimache Yupangui les pararon luego de
tal suerte que, antes que pudiesen huyr mucho trecho avn, se tomaron del
54 camino mal de su grado, derrocandolos de sus cauallos abaxo e traiendolos por ffuerca para hazer dellos sacriffiçio; a todos los quales dieron muy
crudas muertes y avn algunos quemaron; y despues de todo esto, biuio el
dicho mi padre tres dias, el qual antes que muriese mando llamar a todos
sus capitanes y a mi para nos hablar antes que se muriesse, el qual dixo
estas palabras a los capitanes:

A few days and years later, these Spaniards were staying with my father in his house in the town of Vitcos. One day they were merrily playing a game of quoits,[143] alone with my father and me (I was still a boy). Several days earlier, a native woman named Bauba, who was with one of the Spaniards, had told my father that the Spaniards wanted to kill him. But my father had not believed or even remembered what she said. So my father, who suspected nothing, took his leisure with the Spaniards just as he always had. When, during this game I have mentioned, my father went to pick up the quoit to play it, the Spaniards all attacked him with daggers, knives, and some swords. When he knew he was wounded, my father furiously tried to defend himself against one Spaniard and then another. But since he was alone and unarmed—and since there were seven of them—the Spaniards finally brought him to the ground, gravely wounded, and left him for dead. Though I was small, I wanted to go and help my father when I saw him treated in that way. But the Spaniards set upon me angrily, and threw my father's lance, which happened to be there at the time, at me. The lance came so close to me that I was almost killed, too. Afraid, terrified of what I had seen, I fled downhill into some dense growth so that the Spaniards could not find me even if they tried. After leaving my father there to die, the Spaniards left through the gate, rejoicing and saying: "We have just killed the Inca, do not be afraid." Some Andes who were just arriving and the captain Rimache Yupanqui[144] stopped the Spaniards before they could get very far away. They were captured on a steep stretch of road where they were knocked off their horses and brought back by force to be sacrificed. All of these Spaniards suffered very terrible deaths. Some were burned alive. My father lived for another three days after all this took place. Before he died, he ordered that I be brought to him, along with all of his captains, so he could speak to us. He said the following to his captains:

53v

54

---

143. A game in which metal rings are thrown up and down a pitched slope with target pins at each end.

144. Rimache Yupanqui was captured in Vilcabamba in 1572 (Nowack and Julien, 25). He is also one of the witnesses to Titu Cusi's *History* (f. 63v) and a potential source of information about the events Titu Cusi was too young to remember.

Parlamento que hizo Mango Ynga a sus capitanes
quando estaua a la muerte, el qual dixo:

"Hijos, ya me beis de la manera que estoy por aberme fiado tanto desta
gente española, en espeçial destos siete que aqui vosotros aveis visto que
me an guardado tanto tienpo ay que les he tratado como a hijos, por el
qual tratamiento me an puesto desta suerte. Bien creo que no escapare
desta, por vuestra vida que se os acuerde de lo que tantas vezes os he dicho y amonestado en el Cuzco y en Tanbo y en todas las demas partes
adonde os abeis juntado a mi llamamiento y por las partes adonde abeis
andado comigo, lo qual porque see que lo teneis todos la memoria, no me
quiero mas alargar, lo vno porque my dolor ecçesiuo no me da mas lugar
y lo otro porque no ay para que mas os molestar.

54v   "Encomiendoos mucho a mi hijo Titu Cusy Yupangui para que mireis
por el, pues sabeis ques la lunbre de mis ojos y que yo le tenia a ese mochacho no solamente por hijo mas por hermano por el mucho entendimiento
que thiene, y ansy le he encomendado yo mire e tenga quenta con todos
vosotros e con todos mis hijos como yo pudiera tener; y os rruego que
ansy como lo aueis hecho comigo lo hagais con el, que yo tengo del tal
conçepto, que os lo agradesçira y pagaria muy bien; por tanto, llamadmele
aca para que le de mi bendiçion y diga lo que a de hazer".

Parlamento que Mango Ynga hizo
a su hijo al punto de la muerte

"Hijo mio muy amado, bien me bes qual estoy, e por eso no tengo que te
signifficar por palabras mas mi dolor de lo que las obras dan testimonio;
no llores, que si algu[i]en auia de llorar auia de ser yo, si pudiera, por
auerme a mi mismo yo propio parado de la suerte que estoy, fiandome
tanto de semejante [gente] questa y haziendoles tanto rregalo como les he
hecho, no lo meresçiendo ellos, que como tu sabes vinieron aqui huyendo
55   de sus conpañeros por delitos que alla auian de auer hecho, a los quales
rrecoxi, ffauoresçi con entrañass de padre; mira, que te mando que perpetuamente nunca tengas ley perfetta con semejante gente que esta porque

Speech that Manco Inca made to his captains when he was near death. He said:

"Sons, you see me in this way because I trusted these Spanish people, especially the seven who guarded me for so long and whom I treated like sons, as you have seen. And they have repaid my good treatment by doing this to me! I do not think that I will escape from this. By your very lives, remember what I have told you and admonished you about so many times in Cusco, in Tambo, and in all of the other places where you have been gathered together in response to my call and in all the places where you have gone with me. I do not want to go into it now, since I know that you all remember what I have said. The pain will not permit it and there is no reason to bother you with it.

"I charge you with looking after my son Titu Cusi Yupanqui. You know 54v he is the light of my eyes and that I consider this boy not just a son, but also a brother[145] because of his great capacity for understanding. So I have charged him to look after, and be responsible for, all of you and any children I have. I beg you to treat him in the same way that you have treated me. I am so impressed with him that I know he will thank you and pay you well for it. Therefore, call him to me here so that I can give him my blessing and tell him what he must do."

Speech that Manco Inca made to his son at the moment of his death

"My beloved son, you can see how I am, and so I do not have to say any more about my pain in words since deeds have already told the tale. Do not cry. If someone should cry, it should be me, if I could, for having gotten myself into this fix, for believing so firmly in such people as this and treating them so well, even though they were undeserving. As you know, those men came here fleeing from their companions because of crimes they must have committed where they had come from. I took them in 55 and favored them with the heart of a father. Look well: I order you never, ever, to enter into any kind of accord with people such as this, so that what

145. Here again, Manco is using Spanish equivalents for terms that meant something different in the Inca language (see note 114).

no te acontesca a ti otro tanto como a mi; no consienta que entren en tu tierra avnque mas te conbiden con palabras porque sus palabras melosas me engañaron a mi y ansy haran a ti si los crees.

"Encomiendote a tus hermanos y hermanas y a tu madre para que mires por ellos y los rremedies e ffauorescas como yo hiziera a ti, e mira que no des pena a mis huesos, tratando mal a tus hermanos e madre, porque bien saues vosotros que la rresçibiran grande.

"Encomiendote tanbien a estos pobres yndios, que mires por ellos como es rrazon; e mira como me an seguido y guardado y anparado en todas mis neçesidades, dexando sus tierras y naturaleza por amor de mi; no les trauajes demasiado, no les acoses, no les rriñas ni castigues syn culpa, porque en ello daras mucho enojo al Viracochan; yo les he mandado a ellos que te rrespeten y acaten por señor en mi lugar, pues heres mi primer hijo y heredero de mi rreino y esta es mi postrimera voluntad; yo confio de su bondad de todos ellos que te acataran y rrespetaran por tal, y que no haran mas de lo que yo les he mandado e tu les dixieres"; el qual luego ffino y me dexo a mi en el pueblo de Vitcos; y de alli me bine a este Billcapanpa donde estube mas de beinte añoss hasta que me desosogaron [desasosegaron] vnos yndios de Guamachuco por mandado de la justiçia del Cuzco puesta por Gonçalo Piçarro, que a la sazon andaua alterado contra el rrey.

55v

happened to me will not happen to you. Do not allow them to enter your land, even if they approach you with sweet words. Their words deceived me and will deceive you, too, if you believe them.

"I commend your brothers and sisters and your mother to your care, so that you will look after them and take care of them and favor them in the same way I would treat you. See that you do not make my bones suffer by treating your siblings and mother badly, because you know that they will feel it greatly if you do.

"I commend these poor Indians to your care as well. Look after them so far as is reasonable. Remember that they have followed me and protected me and helped me in all my times of need, leaving their lands and environs out of love for me. So do not work them too hard, or harass them, or scold or punish them without reason, because in doing so you will anger the Viracochan. I have ordered them to respect you and honor you as lord   55v in my place, since you are my firstborn son and heir to my kingdom[146] and this is my last wish. I rely on their goodness, and expect them to honor and respect you as their lord and not to do anything other than what I have ordered them or what you would tell them." Then my father died and left me in the town of Vitcos. From there I traveled to this town of Vilcabamba. I have been here for more than twenty years, save for the time when some Indians from Huamachuco upset my peace on the orders of the Cusco authorities named by Gonzalo Pizarro (who was then in open rebellion against the King).

146. Titu Cusi appears to be posing his argument about succession in Spanish terms, since there was no Inca rule that the firstborn son succeed.

[3]

Aqui comiença la manera y modo por la via que yo, don Diego de Castro Titu Cusi Yupangui, vine a tener paz con los españoles, de la qual paz, por la bondad de Dios a quien nosotros antiguamente llamavamos Viracochan, vine a ser cristiano, la qual es esta que se sigue:

En lo sobredicho arriba, por mi declarado, di a entender llana y susçintamente la manera como mi padre Mango Ynga Yupangui ffue señor natural destos rreynos del Piru y el modo y la manera de la entrada de los españoles en su tierra y como y a que effeto se les rreuelo, que fue por sus muchos malos tratamientos, y el descurso y fin de bida; en esta quiero declarar el como yo me he abido despues de sus dias y la manera por donde me he venido a tornar cristiano e tener paz con los españoles, que fue mediante Dios, por ser su Señoria del señor gouernador el liçençiado Lope Garçia de Castro quien rregia e gouernaua los rreynos del Piru, la qual manera passa ansy:

En el tienpo que ffue visorrey de los rreynos del Piru el Marques de Cañete, me enbio a esta tierra donde yo estoy vn padre de la horden de señor Santo Domingo para que tratasse comigo de sacarme alla ffuera al Cuzco, diziendo quel señor visorrey traia mandato del enperador don Carlos para que, saliendo yo alla fuera e queriendo ser cristiano, me darian de comer confforme a mi calidad; e yo, acordandoseme del tratamiento que los españoles les auian hecho a mi padre, estando en el Cuzco en su conpañia, e por lo quel dicho mi padre me dexo mandado al fyn de sus dias, pensando que por ventura me acontesçeria a mi lo que a mi padre, no quise estonçes dar consentimiento a lo quel padre ffray Melchor de los Reeies, que ffue el que vino con la enbaxada, y vn Joan Sierra, su conpañero, por mandado del señor visorrey me dixeron; antes para çertifficarme de lo

[3]

Here begins the manner and method by which I, Don Diego de Castro Titu Cusi Yupanqui, came to have peace with the Spaniards, through which peace and the goodness of God (whom we anciently called Viracochan) I came to be Christian, as follows:

In what I have said above, I have related fully and succinctly how my father, Manco Inca Yupanqui, was the natural lord of these kingdoms of Peru and how the Spaniards entered his territory. I have also related how, and to what effect, he rebelled against the Spaniards because of their repeated mistreatment of him. I have also narrated the course and end of his life. In this history, I want to relate what has happened to me since he died and how I became a Christian and made peace with the Spaniards through the intervention of God and His Lordship the lord governor Licentiate Lope García de Castro, who ruled and governed the kingdoms of Peru. It happened in the following way:

56

    While the Marquis of Cañete was viceroy of these kingdoms of Peru,[147] he sent a Dominican father[148] to this land where I am now in order to try to convince me to leave here for Cusco. The Dominican said that the lord viceroy had brought orders from the emperor Charles V stating that, once I left this land and if I became a Christian, I would be given a source of income commensurate with the quality of my person. But I remembered the way the Spaniards had treated my father during the time they spent with him in Cusco and the orders my father had given me at the end of his life. Because I thought I was fated to have the same experience with the Spaniards as my father, I did not want to consent to what the father, Friar Melchor de los Reyes (who was the person who came with the official communication), and a certain Juan Sierra,[149] his companion, asked me to do by order of the viceroy. I wanted, instead, to ascertain whether

56v

---

147. Viceroy Andrés Hurtado de Mendoza (1555–1559).

148. This person is named below as Friar Melchor de los Reyes.

149. Juan Sierra was the *mestizo* (mixed Spanish-Indian) son of Mancio Serra de Leguizamo, who came with Francisco Pizarro when he first arrived in Cusco in 1533.

quel padre y su conpañero me dezian si hera ansy v no, enbie con el dicho padre çiertos capitanes mios al Marques para que ellos me truxiesen la çertinidad del negoçio, y que, sy hera ansy como me dezian, enbiaria vn hermano mio alla afuera en mi lugar, esto para que expirementase la biuienda de los españoles y me diese auisso de como lo hazian con el, y que, sy lo hiziesen bien, estonçes yo saldria.

Despues de pasado vn año, boluio el dicho padre con los dichos mis capitanes con la sertinidad de todo; e yo, visto que vna persona como aquella me lo rrogaua tanto y que me daua tan çierta çertificasçion de que me darian de comer, enbie al dicho mi hermano llamado Saire Topa, al qual di yndustria de como se auia de auer, y dada, se fue con el dicho padre al visorrey, el qual le rresçiuio muy bien y le dio de comer en el valle de Yucay e otros rrepartimientos adonde murio cristiano; e yo, desque supe

57   su muerte, rreçiui gran pena, pensando que los españoles le auian muerto como mataron a my padre, con la qual pena estube algunos dias hasta que del Cuzco me enbio el liçençiado Polo con Martín de Pando, mi notario que hasta oy dia me guarda, [y] con Joan de Betanços la çertinidad de como my hermano don Diego Saire Topa avia muerto su muerte natural; y por mi visto, detube en mi tierra al dicho Martin de Pando para çertificarme del de cosas que me conbenian y dexe yr a Juan de Betanços con la

the father and his companion were telling me the truth or not. So I sent certain captains with the father to the Marquis, in order that the captains could bring me confirmation of the proposal. If I had been told the truth, I would send one of my brothers to live in the outside world in my place. That way, he could experience life among the Spaniards and could tell me how they treated him. If they treated him well, then I would follow.

The Dominican father and the captains returned a year later and confirmed everything. When I saw how earnestly someone like the Dominican father pleaded with me and assured me that I would be given a source of income, I sent my brother Sayre Tupa [out of Vilcabamba].[150] I had already taught Sayre Tupa how to carry out this task. After being instructed, he went with the father to the viceroy, who welcomed him. Sayre Tupa was given an income in an *encomienda* in the Yucay valley[151] and other such grants, and there he died a Christian.[152] When I learned of his death, I was greatly saddened, thinking that the Spaniards had killed him as they had killed my father. I was troubled by this idea for some time until the Licentiate Polo[153] sent proof to me from Cusco—by means of Martín de Pando,[154] my notary, who is still with me to this day, and Juan de Betanzos[155]—

57

150. According to Juan de Betanzos, Sayre Tupa was chosen Inca by Manco's captains in Vilcabamba after Manco's death (about 1544). Sayre Tupa was then ten years old (Betanzos, *Narrative of the Incas,* pt. 2, ch. 33: 297–98).

151. Sayre Tupa was given part of what had been the *encomienda* of Francisco Pizarro, including the estates of Huayna Capac at Quispillacta near Yucay and coca fields in the Paucartambo region (Julien, "La Encomienda del Inca," 505–6; Hampe Martínez, 89).

152. The date of Sayre Tupa's death is difficult to pinpoint, but he must have died about 1561 (Hemming, 299). He left Vilcabamba in October 1557 (Hemming, 293).

153. Polo de Ondegardo, *corregidor* or royal magistrate of Cusco (1559–1561). The first of the letters of Titu Cusi that have survived was directed to him on June 20, 1559 (Guillén Guillén, "Documentos," 84–85).

154. Pando, of course, is the notary who recorded Titu Cusi's *History,* as well as the known letters of Titu Cusi. Pando was a *mestizo,* but who his parents were is unknown.

155. The interpreter sent to Vilcabamba by Cañete in 1557. He married Angelina Yupanqui, a cousin and wife of Atahuallpa, after Atahuallpa's death, and he also recorded a narrative account of both the pre-Hispanic Inca past and Inca dealings with the Pizarros, right up to the time of his assignment in Vilcabamba (Betanzos, *Narrative of the Incas*).

rrespuesta; y ansy me estube algunos dias hasta que por parte del Conde de Nieua, visorrey subçesor al Marques de Cañete, me vinieron otros mensajeros con cosas tocantes a la paz que de mi pretendian con los españoles, el qual me enbiaua a dezir lo mesmo que el Marques; e yo rrespondi que, como me gratificasen algo de lo mucho quel rrey poseia de las tierras de mi padre, aparejado estaua para tener paz, los quales mensajeros se fueron con esta rrespuesta.

Todas estas pazes entiendo yo que procurauan los españoles por vna de tres vias: o por entender que yo andaua dando saltos en sus tierras e traiendoles mucha gente de los naturales; o porque el rrey se lo mandaua por lo que le ditaua la conçiençia açerca de lo que de mi padre possee; o por ventura seria por quererme tener alla consigo en su tierra para çerteficarse que no les haria mas mal como estubiese alla porque, como yo no estaua yndustriado en las cossas de la ffee, no sospechaua que ffuese la prençipal caussa, como agora sospecho, el quererme hazer cristiano, pero agora despues que los padres me lo dizen, alcanço que fue vna de las caussas dichas y mas prençipal aquella.

Despues de ydos los mensajeros arriba dichos que binieron por parte del Conde de Nieua, boluio otra bez con el mesmo mensaje el tesorero Garçia de Melo a rrogarme que, porque tubiesen sosiego los españoles, me quietase yo a mi mesmo y que no andubiese de aca para alla, que el rrey me daba su palabra de Melo gratifficar como yo consintiesse que entrassen en mi tierra saçerdotes a pedricar [predicar] la palabra de Dios, al qual yo rrespondi, que a lo que dezia de quietarme yo y no hazer mal a los yndios ni ynquietar a los españoles, que yo le daua mi palabra de que no me dando ellos ocassion, que yo me quietaria muy a gusto, como lo veria por las obras; y a lo que dezia de que consintiese que entrasen saçerdotes en mi tierra, que yo no sabia nada de aquel menester, que se effetuase vna bez

57v

58

that my brother Don Diego Sayre Tupa had died a natural death. Once I had seen this proof, I detained Martín de Pando in my territory so I could learn from him some things I wanted to know. I allowed Juan de Betanzos to leave with my response. Many days passed before some other messengers came to me to discuss the details of the peace that the Spaniards were attempting to negotiate with me on behalf of the Count of Nieva,[156] the viceroy who succeeded the Marquis of Cañete. The Count of Nieva sent me the same message that the Marquis had. I replied that if they would grant me something from all of what the Spanish Crown now possessed that had been my father's, I was ready to have peace. The messengers left with my response.

I understand that all these efforts at making peace were motivated by one of three reasons. Either the Spaniards thought I had been attacking 57v them in their lands and bringing many people from those lands back with me, or the King had dictated [this peace] to remedy what my father had lost, or, possibly, because the Spaniards wanted to have me there with them in their land to be more certain that I would do them no harm. Since I had not yet learned about the Christian faith, I did not suspect, as I do now, that the principal reason [for these efforts to make peace] was to make me a Christian. Now that the fathers have told me as much, I have begun to understand that [my conversion] was also a reason, perhaps the most principal one.

After the messengers just mentioned—those who had come on behalf of the Count of Nieva—left, the treasurer García de Melo[157] returned again with the same message. So that the Spaniards would stay calm, he pleaded with me to stay quiet and not travel about. He also said the King had given his word to grant me an income in return for allowing priests into my territory to preach the word of God. I told him that, in answer to his plea that I stay quiet and do nothing bad to the Indians or disturb the 58 Spaniards, I gave my word that if they did not give me any reason [to do otherwise], I would remain as quiet as anyone could wish; my actions would prove this. With regard to what he said about allowing priests to come into my territory, I answered that I did not know why they were necessary. That part of the bargain would be carried out once there was

156. Viceroy Diego López de Zúñiga y Velasco (1561–1565).
157. Melo's embassy took place in 1562 or 1563.

la paz e despues se haria lo que fuese justo, con la qual rrespuesta se fue el tesorero Melo la primera vez.

En estos medios de ydas y benidas del Cuzco a mi tierra y de mi tierra al Cuzco, estando por corregidor en el el Doctor Quenca, oydor de su Magestad, acaesçio que vnos yndios encomendados en Nuño de Mendoça, que rresidian lindes desta mi tierra en vn rrio llamado Acobanba, por çiertos malos tratamientos que rresçibieron de vn español que los tenia a cargo se huyeron del y se pasaron a esta mi tierra a rreconoçerme por señor, lo qual sabido por el Doctor Quenca, pensando que yo los auia traido por ffuerça, me escriuio vna carta muy descomedida, en la qual me dezia que boluiese los yndios a su dueño, y si no, que me auia de dar la mas cruda guerra que se auia dado a honbre, la qual carta, como yo la vi, rresçiui mucha pena con ella; y rrespondi que no hera ansy lo que me ynportunaban, y que si guerra querian, aparejado estaua para cada y quando que biniesen; y con este enojo aperçibi mi jente para el effeto y mande poner espias por no se que partes, porque no me coxiesen descuidado los que me quisiesen hazer mal, el qual Doctor Cuenca nunca mas me rrespondio cosa ninguna, mas antes yo ffuy al camino por donde auia de pasar para ber sy todabia me queria dar la guerra dicha, y desta salida traxe para casa mas de quinientos yndios de diuersas partes; y boluime a quietar a mi cassa, en la qual rresçiui vna carta del dicho Doctor Cuenca, escrita en Lima, que no se por donde se me paso, en la qual se me ofresçia mucho y me rrogaua que lo pasado ffuese pasado.

58v

peace. After we had peace, what was fair would be done. The treasurer García de Melo left with that response after his first embassy.

During these times of comings and goings—from Cusco to my land and from my land to Cusco—and while Doctor Cuenca,[158] one of His Majesty's judges, was *corregidor* of Cusco, it happened that some Indians granted in *encomienda* to Nuño de Mendoza,[159] who resided on the border of my territory on the Acobamba river, fled and came to my territory. They fled because they had been treated badly by a Spaniard who was in charge of them, and [came to me] because they recognized me as their lord. When Doctor Cuenca learned that these people had come to me, he thought that I had taken them by force and wrote me a very disrespectful letter in which he told me that I had to return the Indians to their master, and that if I did not return them he would wage a very cruel war against me, a war worse than any ever waged before. When I saw the letter, I was very upset. I answered that I was not what he insisted I was, and that if war was what he wanted, I was ready to give it to him at any time or place.[160] In this temper I prepared my people and ordered that spies be sent everywhere so that those who wanted to do me harm would not catch me unprepared. But Doctor Cuenca never wrote to me again. Instead, I went out to the road where I knew he would pass, in order to see if he still wanted to make war. I took more than 500 Indians from various areas[161] on this trip and then returned to live quietly at home. Once there I received a letter, written in Lima, from the same Doctor Cuenca, who had somehow gotten past me. He made me an attractive offer and pleaded with me to let bygones be bygones.

58v

158. Doctor Gregorio González de Cuenca, *corregidor* or royal magistrate of Cusco sometime in the years between 1562 and 1564.

159. Nuño de Mendoza had the *encomienda* of Curamba (Cook, 207).

160. This letter has survived but has not been published. It was written in Quechua and translated into Spanish, but only the Spanish has been recorded. In it, Titu Cusi uses fiery rhetoric that shows clear traces of Quechua poetics. He threatens to drink from Cuenca's head, something that earlier Incas had done with the heads of their enemies (Levillier, vol. 2, 200).

161. In the *Memorial* of 1565, Titu Cusi mentions that he attacked the Indians of Sotelo in this period. Sotelo had the *encomienda* of Abancay (Cook, 205), suggesting that Titu Cusi was campaigning in this region.

Despues desto torno otra bez a venir el tesorero Garçia de Melo con despachos de vuestra Señoria, el qual me aconsejo, por lo que yo le adverti, que casasemos a mi hijo don Phelipe Quispe Tito con su prima doña Beatriz; y ansy lo conçertamos, como se hiziesen las pazes que despues hezimos en Acobanba por mandado de vuestra Señoria, el e yo traiendo para ello los testigos que vuestra Señoria señalo, a lo qual se hallo pressente Diego Rodriguez como corregidor y Martin de Pando como secretario, el qual conçierto y capitulasçion, como y de la manera que paso, porque vuestra Señoria lo thiene alla mas por estensso y lo podra enseñar a su Magestad, no lo pongo aqui ni ninguna cosa porne espaçifficada, pues de todo es vuestra Señoria el autor, si no ffuere lo de Chuquichaca de la venida de Hernando Matienço y mi conberssion y bautizmo, lo qual quiero que su Magestad entienda de mi, que fue vuestra Señoria la prençipal causa de todo.

Como vuestra Señoria sabe, quando me enbio a Diego Rodriguez que fuese corregidor desta mi tierra, yo lo rresçiui por mandarlo vuestra Señoria y por ber que conbenia para la rratifficasçion de la paz que yo auia dado mi palabra de tener con el Rey nuestro señor y con sus vasallos, la qual rratiffique de todo en todo, lo vno con el rresçibimiento que hize al oydor Liçençiado Matienço en la puente de Chiquichaca, dandole a entender algunass cossas que en mi tierra me pasauan

59

59v

After all of this, the treasurer García de Melo returned with correspondence from Your Lordship, who counseled me based on what I had told him that we marry my son Don Felipe Quispe Titu[162] to his cousin Doña Beatriz,[163] and so Melo and I agreed to make the peace that we later made in Acobamba[164] by order of Your Lordship, and accompanied by the witnesses that Your Lordship had chosen for that purpose. Diego Rodríguez,[165] as *corregidor,* and Martín de Pando, as secretary, were present. I will not include any discussion here of how or in what manner the agreement and capitulation came into being; nor will I include any of the details from the agreement, because Your Lordship has an extensive accounting of it and can show it to His Majesty, and also because you are its author. I will mention what happened in Chuquichaca[166]—that is, the arrival of Hernando Matienzo[167] and my conversion and baptism—because I want His Majesty to hear from me that Your Lordship was the principal cause of it all.

Your Lordship knows that when you sent Diego Rodríguez to be the *corregidor* of my territory, I received him because Your Lordship ordered it and because I knew it was important to the ratification of the peace I had promised to make with the King, our lord, and with his vassals. I ratified the agreement and everything stipulated in it. I received the judge Licentiate Matienzo at the bridge of Chuquichaca and told him about some of the things that were happening in my territory. I also

59

59v

162. Born about 1557 (Nowack and Julien, 29–32).

163. Beatriz was the daughter of Sayre Tupa and his sister, the Coya Maria Cusi Huarcay. She inherited the *encomienda* that had belonged to Sayre Tupa. The marriage was a linchpin in the agreement later made in Acobamba, although Beatriz was still a small child (see note 164).

164. The Capitulations of Acobamba, dated August 24, 1565 (Guillén Guillén, "Documentos," 62–71).

165. Diego Rodríguez de Figueroa conducted the Acobamba negotiations (Guillén Guillén, *La guerra de reconquista Inka,* 139–43).

166. Chuquichaca was the bridge over the Urubamba river near its confluence with the Amaybamba river. This was where the main Inca road entered the Vilcabamba region, and it marked the effective frontier between the Inca province of Vilcabamba and Spanish Peru from 1539 to 1572.

167. Titu Cusi gives the wrong first name. He means Juan de Matienzo, the *oidor* or judge who had come from the high court (*audiencia*) of Charcas to carry out certain judicial business in Cusco, then subject to Charcas.

y lo otro en rresçibir saçerdotes en mi tierra para que yndustriasen a mi e
a mi gente en las cosas de Dios, como ffue al padre Bera que vuestra Señoria me enbio, el qual bautizo a mi hijo don Phelipe Quispe Tito y estube
[sic: estubo] en la tierra casy año y medio, el qual salio por la venida de los
ffrailes agustinos que binyeron a bautizarme.

Da tanbien testimonio desta paz y conffirmalo en todo la rrenunçiaçion
que yo a vuestra Señoria hize en nonbre de su Magestad, de todos mis
60   rreynos y señorios, ni mas ni menoss que mi padre los poseya, lo qual todo
concluyo el tesorero Melo en Acobanba, pues dexadas todas cosas aparte,
siendo como es vuestra Señoria testigo de todo como prençipal actor, es
esta la manera que yo tube y he tenido en mi cristianismo hasta agora.

Por escriuirme vuestra Señoria muchas cartas, rrogandome que me
boluiese cristiano diziendo que conbenia para seguridad de la paz, procure
de ynquerir de Diego Rodriguez y de Martin de Pando quien hera en el
Cuzco la persona mas prençipal de los rreligiosos que en ella auia y qual
rreligion mas aprouada y de mas tomo; e dixeronme que la rreligion de
mas tomo y de mas autoridad y que mas ffloresçia en toda la tierra, avnque
de menos ffrayles, hera la de señor Sant Agustin y el prior della, digo de
los ffrailes que rresyden en el Cuzco, hera la persona mas prençipal de todos los que en el Cuzco auia; y oydo y entendido ser esto ansy, affiçioneme
60v   en gran manera a aquella horden y rreligion mas que a otra ninguna, y
determine descriuir al dicho prior muchas cartas, rrogandole que me viniese
a bautizar el en persona porque me daua gusto ser bautizado por su mano
por ser persona tan prençipal antes que por otro; y ansy siendo como es
tan honrrado rreligiosso, me hizo merçed de tomar el trauajo y llegarse

received priests in my land to instruct me and my people in the things of God, and specifically, I received father Vera,[168] who was sent by Your Lordship to me. He baptized my son Don Felipe Quispe Titu[169] and was in my territory almost a year and a half. He left when the Augustinian friars, who came to baptize me, arrived.

The renunciation I made of all my kingdoms and lordships[170]—neither more nor less than my father had possessed them—to Your Lordship, act-   60 ing in the name of His Majesty, testifies to the peace and confirms it in every detail. All of this was carried out by treasurer Melo in Acobamba. Leaving everything else aside, since Your Lordship is a witness and principal actor in everything that happened, this is the way I have proceeded and still proceed as a Christian.

Because Your Lordship wrote me many letters in which you pleaded with me to become a Christian and told me that my conversion would help to ensure the peace, I asked Diego Rodríguez and Martín de Pando to tell me who was the most principal member of the religious orders of Cusco; I also asked them to tell me which order was the most approved and accepted and had the greatest authority and most flourished in all the land. They named the friars of the order of Saint Augustine—and I mean the friars who reside in Cusco[171]—even though they were fewer in number than other orders. They also said that the prior of that friary was the most principal member of the religious orders of Cusco. Once I heard and understood that this was true, I became affectionately disposed toward that order more than toward any other. I wrote the prior many   60v letters[172] in which I pleaded with him to come here and baptize me in person. I told him it would please me to be baptized by his hand instead of any other because he was such an important friar. And, since he was such an honorable friar, he did me the favor of taking the trouble to come here

168. He speaks of Antonio de Vera, a cleric in the Cusco cathedral (Hemming, 314–15).

169. On July 20, 1567 (Guillén Guillén, "Documentos," 72).

170. He had sworn to be a vassal of the Spanish crown (Guillén Guillén, "Documentos," 68).

171. The Augustinians were the fourth religious order to arrive in Cusco, coming on the scene in 1560 only after the Dominicans, Franciscans, and Mercedarians. Titu Cusi was trying to select the most important religious leader in Cusco to officiate at his baptism.

172. No copies are known.

a esta mi tierra a bautizarme, traiendo consigo a otro rreligiosso y a
Gonçalo Perez de Biuero e Tilano de Anaya, los quales llegaron a Rayangalla a doze dias del mes de agosto del año de mill e quinientos y sesenta
y ocho, adonde yo sali deste Villcabanba a rresçibir el bautizmo como
entendi que me lo venian a dar; y alli en el dicho pueblo de Rayangalla
estubo el dicho prior llamado ffray Joan de Biuero con su conpañero y los
demas catorze dias, endustriandome en las cosas de la ffee, a cabo de los
quales, dia del gloriosso doctor Sant Agustin, me bautizo el dicho prior,
siendo mi padrino Gonçalo Perez de Biuero y madrina doña Angelina Çiça
Ocllo; y desque me vbo bautizado, estubo otros ocho dias el dicho prior,
rretificandome de todo en todo en las cosas de nuestra santa ffee catolica
y enseñandome las cosas e misterios della; acabado todo vno y otro, sse
ffue el dicho prior con Gonçalo Perez de Biuero y dexome en la tierra al
conpañero llamado ffray Marcos Garçia para que me ffuese poco a poco
adbirtiendo de las cosas quel dicho prior me abia enseñado y porque no
se me oluidassen, y para que enseñase y pedricasse [predicase] a la gente
de mi tierra la palabra de Dios; e yo, antes que se ffuese, les di a entender
a mis yndios la causa porque me auia bautizado y traido aquella gente a
mi tierra y el effeto que de bautizarse los honbres sacaban y para que
quedaua este padre dicho en la tierra; todos me rrespondieron que se hol-
gaban de mi bautizmo y de que quedase el padre en la tierra, que ellos
procurarian de hazer otro tanto en breue, pues el padre quedaua para el
effeto en la dicha tierra.

Pasados dos meses queste dicho padre estubo en Rayangalla, despues
que se ffue el prior, enseñando e yndustriando en las cosas de la ffee y
bautizando algunas criaturas por consentimiento de sus

61

61v

to my territory to baptize me. He brought another friar[173] and Gonzalo Pérez de Vivero and Tilano de Anaya[174] with him. On August 12, 1568, they arrived at Rayancalla,[175] where I had come from Vilcabamba to be baptized, as I understood would happen. The prior, named Juan de Vivero, remained in the town of Rayancalla for fourteen days with his companion and the rest of his party, and instructed me in matters of the faith. At the end of this time, on the day of the glorious Doctor Saint Augustine, the prior baptized me. My godfather was Gonzalo Pérez de Vivero and my godmother was Doña Angelina Sisa Ocllo. The prior stayed another eight days after my baptism, reiterating everything that he had taught me about our holy Catholic faith and instructed me in its principles and mysteries. After this was done, the prior departed with Gonzalo Pérez de Vivero, leaving his companion, Friar Marcos García, with me in my territory so that García could remind me, little by little, about the things that the prior had taught me so that I would not forget them. I would also be able to teach and preach the word of God to the people of my territory. Before the prior left, I told all my followers the reason why I had accepted baptism and why I had allowed those friars into my territory. I also told them how people benefited from receiving baptism and for what purpose this father would remain in the territory. All of my people responded that they rejoiced at my baptism and at the news that the father would remain in the land. My followers said that they also would attempt to accept baptism, since the father had remained for that reason.

    Father García had been in Rayancalla two months (after the departure of the prior), during which time he taught and instructed the people in matters of the faith and baptized some infants with the consent of their

61

61v

173. The other friar was Marcos García, who participated in the composition of Titu Cusi's *History.*

174. Tilano de Anaya would return to Vilcabamba as envoy of the Viceroy Francisco de Toledo in late 1571. He was killed, and the incident sparked the viceroy's campaign to remove the Inca from Vilcabamba, launched in April 1572. While the war was underway, the archbishop Jerónimo de Loaysa wrote to the King that the man the viceroy had sent had been told not to return to Vilcabamba or he would be killed (Lisson, vol. 2, no. 9: 610). Nothing Titu Cusi says about him here indicates any kind of a problem with him.

175. Rayancalla (or Rayangalla) is the "Layangalla" located several miles upriver from Rosaspata, on the road toward Pampaconas (Lee, 227–28).

padres, acorde de yr con Martin de Pando a visitar la tierra que esta de la
otra parte de loss puertos hazia Guamanga, en la qual estube quatro meses
haziendo el mesmo offiçio y poniendo cruzes e haziendo yglesias en los
pueblos adonde llegue, que fueron ocho los pueblos y tres las yglessias, y en
los demas cruzes; bautizo en todos ellos noventa criaturas, lo qual hecho
todo y dexando mochachos para que dixiesen la doctrina, se boluio al
dicho pueblo de Rayangalla adonde estubo solo siete meses, bautizando
y enseñando a los yndios de toda la comarca; y por el mes de septienbre
62   le vino otro padre conpañero y anbos juntos se estubieron en aquella tierra
hasta que yo los traxe a este Billcabanba donde agora estamos; no an
bautizado aqui ninguno porque avn es muy nueua la gente desta tierra en
las cossas que an de saber y entender tocantes a la ley e mandamientos de
Dios; yo procurare que poco a poco lo sepan.

*   *   *   *

Por tanto, porque entienda vuestra Señoria y me haga merçed de lo dar a
entender a su Magestad, he procurado por la via arriba dicha declarar
sumariamente syn espaçifficarlo mas la manera y biuienda de mi padre y el
subçeso y el fyn de mis negoçios hasta el fyn e punto en que agora estoy;
si acasso fuere menester que baya vno y otro declarado mas por estensso
como y de la manera que ffue y a sido hasta agora, quando vuestra Señoria fuere seruido me podra auissar para que yo lo haga como vuestra Señoria lo mandare; por agora paresçeme que basta esto.
62v   Avnque avia otras muchas cossas que auisar e que dezir, en especial
de nuestro origen y prençipio y trajes y manera de nuestras personas, confforme a nuestro vsso, todo lo dexo por euitar prolexidad y

parents. I agreed to go [with him and] with Martín de Pando to visit the territory on the other side of the passes toward Huamanga.[176] There I spent four months assisting the friars and erecting crosses and building churches in the towns I visited. I visited eight towns in all. I built churches in three of them and erected crosses in the rest. The father baptized ninety infants in those same towns. Once all this was accomplished, the father returned to the town of Rayancalla. There he spent only seven months baptizing and teaching the Indians of that region. In the month of September another father, his companion, arrived. Both of these fathers stayed [in Rayancalla] until I brought them to Vilcabamba, where we are now. They haven't baptized any people here because the people are very new to the things they have to know and understand regarding the laws and commandments of God.[177] I will see that they come to know these things, little by little.

62

*   *   *   *

Therefore, because Your Lordship understands and will make His Majesty understand, I have tried to tell above and in summary form, without going into great detail, how my father lived his life and the content and purpose of my own actions to the present moment. If it should be necessary to explain anything in greater detail than it has been explained here, you can let me know and I will do what you tell me. What I have written seems to me at the moment to be sufficient.

Although there are many other things about which I could inform and relate to you—especially about our origins and beginnings and our dress and appearance[178]—I will not discuss them here to avoid being prolific and

62v

176. Huamanga was the colonial name of the present city of Ayacucho.

177. According to an Augustinian chronicler, the two friars were frustrated that they had not been allowed to work in Vilcabamba itself, imagining that Titu Cusi was feigning his interest in Catholicism while preserving idolatrous practices in Vilcabamba (Calancha, *Corónica*, 787–812). Titu Cusi addresses this matter in the *History*, which was composed at Vilcabamba with both friars present.

178. Again, Titu Cusi excuses himself from writing about the Inca past (see note 5). It is interesting to note that this time he mentions communicating something about

porque no hazen a nuestro proposito açerca de lo que bamos tratando; solo suplicare a vuestra Señoria, pues en todo me a hecho merçed, en dar muy de veras y con todo calor a entender esto que aqui va escripto a su Magestad me haga merçed muy grande, pues tengo entendido que sienpre me a de ffaboresçer como mi señor; e porque me paresçe que me he alargado mucho, çesso con esto.

Ffue ffecho y ordenado todo lo arriba escripto, dando avisso de todo el illustre señor don Diego de Castro Titu Cussi Yupangui, hijo de Mango Ynga Yupangui, señor natural que ffue de los rreynos del Piru, por el muy rreuerendo padre ffrai Marcos Garçia, ffraile presvitero de la horden de

63   señor Sant Agustin que rresside en esta prouinçia de Villcabanba, teniendo como thiene a cargo la administrasçion de las animas que en toda ella rresiden a honrra y gloria de Dios todopoderosso, padre e hijo y espiritu santo, tres personas y vn solo Dios verdadero, y de la gloriossa rreyna de los angeles, madre de Dios Sancta Maria, nuestra señora, agora e para sienpre jamas, amen.

Yo, Martin de Pando, escriuano de comission por el muy yllustre señor el liçençiado Lope Garçia de Castro, gouernador que ffue destos rreynos, doy ffee que todo lo arriba escripto lo rrelato y ordeno el dicho padre a ynsistion del dicho don Diego de Castro, lo qual yo escriui por mis manos propias de la manera que el dicho padre me lo rrelataua, siendo testigos a lo veer escriuir e rrelatar el rreberendo padre ffray Diego Ortiz, proffesso presvitero de la dicha horden que juntamente rreside en

63v   conpañia del autor desto, y tres cappitanes del dicho don Diego de

because these matters have nothing to do with my present purpose. I only ask this of Your Lordship (who has favored me in every way): that you would do me a great favor by communicating, as accurately and with as much advocacy as you can, all that I have written to His Majesty (and I understand that, as my lord, you must favor me). I will end here and now because it seems that I have gone on at great length.

All of what was written above (providing information about the actions of our illustrious lord Don Diego de Castro Titu Cusi Yupanqui, son of Manco Inca Yupanqui, natural lord who ruled these lands) was done and ordered by the reverend father Friar Marcos García, a friar of the order of our lord Saint Augustine and priest who resides in this province of Vilcabamba, who is in charge of the administration of the souls who reside in that province for the honor and glory of the all-powerful God, father, son, and holy ghost, three persons in one true god, and of the glorious queen of the angels and mother of God, Our Lady Mary, now and forever, amen.[179]

I, Martín de Pando, notary commissioned by the very illustrious lord Licentiate Lope García de Castro, who was governor of these kingdoms, swear that all of what was written above was related and organized by the said father on the insistence of Don Diego de Castro; and that I write it in my own hand[180] in the manner in which the said father related; having witnessed it being written and related the reverend father Friar Diego Ortiz,[181] a professed member of the same order and a priest who resides in the company of the author,[182] and three captains of the said Don Diego de

63

63v

Inca dress and appearance, suggesting that he thought that this information was necessary to explaining who the Incas were.

179. The rhetorical flourish ends a paragraph written in the third person, in the voice of the notary, in contrast with the preceding narrative, written in the first person. This paragraph marks the end of Titu Cusi's narration.

180. Some facts about the composition of the present text are clearly indicated: Titu Cusi "insisted" that the story be written; Marcos García "related and organized" it; Martín de Pando "wrote" it. What is missing is a precise statement about what information Marcos García received from Titu Cusi, and what language or languages were used in communication.

181. Diego Ortiz was killed in the aftermath of Titu Cusi's death, probably in 1571 (Hemming, 323–26, 417–18).

182. Pando seems to refer to Marcos García as "author," but he might mean Titu Cusi.

Castro, llamados el vno Suta Yupangui e Rimache Yupangui y Sullca Varac; y porque haga ffee todo lo susodicho, lo ffirme de mi nonbre.

Fecho en el pueblo de Sant Saluador de Villcabanba, a seis de hebrero del año de mill e quinientos y setenta años, lo qual para que haga mas ffee lo ffirmaron de sus nonbres el dicho padre ffrai Marcos Garçia y ffrai Diego Ortiz e yo, el dicho Martin de Pando. Fray Marcos Garçia. Digo que lo vi escribir. Por testigo, ffray Diego Ortiz. En testimonio de verdad, Martin de Pando, escrivano.

Yo, don Diego de Castro Titu Cusy Yupangui, hijo que soy de Mango Ynga Yupangui, señor natural que ffue destos rreynos del Piru, digo que por quanto me es neçesario hazer rrelasçion al rrey don Ffelipe, nuestro señor, de cosas conbenientes a mi y a mis subçesores y no se el ffrase y la manera que los españoles thienen en semejantes auisos, rrogue al muy rreverendo padre ffray Marcos Garçia y a Martin de Pando que confforme al vsso de su natural me ordenasen y conpusiesen esta rrelasçion arriba dicha para la enbiar a los rreynos de España al muy yllustre señor el liçençiado Lope Garçia de Castro, para que por mi y en mi nonbre, lleuando como lleua my poder, me haga merçed de la enseñar e rrelatar a su Magestad del rrey don Phelipe, nuestro señor, para que vista la rrazon que yo tengo de ser gratifficado, me haga merçedes para mi e para mis hijos e dessendientes como quien su Magestad es. E porque es verdad lo sobredicho, di esta firmada de mi nonbre. Ques ffecho dia, mes y año susodicho. Don Diego de Castro Tito Cusi Yupangui.

Castro, named Suta Yupanqui, Rimache Yupanqui, and Sulca Huarac.[183] And so that all of the above be convincing, I have signed my name to it.

Done in the town of San Salvador of Vilcabamba, on the sixth of February in the year 1570. And to further confirm it, the said fathers Friar Marcos García and Friar Diego Ortiz signed their names. And I, the said Martín de Pando. Friar Marcos García. I state that I saw it written, as witness, Friar Diego Ortiz. In testimony of the truth, Martín de Pando, notary.[184]

I, Don Diego de Castro Titu Cusi Yupanqui,[185] son that I am of Manco Inca Yupanqui, natural lord[186] who ruled these lands of Peru, say that, because it is necessary for me to relate to King Philip II, our lord, what is in my interest and in the interest of my successors, and I do not know the phrases and the manner Spaniards use for such enterprises, I requested that the very reverend father Friar Marcos García and Martín de Pando order 64 and compose the above narrative, according to their custom, so that it could be sent to the kingdoms of Spain to [sic: with] the very illustrious lord the Licentiate Lope García de Castro, so that he, for me and in my name, and taking with him my Power of Attorney, as he has, could do me the favor of showing and communicating it to His Majesty the King, Philip II, our lord, so that, once the reason for rewarding me is made evident, he will grant favors to me and my children and descendents, since he is the person he is. And because the above is true, I made this statement, signed in my name and dated the same day as that given above. Don Diego de Castro Titu Cusi Yupanqui.[187]

---

183. Rimache Yupanqui was the only one of the three to be taken prisoner in 1572 (Nowack and Julien, 25; Nowack, 157).

184. Since this document is a copy, there are no original signatures. The original document would have borne the signatures of the friars Marcos García and Diego Ortiz. Pando, who wrote all of the original documents, would also have signed with his signature and rubric.

185. The account again shifts to the first person and voice of Titu Cusi.

186. Titu Cusi again identifies himself as the son of the "natural lord" of Peru, using the conceptual repertoire of a sixteenth-century Spaniard (see note 4).

187. The document is a copy, and there are no original signatures. The original document would have been signed in the name of Don Diego de Castro Titu Cusi Yupanqui. Pando makes no indication that he signed for Titu Cusi.

[4]

Poder para el señor gouernador el liçençiado
Lope Garçia de Castro

Sepan quantos esta carta de poder vieren como yo, el *sapai ynga* don
Diego de Castro Tito Cusi Yupangui, hijo mayorazgo que soy de Mango
Ynga Yupangui y nieto de Guaina Capac, señores naturales que ffueron
destos rreynos e provinçias del Piru, digo que por quanto yo tengo neçesidad de tratar en los rreynos de España muchas cossas y negoçios con el
rrey don Phelipe, nuestro señor, y con otras justiçias de qualquier estado
y condiçion que sean, ansy seglares como eclesiasticas, y juntamente con
algunas otras personas que destos rreynos ayan ydo a los de España que
alla puedan rresidir o rresidan, y no podria hallar persona que con mas
calor ni soliçitud pudiese soliçitar mis negoçios como es el señor gouernador el liçençiado Castro, que a los rreynos de España agora ba, ni quien
con mas amor los haga ni pueda hazer, como a tenido e tiene de costun-
bre de hazerme merçed; que por esta, con la conffiança que de su persona
tengo, le doy todo mi poder, bastante, libre y suffiçiente, qual de derecho
mass puede valer ansy como yo lo he e tengo y de derecho en tal caso
se rrequiere, para que por mi y en mi nonbre, y como mi persona
mesma, pueda paresçer ante su Magestad y pressentar a su rreal nonbre
qualesquier petiçion e petiçiones, y dezir y declarar todo lo que le ffuese
preguntado tocante a mis negoçios de la misma manera sy yo lo dixiese y
declarase; e pueda paresçer ante qualesquier justiçias de su Magestad,
ansy eclesiasticas como seglares, y pedir y demandar, anparar y defender,
todas y qualesquier cosas que bea que me puedan y deban pertenes-
çer, las quales pueda poseer, rregir y adjudicar como si yo mesmo las
poseyese, rrejiese y adjudicase con mi propia persona; e para lo que
ansi oviere de pesos de oro e plata, haziendas, rrentas, ganados y otras
qualesquier cossas que vbiere, me las pueda enbiar a estos rreynos a mi
costa y minsion; e para que por my y en mi nonbre, sy le paresçiere,

[4]

Power given to the lord governor Licentiate
Lope García de Castro

Know all who see this Power of Attorney that I, the Sapay Inca Don Diego de Castro Titu Cusi Yupanqui, son and principal heir of Manco Inca Yupanqui and grandson of Huayna Capac, who were the natural lords[188] of   64v
these kingdoms and provinces of Peru, say that because I must deal with various matters in the kingdom of Spain with King Philip II, our lord, and other authorities of whatever jurisdiction and kind these may be, whether secular or ecclesiastical, and also with other persons who have gone from these kingdoms to those of Spain, who may or do live there, and I could not find a person who would handle my business with more care or concern than the lord governor Licentiate Castro, who is now leaving for the kingdoms of Spain, nor anyone who with more affection could or would attend to it, as he has had and has the custom of favoring me, that by this letter, with the confidence in his person that I have, I give him my power, fully, freely, and sufficiently, to the maximum extent allowed by law, just as I have it and by law is required in such cases,   65
that, for me and in my name and as if he were my person: he can appear before His Majesty and present before his royal name any petition or petitions; he may say and declare everything he may be asked with reference to my affairs in the same manner that I would say and declare it; he can appear before any councils, courts, mayors, or city councils and before any other royal justices, whether ecclesiastical or secular, and ask and demand, support, and defend, any and all matters that he sees that could or should be relevant to me; which things he may possess, govern, or adjudicate in the same manner that I would possess, govern, or adjudicate them if I were there in person; and with reference to what there might be in *pesos* of gold and silver, property, income, livestock, and whatever other things there might be, he may send them to these kingdoms at my cost and expense, and for me and in my name; and if it should seem   65v

188. Here, Titu Cusi again claims that the Incas are the "natural lords" of Peru (see note 4).

de qualesquier pesos de oro que me pertenezcan me pueda hazer conpar [conprar] y conpre qualesquier haziendas, rrentas y mercadurias que le parezca que me conbengan, ansy muebles como rraizes; ansymismo para que pueda hazer qualesquier pedimientos, rrequirimientos, juramentos de calunia y desisorio, dezir uerdad, rresponder a lo hecho de contrario, concluyr, presentar testigos, prouanças, escripturas, prousiones, çedulas rreales y otro genero de prueua, y lo sacar, contradezir los de en contrario, poner qualesquier rrecusasçiones, sospechas, objetos, jurarlas, apartarse dellas, tomar y aprehender en mi nonbre qualesquier poseçiones de qua-lesquier mis bienes e haziendas que me conbengan y sobre la aprehension hazer lo que ffuere justo y conbenga a los dichos bienes, oyr sentençia en ffauor y consentir lo de en contrario, apelar y suplicar adonde y con

66   derecho deba seguir la causa hasta la ffinal conclusion, y pedir costas y las jurar en effeto, hazer todo aquello que yo podria avnque aqui no vaya de-clarado ni espresado y sean cossas de calidad que rrequieran mi pressençia; que quan cunplido poder como tengo y de derecho se rrequiere dar y otorgar, otro tal y ese mesmo lo doy e otorgo con todas sus ynçidençias y dependençias, anexidades y conexidades y con libre e general adminis-trasçion, y para que este dicho poder lo pueda sostituyr en vna o mas per-sonas, como le paresçiere, y los rrebocar, a los quales y a el rrelieuo en fforma; e para firmeza dello, obligo los bienes, tributos, rrentas, hazien-das que ansy me conbengan, muebles rraizes, avidos e por auer; e para tes-timonio de lo susodicho, lo firme de mi nonbre; que es ffecho a seis dias del mes de hebrero de mill e quinientos y setenta años, testigos que ffueron presentes a lo uer sacar los muy rreuerendos padres ffray Marcos Garçia e ffray Diego Ortiz, e don Pablo Guallpa Yupangui y don Martin

66v   Cosi Guaman y don Gaspar Xulca Yanac.

Yo, Martin de Pando, escriuano de comission por el muy yllustre señor el governador el Liçençiado Castro, doy ffee de como es berdad todo lo susodicho, y quel dicho Ynga don Diego de Castro dio este poder al di-cho señor liçençiado Castro, gouernador que fue destos rreinos, como y e [repetition in the original] de la manera en que derecho se rrequiere; en testimonio de lo qual puse en su nonbre don Diego de Castro, en su fyrma,

advisable to him, with these *pesos* of gold that belong to me he can pur-
chase property, whether fixed or mobile, rights to income, or merchan-
dise that appears to him to be of benefit to me; and furthermore, so that
he may make any requests, requirements, oaths regarding calumny or
abandonment, tell the truth, respond to that which has been done
wrongfully, see a matter to its end, present witnesses, evidence, writing,
provisions, royal orders, and any other kind of proof, and unseat or chal-
lenge those presented against me, lodge any claims to reject, suspicions,
or objections, and swear to them or remove himself from them, take or
receive in my name possession of any of my goods or belongings that
would be convenient for me, and regarding their receipt, do that which
is fair and convenient with regard to such goods hear sentences in my favor and consent to those against me, appeal and plead wherever he right-
fully should, follow a lawsuit to its end, ask for costs and swear to be   66
responsible for them, and do all that I would do if it concerns matters of
quality that require my presence, whether it be declared here or not, that
whatever power I may have and that by law is required to be given or
granted, I grant both that power and this one, with all their incidences
and dependencies, annexes and connections, and with free and general
administration, and so that this power may be substituted in one or more
persons, as he sees fit, and may be revoked; and in a manner that affirms
this agreement, I obligate my goods, tribute, income, any property that
may be convenient to me, land, and other fixed assets that I have now or
may yet have; and as testimony of the aforesaid, I signed my name to this
document. Done this sixth day of February 1570. Witnesses who were
present to see it copied, the very reverend fathers Friar Marcos García and
Friar Diego Ortiz, and Don Pablo Huallpa Yupanqui,[189] and Don Martín
Cusi Guaman and Don Gaspar Yulca Yanac.   66v

I, Martín de Pando, notary commissioned by the very illustrious lord
governor Licentiate Castro, who was governor of these kingdoms, attest
that the aforesaid is true and that the said Inca Don Diego de Castro gave
this power to the said lord Licentiate Castro, who was governor of these
kingdoms, in the form and manner in which the law requires it, in testimony of which I put in his name, in his signature, Don Diego de Castro,

---

189. One of the generals pardoned in 1565 (Nowack, 157).

como abaxo paresçera en el original. Don Diego de Castro Tito Cussi Yupangui. Por testigo, ffrai Marcos Garçia. Por testigo, ffrai Diego Ortiz. Y en testimonio de berdad, fiz aqui este mio signo. Martin de Pando, escriuano de comission.

as it appears below in the original. Don Diego de Castro Titu Cusi Yupanqui.[190] By a witness, Friar Marcos García. By a witness, Friar Diego Ortiz. And in testimony of the truth, I made this my sign. Martín de Pando, commissioned notary.[191]

190. Pando states that he signed Titu Cusi's name to the Power of Attorney.

191. The Power of Attorney is a copy. The original would have been formally signed in the name of Don Diego de Castro Titu Cusi Yupanqui, by Martín de Pando, and by the friars Marcos García and Diego Ortiz. Pando, who wrote all of the original documents, would also have signed with his signature and rubric.

Appendix

Memorial, Chuquichaca, 18 June 1565. Translated from a transcription published by Guillermo Lohmann Villena (1941: 13–14)

Illustrious lord. It seems that the honor of those absent perishes, and because some evil-minded individuals have dealt with things in my absence that they should not have, and because my intention is to satisfy Your Lordship (since you seem willing to grant me every favor), it is best that I tell you about my affairs beginning from some years back, so that Your Lordship can truly understand what has happened.

At the time and after the Christians came to this land, my father Manco Inca was imprisoned under the pretext that he wanted to usurp the kingdom after the death of Atahuallpa, with their only motive and purpose being to make him give them a hut filled with gold and silver. During his imprisonment they treated him very badly in both word and deed: placing a collar around him like a dog and chaining his feet; taking him by this collar from one place to another, in full view of his subjects; questioning him every hour; and keeping him imprisoned for more than a month. And because of the bad treatment they gave him and his children and people and women, he got himself released from this imprisonment and went to Tambo, where he confederated with all of the caciques and principal lords of the land to surround Cusco and make war against the Spaniards for the reasons given above. Afterward, he retreated to the Andes. Then there was the battle against the Spaniards in Jauja, where many died, and also the battle of Oroncoy, where more than 400 Spaniards died; then there was the battle in Pucara with Gonzalo Pizarro, where Guaypaty [Huaypar] and Ynguilli [Ynguill], sons of Huayna Capac, died. No one remained except Paullu, who coveted [my father's] estates and women from here to Quito. No one escaped. And afterward, there was a battle in Pillcosuni between the Indians of this kingdom and the Spaniards with a great deal of killing of people on both sides. And, the active campaign having ended and my father having withdrawn to live peacefully in the miserable outpost of Vitcos, seven Spaniards who had rebelled with Gonzalo Pizarro against the authority of the king took refuge there. My father treated them well

170

and made them comfortable. And because they coveted what little there was there, they mutinied and plotted among themselves and treacherously murdered him. And they struck me with a lance. If I had not been able to escape into the steep and harsh country near there, they would have killed me, too.

Afterward, we had peace for a few days, but then the Indians of Tambo, Amaybamba, and Guavyacondos took many Indians from Vitcos, and for that reason we went to war with them. After that, and being at peace, we were advised that a certain Tordoya had asked to be allowed to come here and go to war against us. For that reason, we attacked Amaybamba and the Indians awarded to Barrios and Garci Martínez of Huamanga. Afterward, the Indians awarded to Nuño de Mendoza came here of their own free will. Because of a letter that Doctor Cuenca wrote to us saying that he would wage a cruel war against us, we attacked Marcahuasi. Afterward, being at peace again, Treasurer Melo came to speak to us at this bridge [Chuquichaca], where he promised us and told us that, since the King wanted peace he would give me a good living and that, once he [Melo] got back to Cusco, he would write me and tell me everything. I waited a month for word, and thinking he had only tried to deceive and humiliate me and that this deceit was to cover up an attack that was being planned, I attacked the Indians awarded to Sotelo. From that time until now, we have written each other, and he required me to send some messengers to Lima. And in this same time, I received letters from Your Lordship, and Diego Rodríguez came to speak with me, at which time I saw a letter that the President sent to Treasurer Melo, addressed to him, and another to me, in which the President wrote that he had sent me the Treasurer's letter so that I would see it. And it said that there was a gentleman in Lima, sent there by the city of Cusco, who wanted to go to war against me. And there was also a letter from the Treasurer in which they told him that [this gentleman] had sworn for hours on end that I had gathered together 700 Andes (who eat human flesh) and more than 2,000 Indians, all armed, to attack Tambo and Limatambo and Jaquijaguana and Curahuasi and Cochacajas and Abancay and do a great deal of damage. And Diego Rodríguez tried to placate me saying that it was the will of the King and Your Lordship to grant me favors and not to make war against me, and that for this reason, I should send my messengers to Cusco, because they would be very well treated there. And if it did not happen in this way, I would

be hanged. And so I sent them, and because they took two days longer than the eleven I allowed them to go and come back (and when I learned they had taken more time, I wanted to kill them and give them to the Andes to be eaten), but taking the circumstances into consideration, I renegotiated with them and gave them the two additional days. And then the messengers came and I saw that everything I had written about to Your Lordship had been done and I gave you great credit, and I still do. And I have tried to accept the Holy Gospel and the law of our lord Jesus Christ. And I attempted to undo the pact and conspiracy to rebel, whenever I gave the order, that had been made with all of the caciques of the kingdom. I had already made the decision that no one should enter my territory nor would I return to this bridge, but, to see the Treasurer again, and knowing your caliber, honesty, and nature, and also because Diego Rodríguez had made me understand it, I decided to make peace and to accept your authority and make you the godfather of my son Tito. And the order and manner for my departure is what Your Lordship will see in this memorial, signed in my name. And because everything is as I have said, I have signed my name. Çapa Ynga Tito Cusi Yupanqui.

Index